Marketing Fashion

Second Edition

Strategy, Branding and Promotion

Harriet Posner

Laurence King Publishing

LAURENCE KING

First published in 2011
Second edition published in 2015
by Laurence King Publishing Ltd
361–373 City Road
London EC1V 1LR
Tel: +44 20 7841 6900
Fax: +44 20 7841 6910
email: enquiries@laurenceking.com
www.laurenceking.com

A catalogue record for this book is available
from the British Library

ISBN: 978 1 78067 566 4

Design: Alexandre Coco

Picture research: The author and Louise Thomas

Printed in China

Front cover illustration by Jason Brooks

*Dedicated to the memory of Rhona Posner,
my dear mother who first ignited my passion
for the world of retail and beautiful design,
and Boris Trambusti, a unique force in
fashion, an inspiration to students and the
person responsible for getting me into fashion
education in the first place.*

Introduction

1   The Fashion Market

2   Marketing Strategy

3   Research and Planning

4   Understanding the Customer

5   Introduction to Branding

6   Fashion Promotion

7   Careers in Fashion Marketing

Related study material is available on the
Laurence King website at www.laurenceking.com

Introduction

"Today, a designer's creativity expresses itself more than ever in the marketing rather than in the actual clothes."

Teri Agins

Marketing and branding play a critical role in today's fashion industry; they are stimulating and exciting disciplines that inform many of the strategic and creative decisions involved in design and product development. Marketing bridges the gap between the intangibilities of fashion and the concrete realities of business. It can be viewed as a holistic system connecting the commercial goals and value system of a business organization with the personal ideals, desires and actual needs of consumers.

Fashion is by its very nature a marketing tool. Marketing is part of its DNA; it is inherent in its substance and spirit. Think about it; if it was not called fashion, it would be plain apparel or garments, and these words contrive to kill the very essence and flamboyance of fashion itself. Fashion allows us to dream; it can transport us from the mundane to the glossy world of models, catwalks and fantasies. In the magical realm of fashion, clothes transmute into the season's must-haves, a garment's shape and proportion becomes a silhouette, a colour transforms from plain brown into glamorous mocha and a simple sheath of black fabric becomes a little black dress. It is hardly surprising that fashion is so seductive, when so much of the media focus centres on the more glamorous aspects of the industry. Swathes of media coverage are dedicated to the reporting of every aspect of the fashion world; beautifully styled fashion spreads display tantalizing looks created from the new season's collections and magazines flaunt innumerable glossy adverts promoting an assortment of fashion, accessories and perfume. The fashion industry has embraced digital media, using it to increase awareness and connections between brands, labels and customers. Fashion is a complex cultural phenomenon but it is also a global manufacturing and retail industry, the scope of which is immense. The industry extends to the agricultural, chemical and fibre industries that produce and supply the raw materials for textile manufacturing through to those working at the more glamorous end of the spectrum in the world of styling, art direction, photography, advertising, media and digital marketing.

Marketing operates at every level of the fashion system and affects the entire industry **supply chain** from product development through to retail; it is as relevant to couture, luxury labels and designer brands as it is to independent niche labels or to the mass-market and volume apparel businesses. Marketing is the common denominator that ties it all together.

Opposite
Couture dress by Alexandre Vauthier.

"When clothes leave the factories where they are made, they are merely 'garments' or 'apparel'. Only when the marketers get hold of them do they magically become 'fashion'."

Mark Tungate

What is in this book?

Marketing Fashion aims to offer you a contemporary visual guide to the fundamental principles of marketing theory and branding practice. The book explains key theoretical concepts, illustrating how these might be applied within the ever-evolving context of the global fashion and retail industry. Readers are led through the marketing process from initial research through to the creation of marketing and branding campaigns. Examples and case studies drawn from a broad range of fashion businesses help explain key concepts, and comprehensive lists of industry resources and suggestions for further reading are provided at the end of the book.

Marketing Fashion provides many useful tips and inspirational ideas aimed at assisting the reader to:

» Study and understand marketing theory and practice

» Understand how fashion marketing and branding principles are put into action

» Design fashion products that can be marketed with ease

» Recognize the importance of research and market analysis

» Analyse fashion consumers and understand their needs

» Create exciting and effective marketing and promotional campaigns

How the book is structured

Chapter 1

The Fashion Market sets the scene, outlining the basic structure of the fashion industry and offering definitions of marketing. It explains the different levels of the market and provides information on emerging fashion markets and important industry trade fairs.

Chapter 2

Marketing Strategy introduces the fundamentals of marketing strategy, explains key theoretical marketing tools and concepts, and gives examples of how they are applied in practice within the context of the global fashion and retail industry.

Chapter 3

Research and Planning explains how key marketing tools are utilized within the planning process. The chapter emphasizes the importance of thorough research and analysis and examines the purpose and value of both primary and secondary research, outlining key areas to consider when gathering market and trend intelligence.

Chapter 4

Understanding the Customer focuses on research and analysis of customers. It explores ways in which a business can analyse its customer base so they are best able to understand customer requirements and target products and marketing strategies accordingly. It explains customer segmentation – how to group consumers into clusters that have broadly similar characteristics, needs or fashion traits. The reader will gain an understanding of the impact of psychology on consumer purchasing behaviour and learn techniques for creating customer profiles.

Above
From catwalk to store, the fashion dream must be promoted and maintained.

Chapter 5

Introduction to Branding introduces readers to the fundamentals of branding and explains why brands are such valuable assets. The chapter shows how brands are created and explains the importance of brand identity as a strategic tool for building a relationship between a brand and its customers.

Chapter 6

Fashion Promotion covers the main types of promotional activities employed within fashion and retail. A broad selection of case studies highlights current trends in contemporary fashion promotion.

Chapter 7

Careers in Fashion Marketing outlines potential career paths and provides information on a selection of key roles relevant to those seeking a career in fashion design, marketing, PR or fashion management, and details the skills and competencies required.

Who is this book for?

Fashion marketing is now an essential area of study for all who plan a career in the industry. Students studying fashion, textile or accessory design, fashion management or buying and merchandising will all find that marketing is included as part of the curriculum. Fashion, however, is never static and fashion marketing does not always conform to standard theoretical formulae. To be successful within the world of fashion marketing you need to build upon basic principles and adapt ideas so as to meet the challenges of each new market situation. The book aims to educate but also to inspire, and readers are encouraged to use the material as a platform for further research and enquiry.

Below
The adidas '60 Years of Soles and Stripes' launch event in Milan, Italy. Rather than using a runway show, the adidas Originals 60th anniversary collection was promoted at a unique house party event which provided a sneak preview into the global brand campaign.

1

The Fashion Market

"Marketing is not the art of finding clever ways to dispose of what you make. Marketing is the art of creating genuine customer value."

Philip Kotler

Fashion is a global market with a complex structure that operates on many different levels to reach everyone from fashionistas to those who just purchase clothing as a necessity of everyday life. The range and scope of fashion is immense, from an ornate haute couture gown made by hand in a Paris atelier to a simple mass-produced T-shirt manufactured in China. This opening chapter is divided into two sections. The first will provide you with an outline of the basic structure of the industry, explain the different levels of the fashion market and discuss examples of global markets. The second section gives key definitions of marketing and explains why marketing is such an important element of the fashion industry.

Fashion market sectors

The fashion market can be subdivided in a number of ways depending on what aspect of the market or industry is being analysed. For example, by product sector such as clothing and apparel or accessories; by geographic market such as Europe, US, Asia or South America; by market level, haute couture or ready-to-wear; or by function such as sportswear, performance wear, formal wear and so on. Information is broken down in this way so that companies are better able to analyse market data and monitor their business results more effectively. Market statistics can be compiled and analysed by one or more of these criteria. The list and diagram below outline some of the criteria that can be used.

» **Market or product category**

Apparel, accessories, perfume or homeware.
The apparel market can be further subdivided into womenswear, menswear and childrenswear

» **Product type, end-use of product or fashion style**

Denim, lingerie, sportswear, formal wear or contemporary fashion

» **Market level**

Couture, luxury, mid-market or value market

» **Location of market**

Global, international, national or regional

FASHION MARKET SECTORS

CLOTHING AND APPAREL			ACCESSORIES AND FOOTWEAR	PERFUME AND COSMETICS	LIFESTYLE AND HOMEWARES
WOMENSWEAR	MENSWEAR	CHILDRENSWEAR			
Evening wear	Bespoke tailoring	Baby	Shoes		
Formal work and office	Formal work and office	Toddler	Bags		
Wedding and occasion	Wedding and occasion	Boys	Sunglasses		
Contemporary fashion	Contemporary fashion	Girls	Gloves and scarves		
Casual wear	Casual wear		Wallets and purses		
Denim	Denim		Hats		
Streetwear	Streetwear		Men's ties		
Resort or cruise wear	Sportswear		Luggage		
Sportswear					
Slouch or loungewear					
Lingerie					

The diagram gives an indication of some of the key market and product sectors within womenswear, menswear, childrenswear and accessories. As new niche markets develop, so the chart can be adapted to include emerging sectors, for example, clubwear, urban wear, and performance wear.

Above
Matthew Zorpas, seen here wearing a suit by Hardy Amies, is a London-based fashion consultant who blogs at www.thegentlemanblogger.com. He has become an authority on men's style. There is a growing demand for designer and trend-led men's fashion. The UK menswear market, for example, is predicted to increase by nearly 30 per cent by 2019.

Right
A young Emirati couple shopping for sunglasses, Dubai.

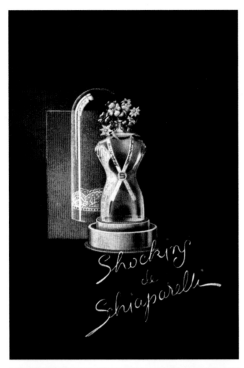

Fashion market levels

Fashion can be divided into two overarching levels:

> » Haute couture and couture
>
> » Ready-to-wear

Haute couture

Haute couture is literally defined as 'high sewing' or 'fine sewing' and is fashion at its highest level. Haute couture operates at a quality and standard way above that of luxury designer ready-to-wear. Prices are extremely high (an haute couture dress can sell for a six-figure sum) so there is an unwritten rule of limiting sales of any garment of over £100,000 to one per continent to ensure the exclusivity that clients expect. For lesser-priced garments, sales are usually confined to no more than three per continent. Haute couture clients view themselves as art patrons and consider these clothes to be a collectable form of art and an investment. The term 'haute couture' is protected by law and governed by very strict rules set by the Chambre Syndicale de la Haute Couture in Paris. To be classified as a bona fide haute couturier a fashion house must create made-to-order garments for private clients. They must also produce two collections a year in January and July, employ a minimum of 20 full-time staff, run an atelier in Paris and show a set minimum of runway looks, or 'exits', as they are known, of evening and daywear. In the 1980s and 1990s the Italian designer Valentino showed over 180 exits for his haute couture show, now he produces only 40. Very few design houses are approved as haute couture establishments showing at the official Paris haute couture; Chanel, Dior, Jean Paul Gaultier, Valentino, Giorgio Armani, Jean-Louis Scherrer, Elie Saab, Dominique Sirop, Giambattista Valli, Stéphane Rolland and Franck Sorbier are all recognized as true haute couturiers. Maison Martin Margiela and Alexis Mabille were awarded haute couture status in 2012.

Haute couture relies on the expertise of many highly skilled artisans and craftspeople who labour behind the scenes to produce all the luxurious embroideries, trimmings and accessories required by the haute couturiers. Traditionally Paris has been home to a large number of studios or ateliers specializing in millinery, shoemaking, embroidery, beading, creating decorative flowers, buttons and costume jewellery. In 1900, Paris had over 300 *plumassiers* or feather specialists; today the Lemarié atelier is virtually the only one still in existence. Chanel bought the business along with five other specialist craft ateliers: Michel, specializing in millinery; shoemakers, Massaro; embroidery house, Lesage; button and

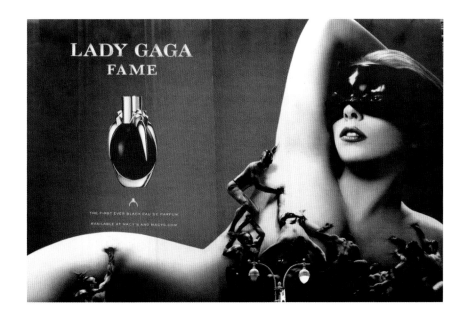

BASIC HIERARCHY OF FASHION

TRICKLE DOWN
Ideas from couture and designer catwalk shows filter down through the fashion market and are used as inspiration for ranges created by high-street retailers.

BUBBLE UP
Ideas from street fashion and cultural subgroups gain momentum to become a trend that bubbles up through the hierarchy of fashion, eventually reaching the top when expensive designer versions are created.

HAUTE COUTURE AND COUTURE

HIGH-END FASHION
LUXURY DESIGNER AND PREMIUM BRANDS

MIDDLE MARKET
DESIGNER DIFFUSION OR BRIDGE LINES
AFFORDABLE LUXURY RETAIL BRANDS
MIDDLE-MARKET RETAIL CHAINS

MASS MARKET
HIGH-STREET MULTIPLE RETAILERS

VALUE MARKET
VALUE FASHION RETAILERS
DISCOUNT RETAILERS

Haute couture sits at the pinnacle of fashion. Although only a small sector of the overall market, its influence on designer and high-street fashion is of great importance. Designers distil ideas from their own couture collections and use them in a more commercial format for their ready-to-wear collections.

In turn the designer and luxury brand ready-to-wear collections set the trends followed by mass-market fashion retailers. When trends work their way down from the top of the market to the bottom, it is known as a trickle-down effect.

Above
Alexis Mabille Haute Couture Autumn/
Winter 2013. A dramatic robe-style silk
coat with a large collar and back draping
into a bow.

costume jewellery makers, Desrues; and the gold- and silversmith, Goossens. While many argue that something as arcane and extravagant as haute couture cannot or should not survive, it seems that demand has not diminished, but shifted to a new set of younger, more fashion-conscious clientele from emerging rich nations such as China, Russia and the Middle East. For the Christian Dior show in July 2013, Belgian designer Raf Simons, responding to this growing international audience, divided the collection into segments for Asia, Africa, Europe and the Americas. Haute couture is a relatively small business in terms of the overall fashion market; the real value is its power as a marketing tool. Global names such as Chanel, Armani and Dior receive valuable press coverage of their haute couture collections, raising the status and desirability of their **brand** and keeping it in the public eye.

Fashion designers that are not recognized by the Chambre Syndicale can still produce exclusive custom-made clothing but this must be marketed as couture rather than haute couture. Prices for couture can still be high. The British designer Giles Deacon produces two or three couture pieces a year and a dress may cost more than £40,000. The price of a Vera Wang wedding dress can be in the region of US$25,000, although in an attempt to keep customers happy during the recession, Wang introduced what she calls **demi-couture** with a lower price tag.

Ready-to-wear

Fashion product that is not custom-made for an individual client is known as **ready-to-wear** or off-the-peg clothing. Ready-to-wear garments are premade, come in predetermined sizes and are usually mass-produced and industrially manufactured. Ready-to-wear fashion is available at all levels of the market including:

> » High-end fashion

> » Middle market

> » High street

> » Value fashion

Middle-market fashion product is designed and priced to cater for customers wishing to purchase at a level between luxury and mass market. A designer or fashion brand that has established itself within the high-end market may decide to introduce a secondary **diffusion line** or **bridge line**, as it is known in the United States, so that they can extend their brand into the middle market. Examples are See by Chloé, Moschino's Cheap & Chic, Donna Karan's DKNY line and Emanuel Ungaro's Emanuel line. Another example of designer diffusion lines are the affordable collections created for stores such as Target, The Outnet, Payless and J. Crew in the US and Debenhams in the UK. High-street retailers such as Banana Republic, Cos, Hoss Intropia and Whistles can also be considered mid-market. The term middle market is not particularly inspiring and is not always perceived by retail brands as a position they wish to aspire to. Some combat this by re-stating their market level, claiming they offer affordable luxury or masstige (prestige for the masses, or mass luxury) rather than mid-market fashion. Affordable luxury is seen as an important market opportunity now that so many fashion consumers view luxury as something that should be available to all, even those with limited budgets.

Mass-market fashion refers to high-street multiples or fashion retail chains such as Gap, Topshop, H&M or Zara, available on high streets in most major cities or towns, or internationally. At this level of the market, terminology can become slightly confusing as 'high street', 'fast fashion' and 'mass market' are descriptions also used in reference to British retailers Primark and New Look, French value chain Kiabi and Germany's Takko. Value retailers have expanded throughout Europe. Primark already has stores in Spain, Germany and the Netherlands, and Takko in Austria, the Czech Republic, Hungary, the Netherlands, Lithuania and Estonia. Worried by the increasing number of value retailers encroaching on its market, the Spanish fashion chain Mango produced a new low-cost line called 'Think Up' in a bid to stay competitive. The 90-piece range was marketed with the slogan, 'Special prices for creative living'.

The demarcation between different levels within the fashion market is becoming ever more complicated and hard to pin down with clarity. An increasing number of fashion companies are implementing strategies to extend their businesses or brands in a bid to appeal to a wider range of customers. As the Mango Think Up example illustrates, a retailer or fashion brand can extend its appeal by introducing more affordably priced products. Alternatively they can reposition upwards by offering luxury and premium products aimed to attract a more discerning customer willing to pay a higher price.

Other fashion markets

In addition to the basic fashion sectors described so far, there are other markets, such as vintage fashion and sustainable fashion, which have emerged and grown over recent years. Vintage or thrift fashion refers to collectable second-hand garments, shoes or accessories from the past sold in specialist vintage stores and on websites or in charity shops.

Above
In 2013 Oscar de la Renta teamed up with The Outnet to produce a 24-piece range selling at more accessible prices than the label's main line.

BRAND PYRAMID

A fashion brand is constructed to make money from merchandise designed for different levels of the market. At the top of the range, the most expensive and luxurious product may be exclusive and available in limited quantity. These couture and ultra-premium ranges may operate as a loss leader but act as a promotional tool to secure the brand's status. To make money, brand companies must extend their offering to a wider range of customers. An example is the **brand architecture** of Armani described below.

Armani Privé: couture and ultra-premium, top-of-the-range product with very high price points. Targets customers in the 35–60 age bracket. Armani Collezioni: priced approximately 20 per cent lower than the main line, this collection is aimed at the discerning customer who cannot afford the signature price points. Emporio Armani: targeted at the young professional aged 25–35. Diffusion line providing contemporary Armani designs. Armani Jeans and A/X Armani Exchange: both aimed at a younger age bracket of 18–30. These collections have a more casual and relaxed style; they make the Armani brand accessible to more consumers.

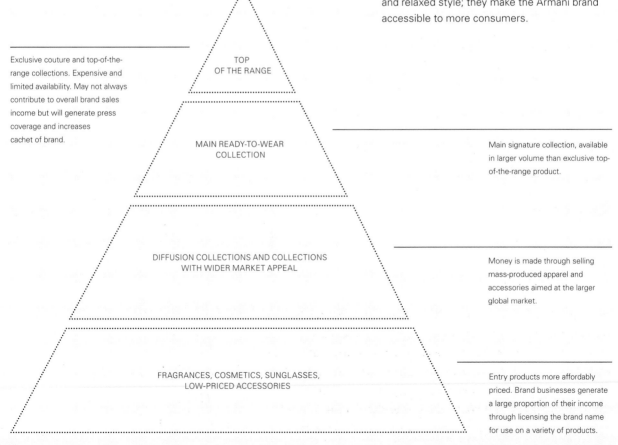

Exclusive couture and top-of-the-range collections. Expensive and limited availability. May not always contribute to overall brand sales income but will generate press coverage and increases cachet of brand.

TOP OF THE RANGE

MAIN READY-TO-WEAR COLLECTION

Main signature collection, available in larger volume than exclusive top-of-the-range product.

DIFFUSION COLLECTIONS AND COLLECTIONS WITH WIDER MARKET APPEAL

Money is made through selling mass-produced apparel and accessories aimed at the larger global market.

FRAGRANCES, COSMETICS, SUNGLASSES, LOW-PRICED ACCESSORIES

Entry products more affordably priced. Brand businesses generate a large proportion of their income through licensing the brand name for use on a variety of products.

An increasing number of consumers choose vintage or thrift as a way to make a fashion statement, stand out from the crowd, save money or be more sustainable and consume less. The scope of the market varies from second-hand merchandise in a thrift or charity store to rare designer dresses. Buying luxury vintage fashion has become an interesting way of investing, as many people now view vintage items as tradable assets. Stores such as Liberty in London and Bergdorf Goodman in New York recognize the potential of vintage, with both retail establishments housing curated selections of vintage fashion. The online world of vintage has also had a makeover. Sites such as It's Vintage Darling or Juno Says Hello offer luxury vintage fashion online.

Eco-fashion, also known as ethical fashion or sustainable fashion, is another growing sector of the market. An increasing number of fashion companies endeavour to ensure their collections are ethically sourced, or at least some elements of their product offer are produced sustainably. Issues of sustainability and ethics affect every aspect of the fashion supply chain, from production of raw materials, clothing manufacture, distribution and marketing through to retail. Determining what is or is not sustainable is extremely complicated, not helped by the fact that sustainable fashion, or eco-fashion, is used as an umbrella term to describe a range of practices that include:

  » Use of certified organic fibres such as cotton or linen

  » Use of renewable fibres such as bamboo and maize

  » Recycling of fibres and garments

  » Use of natural dyes or low-impact dyes

  » Breaking the cycle of consumption by creating a long-lasting product

  » Fair-trade raw materials and fibres

  » Ethical labour and ethical farming practices

  » Reduction in energy consumption

  » Minimal or reduced packaging

It is claimed that the fashion industry is 10–15 years behind the food industry in terms of public understanding and with so many issues to grasp many consumers find the topic confusing. The biggest problem is establishing what can or cannot be termed eco, sustainable or ethical fashion. A growing number of designers, fashion retailers and industry bodies are working together to clarify the issues, set clear standards, introduce regulation and clear labelling and raise

Left, top to bottom
Armani Privé
Armani Collezioni
Emporio Armani
A/X Armani Exchange

Vintage paradise

Beacon's Closet

The three Beacon's Closet stores are well-known destinations for those seeking original vintage finds in New York. The Manhattan store, located near Parsons New School for Design and New York University, is a favourite spot for emerging designers to source inspiration for their work and has featured in *Vanity Fair*, Italian *Vogue* and French *Vogue*. The website has a fresh contemporary vibe and the Beacon's Blog is kept up-to-date with posts on essential fashion information and trends. Key seasonal fashion looks are promoted on the Beacon's Closet homepage with a styled photo shoot worthy of a top fashion magazine.

Stylist Bunny Lampert created this New Year's Eve themed look to promote the holiday season on the Beacon's Closet website. The models are all staff members, including one of the co-owners, Cindy Wheeler. The photograph was shot by Carly Rabalais, who runs the online store.

the profile of sustainable fashion. Opportunities to sell and promote wholesale collections of eco-fashion are improving, with London Fashion Week, Prêt à Porter Paris®, Berlin Fashion Week, New York Fashion Week and Portland Fashion Week in the US all incorporating sustainable fashion within their remit. There is also an increasing number of dedicated eco-fashion weeks, conferences and related trade initiatives designed to educate and support the growth of this sector, for example Vancouver Eco-Fashion Week and Dublin's Better Fashion Week.

There is evidence of a new kind of luxury consumer seeking out eco-friendly fashion products. In Brazil, Oskar Metsavaht created Osklen, a luxury brand that since 1999 has been producing pieces with an 'e-fabrics tag', created to inform the buyer about the sustainable origin of the products.

The global fashion market

Fashion is a global industry with a market value in the region of US$1.7 trillion. The market encompasses all levels of fashion, from mass-market to haute couture, and all types of apparel from a cheap T-shirt to a hand-made dress. Millions of people worldwide are employed in designing, manufacturing, marketing and selling fashion, accessories and textile products. For the majority of designers and businesses, fashion is an international enterprise. Even brands that uphold the value of local design and manufacture, such as 'Made in America' premium denim brand 3Sixteen, may buy the traditional selvedge denim from Japan, and sell the finished jeans in North America, Europe, Asia and Australia.

Global fashion weeks and trade fairs

Traditionally the main centres for fashion were Paris, London, Milan and New York, with each hosting bi-annual Fashion Week events to showcase the women's collections. Menswear collections are shown twice a year in Paris, London and Milan. There is growing pressure to mount a New York showcase for menswear.

Perhaps less well known is the full range of cities that host Fashion Week shows and events: Amsterdam, Beijing, Berlin, Brisbane, Cape Town, Istanbul, Johannesburg, Kiev, Lagos, London, Miami, Milan, Moscow, Mumbai, New York, Paris, Stockholm, Sydney, Tokyo, Toronto and Zurich. Added to this is an enormous number of trade fairs. In Europe for example, Berlin hosts Bread & Butter, an international fair for streetwear, denim and sportswear brands. Düsseldorf holds the CPD womenswear and accessories fair. Spain

Treasure from trash

Michelle Lowe-Holder

Michelle Lowe-Holder is driven by the desire to produce beautiful, dramatic accessories using sustainable and ethical practices. A philosophy of zero waste and ethical production underpins her manufacturing methods. Lowe-Holder's **upcycled** collars and cuffs are made using ends of lines and 'cabbage' (scraps from previous collections), biodegradable paper and vegan leather. Techniques like **flocking** are used to velvetize, revive and recolour thrift-shop bangles, necklaces and rings. Collaboration with SEWA, the Self-Employed Women's Association, an initiative that gives women homeworkers living in the city slums of India regular work and fair rates for their skills, has enabled Lowe-Holder to add beading to the repertoire of intricate artisanal techniques such as smocking, pleating, folding and foiling used to create her hand-made contemporary pieces. The collection is exhibited in Paris at Première Classe and stocked in boutiques worldwide.

A new modern opulence of metallic leather cut-offs and vintage ribbons highlighted by gold and silver accents: Michelle Lowe-Holder's Elizabeth collection is inspired by Queen Elizabeth I. Delicate scalloped edges mixed with lacquered wood and marbled cork embody Tudor detailing in these modern hand-embellished pieces.

is well known for the manufacture of footwear and leather goods. The country holds an international leather goods trade fair, MOMAD Metropolis incorporating Modacalzado + Iberpiel in Madrid and Futurmoda in Alicante. This is only a minute selection of what is on offer; there are also international bridal shows, swimwear collections, denim and sportswear trade events, dance fashion and full-figured fashion collections.

The emergence of global fashion in so many locations is good news for new designers in markets around the world, giving them a platform to show to local and regional press and buyers as well as an increasing number of international fashion professionals who attend. However, the sway of the big four fashion nations, France, the UK, Italy and the US, and their fashion capitals should not be underestimated. The following section outlines the main points.

Paris

Paris is the spiritual home of fashion and the epicentre of haute couture. The haute couture shows take place each year; Spring/Summer collections are shown in January, and Autumn/Winter in July. Men's ready-to-wear works on a different timescale: shows in January feature collections for the following Autumn/Winter; June is the showcase for the next Spring/Summer. There are fewer menswear shows so this is a much smaller event than Paris Fashion Week; however, the menswear market is growing. The women's ready-to-wear shows are Autumn/Winter in March and Spring/Summer at the end of September/early October. Paris Fashion Week is extremely important and many designers from all over the world choose Paris to show their seasonal ready-to-wear collections, knowing that the fashion press and buyers from the most prestigious boutiques and department stores will flock to the city to view the runway shows. Rick Owens, from the United States, Ann Demeulemeester and Dries Van Noten from Belgium, Viktor & Rolf from Amsterdam, Vivienne Westwood and Stella McCartney from the UK, Costume National from Italy and Zucca, Comme des Garçons and Junko Shimada from Japan are just some of the foreign designers showing in Paris.

As well as Paris Fashion Week, there is also Prêt à Porter Paris® at the Porte de Versailles, a trade show where over a thousand exhibitors from a variety of different fashion markets exhibit their product. Prêt à Porter Paris® is an international brand with several sub-branded shows: Atmosphère's in Paris; The Box, an accessory fair that takes place in both Paris and New York; The Train, a fashion and accessory trade fair held in the Terminal Warehouse building in New York's Chelsea district; and Living Room, held in Tokyo for womenswear, menswear, fashion accessories and lifestyle products. Première Vision, or PV, held twice a year – in February for the following Spring/Summer season and September for the next Autumn/Winter – is the largest European textile trade show and a major date in the calendar for international designers and buyers. The fair is an important trade opportunity for textile suppliers from all over the world but fashion designers and buyers visit because of its focus on colour and trend prediction. Paris also hosts Première Classe, Le Cuir à Paris, Paris sur Mode and Woman Paris.

Above
Prêt à Porter Paris® is a leading international fashion trade fair and recognized brand name associated with several key fashion industry trade events in Paris, New York and Tokyo.

London

Ever since the Swinging Sixties and Mary Quant, London has been famous for its street style and avant-garde fashion and this remains one of the city's biggest claims to fashion fame. During the 1990s and up to 2011, it was the designers themselves who became London's greatest fashion export. John Galliano, Alexander McQueen and Stella McCartney worked in fashion houses in Paris, and many other hard-working British or London-trained designers continue to find employment in New York, Milan, Hong Kong, China, India and Japan. London is a magnet for fashion students from around the globe. After graduation some stay on, start their own labels and make London their base.

London Fashion Week is a major event on the fashion circuit. British designers and brands such as Paul Smith, Vivienne Westwood Red Label, Jasper Conran, Julien Macdonald, Christopher Kane, JW Anderson, Matthew Williamson, Daks, Temperley London, House of Holland, Margaret Howell, Mulberry and Burberry all show in London, as well as some overseas labels and international designers who have made London their home.

For wholesale brands there are trade shows such as Pure London, which gives a platform to over 800 brands. Although not traditional fashion trade fairs, the Spring and Autumn fairs at the NEC in Birmingham and Top Drawer and Pulse in London showcase companies selling gifts and fashion accessories, such as bags, scarves, hats or jewellery.

Milan

Italian couture, or Alta Moda, can be traced back to 1951 when the Marquis Gian Battista Giorgini held the first haute couture fashion show in Florence for a select few designers and clients. Rome took over as the centre for high fashion in Italy during the 1960s but lost ground during the 1970s and 1980s to Milan, which became the commercial capital for Italian ready-to-wear. Today, Italy is an important country for the design and manufacture of luxury and mid-market fashion, with particular expertise in leather goods, footwear, knitwear and high-quality ready-to-wear for both men and women. Milan is a major trade centre where most of the design houses have their headquarters and where the majority of Italian fashion shows take place. It is also an important location for Italian fashion magazine publication, so satellite industries such as styling, photography and modelling also gravitate to the city. Italy is well known for its textile industry; Florence and Prato are important

Below
Musician Graham Coxon of rock band Blur wears British tweed from Cordings, a traditional outfitters selling fine-quality British clothing.

centres for the manufacture of yarn and knitwear, Como produces silk fabrics and the Piedmont area manufactures wool textiles. Key industry trade fairs and catwalk shows are held in Milan, Florence and Rome. Milan hosts Milano Moda Donna for women's ready-to-wear and Milano Moda Uomo for menswear. AltaRomaAltaModa in Rome shows Italian couture and high-level ready-to-wear and Florence is the location for the Pitti Filati knitwear and yarn fair, Pitti Uomo menswear and Pitti Bimbo childrenswear trade fair.

New York

New York is the heart of the US fashion and apparel industry and some of the world's most recognizable brands, like Donna Karan, Ralph Lauren, Tommy Hilfiger and Kenneth Cole have their offices and design studios in the city. American fashion is renowned for its relaxed, fluid, casual and chic style, epitomized by designers like Lauren and Donna Karan as well as Michael Kors and Calvin Klein. Retailers like Gap and Banana Republic also have strong global appeal for their accessible and desirable fashion.

Historically, apparel and textile manufacturing was one of the US's largest sectors. It has suffered a decline due to competition from manufacturing countries like China. There is a drive to support a renaissance for American apparel manufacturing. However, 'Made in America' fashion is more expensive to make and needs to sell at a premium to be viable. Nanette Lepore is a designer who champions the cause of local production. She sells her contemporary women's collection in stores like Saks Fifth Avenue and Bloomingdale's; the garments are manufactured in six sewing factories situated in New York City's garment district. Her company occupies six floors in a building on West 35th Street, evidence enough that her strategy for premium-priced, locally designed and produced fashion is working.

Fashion Week in New York attracts 100,000 trade and press visitors and provides huge economic benefit to the city, generating US$850 million in visitor spending each year. Calvin Klein, 3.1 Phillip Lim, Anna Sui, BCBGMaxazria, Carolina Herrera, Nanette Lepore, Diane von Furstenberg, Donna Karan, J. Crew, Tory Burch, Michael Kors, Zac Posen, Reem Acra and Clover Canyon are just some of the names that show at this prestigious event.

In the US, Los Angeles plays a vital role in promoting fashion on the West Coast. Los Angeles also holds two major international textiles and sourcing fairs, GlobalTex and L.A. Textile. Portland, Oregon is an important centre for fashion and active sportswear companies. Nike, adidas, Columbia Sportswear, Jantzen swimwear and Keen footwear all have headquarters there.

London Edge

The London Edge trade fair caters for the alternative clubwear market. Within this market there are several niche categories such as gothic, punk, cyber, techno, glam rock, heavy metal, rockabilly, industrial, underground, festival ethnic and biker. London Central trade fair focuses on urban streetwear, showcasing brands covering the skate, hip hop, surf and hippy end of the youth market.

Fashion seasons and the global market

There is much debate concerning the global market and its effect on the demarcation of the Spring/Summer and Autumn/Winter fashion seasons. Seasonality becomes less relevant when collections are sold globally. Designers must service customers in both the northern and southern hemispheres and be able to sell in stores in the Middle East, Far East, Russia, North America and South America. This has led to the pre-season collections – resort and pre-fall. Resort hits stores in November and is aimed at customers heading for warmer climes during the winter, but also those who live in the southern hemisphere. Pre-fall, arriving in store for May, offers transseasonal products, usually in lightweight materials but in colours that give a foretaste of the Autumn/Winter season to come.

Emerging global markets

There are several options for a company looking to grow its business. One is to be more effective in selling to existing markets, by increasing the number of customers and/or raising prices or lowering costs. Another is to increase the number of markets in which its products are sold. Developing global markets are an important source for growth for fashion companies. According to a McKinsey & Company report published in 2013, emerging countries will have 25 per cent of the women's luxury apparel market by 2015 and mid-market apparel will rise from 37 per cent to 50 per cent in the period from 2013 to 2015. The increase will be fuelled by the growth

Opposite
The Canadian designer Erdem Moralioglu showcases his eponymous fashion label on the catwalk at London Fashion Week. Spring/Summer 2014.

Top
A digital screen displays images from the shows outside New York's Fashion Week, formerly sponsored by Mercedes-Benz.

Above
The Proenza Schouler Spring/Summer 2014 show at New York Fashion Week.

of wealthy middle-class consumers and the emergence of megacities such as Shanghai, São Paulo and Moscow, and middle-weight cities such as Harbin (China), Luanda (Angola) and Puebla (Mexico).

Brazil, Russia, India, China (BRIC)

The key regions for this growth are the countries collectively known as BRIC: Brazil, Russia, India and China. The Global Retail Development Index™ (GRDI), researched and published by A.T. Kearney, is an annual study that ranks the top 30 developing countries for retail expansion worldwide. The results for 2013 ranked Brazil number one for retail growth for the third year in a row. Brazil is South America's largest apparel market.

Although Russia's gross domestic product (GDP) slowed during 2013, retail spending was still developing. Russia is a key market for most global luxury brands but the main driver of growth is the middle-class consumer who looks for affordable luxury.

From 2012 to 2014 there was a slowdown in the Chinese luxury market. According to industry analysts Bain & Company, China's luxury consumers tended to do more shopping abroad. The Bain & Company report stated that women, mainly middle-income professionals in larger cities, now account for 50 per cent of China's high-end purchasing (Bain & Company 2013).

China was ranked number four on the GRDI. Even though this was a drop in position, sales of Western apparel in China benefited from the expansion programmes of fashion mass-market retailers including Uniqlo, H&M, Zara and Gap. E-commerce is also driving growth for sales; according to analysts from Citigroup Inc. the Internet shopping market in China will double from 2012 to 2016.

A report published in 2013 by the Confederation of Indian Industry and market research firm IMRB International announced that the Indian luxury market grew approximately 15 per cent over the preceding three years, although this market is still considerably smaller in size than that in China. Luxury-only shopping malls are opening in India's major cities to service India's new wealthy middle-class consumers, who have a penchant for luxury watches and women's fashion accessories. Trading legislation is complicated in India but in 2012 the situation improved when the Indian government allowed for 100 per cent foreign investment for single-brand retailers; this enabled Brooks Brothers, Kenneth Cole and Armani Junior to open, and Roberto Cavalli and Christian Louboutin opened standalone boutiques.

United Arab Emirates (UAE)

Dubai aims to become a global fashion hub by 2020. Visitor numbers to the region are expected to rise to 20 million, fuelling the potential for the development of an indigenous fashion and retail industry. Dubai is the financial centre of the UAE and location of the world's largest shopping mall. Naturally most of the world's prestigious luxury and fashion brands are housed in the UAE shopping malls. Chinese customers are so important that most retailers recruit a proportion of their sales staff from China. In terms of mid-market retailers UAE has the usual range of European brands like H&M, Topshop and Zara and American retailers such as Victoria's Secret, Abercrombie & Fitch and Hollister. A further wave of growth is expected to develop in Abu Dhabi, the region's capital and second-largest city.

Future markets

As the markets described above mature, so further growth for luxury fashion brands and mass-market retailers will spread to newer, less developed markets in Latin America, Asia Pacific and Africa. According to market analyst Euromonitor, Asia Pacific could become the biggest region in the world for luxury goods by 2018. Africa is also experiencing growth in the number of high net worth individuals and an increasingly wealthy middle class, with Angola and Nigeria emerging markets for luxury. Ermenegildo Zegna and Hugo Boss have stores in Lagos, Nigeria. Prada has a store in Luanda, the capital of Angola, and two stores in Casablanca, Morocco, one for womenswear and one for menswear. In addition, as consumers' taste for more affordable or less ostentatious brands increases, so a second wave of mid-level luxury brands will continue to grow. An example is Michael Kors with stores in China, South Korea, Singapore, Japan, Indonesia and the Philippines.

What is marketing?

Marketing is intriguing in that it has been variously described as a business function, business philosophy and also as a management or social process. Marketing should really be viewed as a holistic system connecting a business with its customers. Professor Philip Kotler, who has been described as the godfather of modern marketing, believes that what makes a company is its marketing. Kotler considers marketing to be both a science and an art. It is strategic and creative, requiring systematic research and analysis as well as innovation, intuition and gut instinct.

Below
Sweden has a strong reputation for cutting-edge and directional denim brands. Dr. Denim, started in 2004 by the Graah family in Gothenburg, exhibit their collection at trade events such as Terminal 2 in Copenhagen, Bread & Butter in Berlin and Modefabriek in Amsterdam.

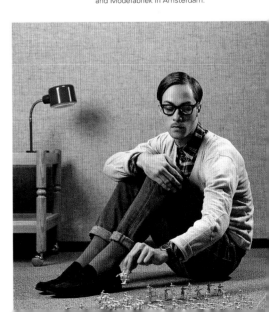

The range and potential of marketing can be almost limitless; it may start way before any product has been designed and continue long after a customer has purchased. This scope and multi-dimensional nature could make a clear definition appear rather elusive. However, the next section will address this by presenting four definitions that capture the essentials and simplify the complexities of marketing. The key points raised by the individual definitions are then examined in more depth.

Marketing definitions

Each of the definitions chosen below highlights a particular facet of the marketing dynamic. Viewed together they reveal the broad scope of marketing.

> *"Marketing is the management process responsible for identifying, anticipating and satisfying customer requirements profitably." Chartered Institute of Marketing (CIM) UK*

> *"Marketing is the human activity directed at satisfying needs and wants through an exchange process." Kotler (1980)*

> *"Marketing is the social and managerial process by which individuals and groups obtain what they need and want through creating and exchanging products of value with others." Kotler (1991)*

> *"Marketing is creating, communicating and delivering value to a target market profitably." Kotler (2008)*

Collectively these definitions summarize the fundamental elements of marketing as:

» An understanding of customer requirements

» The ability to create, communicate and deliver value

» A social process

» An exchange process

» A managerial and business process

While the fundamentals of marketing may be similar for any industry, the exact nature of their application will differ from one sector to another. In the following pages we will see how each of these elements of marketing can be applied in the context of fashion, and, in particular, how they relate to the connection between the consumer and their clothing.

Below
A Vivienne Westwood bag promoted in-store as an exclusive gift at Christmas.

An understanding of customer requirements

The definition from the Chartered Institute of Marketing draws attention to the significance of identifying and anticipating the needs of customers. Naturally this is an important first step in being able to design, produce and deliver merchandise that satisfies or indeed exceeds consumer desires, requirements or expectations. However, it is not just in relation to product that customer requirements need to be considered. The visual and written **content** that consumers expect as part of their engagement and relationship with fashion brands must also be factored into the marketing equation. Content in the form of a constant stream of up-to-date material on a website, Twitter feed, Facebook, Instagram, Tumblr or Pinterest page is now essential marketing currency.

An underlying concept of marketing is to produce what people want. It is therefore important to carry out research in order to identify who the consumers are and determine what they might require. While it is true that many professionals within the fashion industry might have an intuitive understanding of their customers, this in itself does not eliminate the need for research. Predicting future fashion and market trends and working to anticipate consumer demand is a significant element of marketing and a key issue for the fashion and apparel industry. Some high-street fashion retailers can go from design to delivery in a matter of weeks, but the reality is that many apparel and manufacturing businesses start their initial research and design developments months in advance of a season or product launch; adidas, for example, can take 12–18 months to develop and produce a new product. This lengthy process time, also known as the **lead-time**, and the cost of prototyping or sampling a collection are the reasons why anticipating the future is so crucial. Marketing research, forecasting and consumer research will be explained in more depth in Chapters 3 and 4.

Creating, communicating and delivering value

Successful business relies on a strong and effective interrelationship between the activities of creating, communicating and delivering. If one of these aspects fails, it will affect the efficacy of the total result. It is no good generating engaging content and advertising wonderful products if they are not delivered. Similarly if the online experience or physical products do not match the quality levels expected by customers, or service is not up to standard, then value will not have been delivered.

So what exactly is value? Value does not just refer to low price or what might be termed 'good value'. In this instance it is used to

"Marketing should be an ethos (rather than a department) that pervades every facet of a business."

Martin Butler

express a much larger concept and refers to the range of potential issues that customers might value, care about or connect with emotionally. Value may be contained within the product offering – the actual fashion range or collection – but it can also relate to the total **brand experience** at every stage of the consumer journey and the inherent status of a brand. Value is also linked to the overall service a company might provide and to customer experience and satisfaction. The concept of value works both up and down the supply chain; whatever is delivered must not only be of value to consumers but it must also create profit and value for the business as well.

Remarkable marketing

"Remarkable marketing is the art of building things worth noticing right into your product or service. Not slapping on marketing as a last-minute add-on, but understanding that if your offering itself isn't remarkable, it's invisible." Seth Godin

The company LittleMissMatched was founded in the US by three entrepreneurs who recognized a great marketing opportunity – how to solve the age-old problem of the disappearing sock.

"Why do we have to wear socks that match?" the entrepreneurial friends pondered. "Why not start a company that sells socks that don't match, why not sell them in odd numbers so even if the dryer eats one, it doesn't matter."

LittleMissMatched only ever sells socks in odd numbers, three in a pair! Now that is remarkable. And if you get three odd socks that co-ordinate in fun and colourful ways then in essence you get three combinations per pair instead of just one. Revolutionary! Not just boring socks but a crazy way to express yourself and be creative. With a core philosophy of 'nothing matches but anything goes', the kooky founders of Miss Matched Inc. thought they had created tweenie sock heaven. They saw their market as girls from four years to teens, but to their surprise the idea caught the imagination of a much wider audience. Now LittleMissMatched is a full lifestyle brand with a range of products for children and adults, including colourful and mismatched gloves and hats, sleepwear, flip-flops, bedding, stationery, gifts and hair accessories.

Below
LittleMissMatched has a unique take on marketing. They offer three socks in a pair; while each of the socks co-ordinates with the others in the set, none of them are a complete match. This novel approach solves the problem of 'the missing sock'.

Marketing as a social process

Fashion has a unique ability to be used as a vehicle for social connection and communication. Individuals often choose to dress in a specific and recognizable style so that they can express their ideas visually and signal membership to a like-minded group, joining

Communicating value

The Boden Owner's Club Manual

Boden is a British online and mail order clothing brand selling to over a million customers in the UK, Europe and the United States. Boden produce colourful, quirky and distinctive womenswear and menswear collections and lines for children and teens. Inspired by the high standards of US mail order companies, Johnnie Boden started his pioneering upmarket catalogue in the UK in 1991. A website launched in 1999. The brand owed its initial success to the fact that it broke new ground by delivering directly to the customer's home. It is amazing to think that when the company started, online retailing was a novel idea. Now overseas sales count for over half the business, with US sales a third of the revenue.

The website and catalogue are used not only to sell product but also to communicate the Boden brand ethos. Online this is easier to accomplish; the challenge is how to include extra content in a printed catalogue. One tool used to great effect by the company is to insert a special edition brand booklet. Each edition is unique, beautifully designed and jam-packed with information on the details and quality of garment design and the value of the Boden product.

Right and below left
The designers behind the Boden brand believe design details make a difference, so The Boden Owner's Club Manual is used to highlight the hidden extras that make a Boden trenchcoat so special.

Below right
The cost-per-wear principle is used to calculate and communicate the true value of a pair of Boden chinos. By dividing the retail price by the number of times the trousers have been worn over the years, it is possible to determine their value per wear. The message is that although the chinos might not be the cheapest on the market, they are good quality and will stand the test of time.

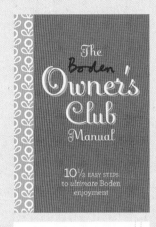

The Boden Owner's Club Manual

10½ EASY STEPS to *ultimate* Boden enjoyment

Step 4:
Appreciate the hidden **extras**

We believe that when it comes to clothing, no detail is small enough to be overlooked.

We're never happier than when we're agonising over an unexpected feature others might find trifling – such as the contrast trim on the reverse of our Trench Coat belt. Some of the detail we've created in a whole host of our products is purely for an 'audience of one'. But *you'll know it's there* and that's reason enough for us.

8

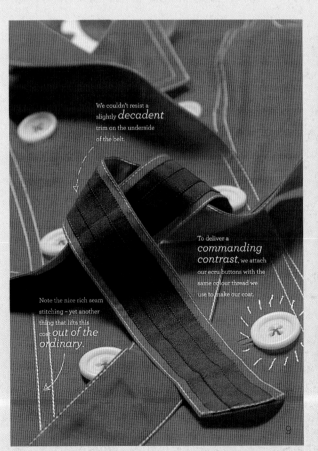

We couldn't resist a slightly *decadent* trim on the underside of the belt.

To deliver a *commanding contrast*, we attach our ecru buttons with the same colour thread we use to make our coat.

Note the nice rich seam stitching – yet another thing that lifts this coat *out of the ordinary.*

9

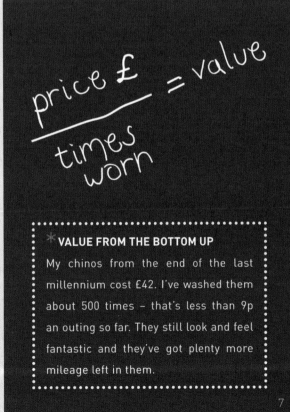

price £ / times worn = value

* **VALUE FROM THE BOTTOM UP**
My chinos from the end of the last millennium cost £42. I've washed them about 500 times – that's less than 9p an outing so far. They still look and feel fantastic and they've got plenty more mileage left in them.

7

"Buzzmarketing captures the attention of consumers and the media to the point where talking about your brand or company becomes entertaining, fascinating and newsworthy."

Mark Hughes

Opposite
Exactitudes, a project by Rotterdam-based photographer Ari Versluis and stylist Ellie Uyttenbroek, documents the dress of fashion tribes from around the world.

Top row
Geeks – London 2008
Skinny boys in V-necks and specs display their fashion geek credentials.

Second row
Charitas – Rotterdam 2007
Power ladies dressed to impress in suits or skirts and structured jackets; handbags at the ready, these women mean business.

Third row
Yupster boys – New York 2006
Yupster = yuppie + hipster. Grown-ups that don't grow up, this tribe of urban creative professional hipsters came of age during the first wave of indie rock and hip hop. Yupster uniform: T-shirt that communicates values or affiliations, zippered hoodie and all-important cross-body bag.

Bottom row
Pin-ups – London 2008
Girls inspired by 1940s and 1950s pin-up style. Pencil skirts and blouses with cinched-in waists accentuate the figure. Retro-styled hair is adorned with accessories or hats.

what is known as a **style tribe**. This is a term for a collection of people who dress in a common distinctive style. They may not actually know each other directly but might share similar values and cultural attitudes; by adopting a specific mode of dress, tribe members can shape their identity and gain a sense of belonging. **Social networking services (SNS)** such as photo-sharing apps Today I'm Wearing, Whatyouwear.in, StyleTag or StyleShare make it easy to share and compare looks and fashion tips with others.

The social style community network Polyvore, for example, enables members to be an online fashion stylist. By piecing together an outfit using images from the Internet, members can create and share fashion collages, or Polyvore sets, as they are known. Formed in the US in 2007, and with more than 15 million users visiting the site each month, Polyvore is a powerful tool for brands to employ as part of their social media strategy. Most key fashion brands have a presence on Polyvore, with a dedicated page showcasing their products and links to their own selling site or an online stockist. This has proven a successful tactic for driving sales.

Style tribes – Exactitudes

Exactitudes (a contraction of exact and attitudes) is a project by Rotterdam-based photographer Ari Versluis and stylist Ellie Uyttenbroek. They work together to systematically document the conspicuous dress codes of numerous fashion style tribes around the globe. Selected individuals are photographed standing in an identical pose in a studio setting. The resulting photographs are placed in a grid framework that serves to amplify the striking similarities of each member of the style tribe.

The Exactitudes project illustrates clearly the subliminal influence and pull of a style tribe. The people photographed by Versluis and Uyttenbroek were spotted in the street and had no personal knowledge of the others photographed in their tribe. Although only 12 individuals appear in each tribal collective, responses to the work indicate that many people who viewed the photographs were able to identify themselves in one of the featured tribes.

We frequently purchase clothes either consciously or subconsciously based on what peers, friends, colleagues or celebrities are wearing. When consumers promote products or pass on style ideas to each other it is known as **peer marketing**. In many cases this can prove to be a far more powerful marketing tool than advertising or promotion controlled directly by a company. When a marketing message spreads rapidly from person to person it is known as **viral marketing**. Social media and digital

communication are instrumental in the impact and potential of this marketing medium. By taking advantage of already established online resources, such as Facebook and YouTube, viral marketing utilizes the connectivity among individuals to capture attention and create a buzz.

Exchanging products and value with others

Marketing is an exchange process. The commodities for exchange are the goods and services and the currency is of course money. However, as stated previously, there are other commodities of value to bear in mind, such as creative ideas, information and content, generated both by a brand and its customers. The purpose is to generate engagement, connectivity and positive emotion. Viewed creatively, the exchange process can be seen as a trade system with exciting potential to generate a diversity of assets for both consumers and businesses. A business model that incorporates this wider view is **co-creation**. This is when a company creates products or generates content in co-operation with consumers or social media followers. There are several types of co-creation. **Crowdsourcing** is when ideas, services, content or design tasks, which would normally be carried out by company employees or suppliers, are outsourced to the public, especially the online community, thus allowing the larger collective or 'crowd' to get involved. Crowdsourcing projects are usually achieved through collaboration, competition or popularity vote.

MARKETING AS AN EXCHANGE PROCESS

Marketing can be viewed as an exchange process or system. The purpose is to generate a diversity of assets for both the company and its customers.

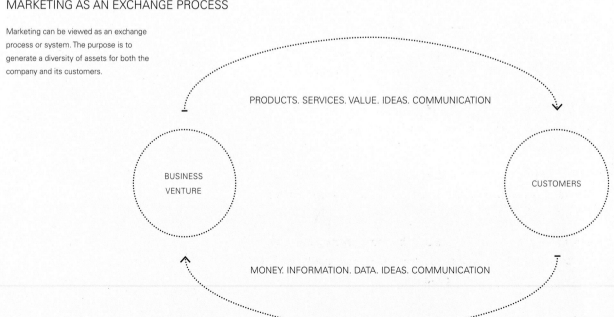

PRODUCTS. SERVICES. VALUE. IDEAS. COMMUNICATION

BUSINESS
VENTURE

CUSTOMERS

MONEY. INFORMATION. DATA. IDEAS. COMMUNICATION

An example is Krush, a crowd-curated marketplace for lifestyle and performance fashion that caters to both brands and consumers. The site allows users a sneak peek of products before they go into production. Members can 'upvote' or 'downvote' designs and share products on a variety of social networks. The member that generates the most feedback on a particular garment wins that item once it is produced. Brands using this platform gain valuable insight into consumer preferences, enabling them to evaluate a product's popularity before investing in full-scale production. Krush.com revenue is derived from selling tailored data reports to brands and by pre-selling branded products to their members, from which Krush retains a percentage.

Crowdsourcing allows value to be created jointly by a company and its users. It opens up the possibilities for exchange and brings diversity and new ideas into a company. The benefit is that it allows a company to communicate with its consumer base, gain knowledge of their needs and preferences and reduce risk by producing product or designs that consumers want. Users and consumers of the online community have been termed Generation C by analysts at trendwatching.com (the C stands for content). They are not related by age but by an attitude to sharing creative content via the Internet. The benefit of crowdsourcing is that it democratizes the process of design, shifting emphasis from manufacturers towards consumers. This user-centred approach has advantages over manufacturer-centred innovation in that users can create exactly what they want rather than relying on manufacturers to do it for them.

A managerial and business process

It is important not to lose sight of the purpose of marketing, and remember it is designed to ensure a business can flourish and generate a profit. Marketing must therefore be managed as an integrated function of business. The ultimate aim is not only to satisfy customers but also to ensure an advantageous result for the business. As the Chartered Institute of Marketing's definition states:

> *"Marketing is the management process responsible for identifying, anticipating and satisfying customer requirements profitably."*

Chapter 2 explains the main concepts behind marketing strategy and examines the key strategic tools available to the marketer. The first of these is the **marketing mix**.

Crowdfunding

Raising finance is one of the main challenges facing independent fashion designers and new businesses. Instead of trying to obtain large sums from limited sources or going to the banks for investment, **crowdfunding** switches the idea around by asking a large number of people to invest a small amount of money. Kickstarter and Indiegogo, early pioneers of this revolutionary concept, saw the Internet as a tool for tapping into the potential of the crowd. A second wave of funding sites includes sites specializing in art and design projects. FashionStake, Catwalk Genius, I Am La Mode and AudaCity of Fashion were set up specifically to launch fashion ventures. There are three main types of crowdfunding: donation, debt and equity.

Donation crowdfunding

Investors donate money because they believe in a project or cause. Rewards are offered in exchange for the investment, such as a small gift product from the collection. Once the recipient reaches their target, their responsibility is to complete the project and ensure investors receive their reward in a timely manner.

Debt crowdfunding

Also known as peer-to-peer (p2p) lending. The return for investing is financial. Investors receive their money back and gain interest on their loan. A fashion collection can be sold online and the proceeds will be split between the designer, the crowdfunders and other investors. The recipient's responsibility is to achieve reasonable sales of a collection so that all parties can be suitably rewarded.

Equity crowdfunding

People invest in a business in exchange for equity, which means they receive shares and own a stake in the business. The incentive for investment is to see the business flourish; higher profits will secure higher dividends for investors. This is an ongoing relationship. The recipient needs to run the business effectively, and consult with stakeholders, with updates on business performance.

The benefits of crowdfunding

With donation or debt crowdfunding, you retain control of your company and don't have to sell a financial share.

You may be able to avoid taking a high-interest bank loan.

You will learn quickly if your business idea appeals to investors and consumers.

On many sites the community can post comments and question you on your intentions. This will force you to set achievable goals, be held accountable and possibly alter your approach.

There is good potential for PR if you get fully funded.

Funders often share about the projects they back, which can lead to more potential backers for your business.

Fully funded

AudaCity of Fashion and Ada Zanditon

Words from Benjamin Disraeli, "Success is the child of audacity", are the inspiration behind the naming of crowdfunding site AudaCity of Fashion. The site acts as a direct channel for funding for new designers and those with innovative fashion concepts they wish to launch. Being able to collaborate with an audience from the initial stages of a project, receive feedback and be supported by the energy and resources of a passionate community is the recipe that founder Muriel Dupas believes will spur a new generation of aspiring fashion entrepreneurs to success. One designer who gained full funding through the site is Ada Zanditon. She made her debut at London Fashion Week in 2009 and her work now sells in boutiques worldwide. Each season Ada Zanditon creates innovative fashion films, showcased at London Fashion Week and the Berlin Fashion Film Festival, in a number of genres. The films have become part of the brand's signature; they help create a talking point and provide a fresh avenue for promotion with fashion, arts and lifestyle press hosting the videos on their sites. The funding target was set at £5,000 with twelve pledge levels available from £5 to £1,300. Rewards included a logo keyring, a signed Ada Zanditon illustration, a limited-edition printed silk scarf and an invitation to London Fashion Week.

Ada Zanditon swimwear on the catwalk at London Fashion Week.

The crowdfunding community can potentially become your customer base.

It can be a great way to see if there is a market for a new product.

The disadvantages of crowdfunding

You might only raise small amounts from a large number of funders. Significant amounts of capital from targeted investors may be preferable.

You are required to expose inside information about your business on the Internet, potentially giving competitors an advantage.

If your product sells well but you cannot meet demand promptly, you risk hurting your professional reputation and brand.

Crowdfunding is not viable as a long-term strategy for funding the growth of a small business.

Top tips for getting funded

Have a compelling story and clear project – funders have to understand who you are, what you want to achieve and why they might want to support you.

Set a realistic funding target – assess this carefully, as you get nothing if you don't reach your target. Check out projects that have been fully funded; analyse what made them appealing.

Great photos and an engaging video – projects with a video have a much higher rate of success. Make sure yours is high-quality; good content is more likely to go viral.

Offer attractive rewards – the motivation for most backers is the satisfaction of supporting an exciting project. However, the rewards are an added incentive.

Strong communication and marketing – be active in promoting your project. The success of your campaign is linked to the 'buzz' around it. Consider marketing prior to launching your project.

2

Marketing Strategy

"Are you at the store? Or is the store at you? And then there's mobile, the store is in your pocket. The game is to satisfy demand wherever and whenever it is."

Tige Savage

This chapter introduces the fundamentals of marketing strategy and explains the essential toolkit available to the marketer. The key strategic principles of market **segmentation**, **targeting**, **positioning**, **differentiation** and **competitive advantage** are explained and illustrated with examples and case studies detailing how fashion designers determine a **unique selling proposition** and create a distinctive **signature style** for their brands. The final section of the chapter introduces the concept of strategic planning and explains the rationale behind writing a **marketing plan**.

Below
Kate Moss appears as a mannequin in the window of Topshop during the launch of her first collection for the retailer. Signing the supermodel was a strategy designed to appeal to the young, fashion-conscious customers that the retailer aimed to attract. Topshop positions itself as a brand offering cutting-edge fashion at affordable prices.

What is marketing strategy?

A marketing strategy outlines how a business intends to market its brand, products and services to existing and potential customers. The initial step in devising a strategy is to define the marketing objectives the business wishes to achieve, set out principal strategic targets and establish the time-frame in which they should be accomplished. The objectives and strategies for achieving them will vary according to the size and goals of the business concerned. A large global corporation, for example, may have a significantly different structure or way of operating compared to an independent niche company or self-employed designer operating out of a tiny studio. However, the overall processes involved in marketing are in fact very similar and can be summarized as:

> » 1. Identifying business opportunities
>
> » 2. Developing products and services
>
> » 3. Attracting customers
>
> » 4. Retaining customers
>
> » 5. Delivering value
>
> » 6. Fulfilling orders and business agreements

Each process is intimately linked to the others, so the failure of one has the potential to jeopardize the business as a whole and negatively affect customer perception of the company or brand. To be successful a business venture must therefore carry out all these processes effectively. This is where the marketing mix comes into play. It is instrumental in supporting a unified approach to the business and marketing. This blend of criteria details the way in which the business will achieve its unique place in the market.

The marketing mix

The marketing mix provides a framework that can be used to manage marketing and incorporate it within a business context. The concept of the marketing mix is that several strategic ingredients need to be considered and blended effectively to achieve the marketing and strategic goals of a company. The principles that underpin the marketing mix were first shaped in the US during the 1940s and 1950s. The term was originally coined in response to the idea that marketing managers were considered as "mixers of ingredients". Neil H. Borden, Professor of Advertising at Harvard

Business School, originally listed 12 marketing variables, but in the 1960s, E. Jerome McCarthy rationalized these into four simpler variables – product, price, place and promotion – known as the 4 Ps of marketing.

The marketing mix can be thought of in a similar way to a recipe where the four ingredients of product, price, place and promotion can be blended in varying proportions giving emphasis to whichever aspect is most appropriate to the company, brand or product.

The mix employed will be unique to each company or situation, so there is no correct formula. Fundamentally it comes down to ensuring that the product is right for the specified market, that it is priced correctly, that the balance of merchandise is correct, that it is in the right place at the right time and that customers are aware of the offer or service through appropriately targeted promotions. Whatever the market level, an effective marketing mix will need to weigh up a company's overall objectives while also taking into account any changes and challenges operating in the market at any given time.

The drawback of the traditional 4P marketing mix is that it tends to focus on the internal needs of the company rather than the ever-changing requirements of customers. This more limiting version of the mix was primarily developed during the rise of mass consumerism to market the physical benefits of a product – the limelight falls on issues surrounding producing, pricing and promoting product. Newer thinking believes the consumer should be at the heart of the matter. An expanded 7P version of the marketing mix has been developed to address this change in emphasis; it includes three further criteria, physical evidence, process and people. It can be a common mistake to consider fashion as a product-based industry, however – it should really be viewed as service- or people-based, which is why the extra criteria are so necessary. As discussed in Chapter 1, digital content is now a key constituent of this service. Brands need to be excellent in designing and producing desirable fashion products, but also in harnessing the power of social media and e-tail platforms to generate engaging content and satisfying shopping experiences in-store and online. Each of the 7Ps is discussed in detail below.

"Marketing is still an art, and the marketing manager, as head chef, must creatively marshal all his marketing activities to advance the short- and long-term interests of his firm."

Neil H. Borden

Product

For apparel, 'product' relates to product design, style, fit, sizing, quality, fashion level as well as performance and function. In the fashion and textile industry, product is rarely a singular item. Commonly it will be a complex range or integrated collection of product. Designers are generally required to construct well-balanced collections or wholesale or retail ranges that include a variety of different product categories offered at appropriate **price points** for specific target markets. When taking a strategic marketing approach to product, some useful questions to consider are:

» Are the products suitable for the specified market?

» Do the products meet the tangible needs of consumers?

» How will the products satisfy the intangible desires or aspirations of customers?

» Does the total product offer or range address the variety of needs relating to the target customers?

» Is the balance of the range or collection correct? Does it have enough choice and variety within it?

Product attributes and benefits

Product attributes refer to the features, functions and uses of a product. **Product benefits** relate to how a product's attributes or features might benefit the consumer. At the most basic level, clothing has core attributes, which offer protection, and safeguard against exposure and nudity. At the next level there are the tangible attributes, integrated into the design, manufacture and function of the garment. These are intrinsic to the product itself and offer concrete and physical benefits to the consumer. So a raincoat made from a water-repellent fabric will have the intrinsic attribute of being waterproof and have the benefit of keeping a wearer dry. Such a garment may be presented in-store with accompanying marketing material informing consumers about the specific attributes and benefits of the design or waterproof material. An item of clothing can also have what are known as intangible attributes. These are more abstract in nature and connect to the ideals, perceptions and desires of the consumer. These intangibles are extremely important for fashion as consumers do not really buy a product but a set of expectations and interpretations, each person perceiving a product's combination of attributes and benefits according to their own particular needs and viewpoint.

The total product concept

The example of the waterproof coat illustrates what Theodore Levitt called the augmented product or the **total product concept**. Levitt's model describes four different levels to a product.

Below
The Regatta women's jacket (top) and men's jacket (bottom) have several important functional product attributes: made from Isotex 1000 XPT, an extreme performance fabric, the jackets are waterproof, breathable and windproof. The jackets also incorporate technical and functional design details such as taped seams, a detachable hood, a centre front zip with storm flap and a map pocket.

» The generic or core product

» The actual or expected product

» The total or augmented product

» The potential product

If we consider a waterproof coat such as a classic trench, at the most basic level the product is a coat. At the next level it is a waterproof coat with specific design features and styling details offered at a particular quality and price. The next tier up is the total or augmented product. This represents everything that the customer receives when they purchase the raincoat, including all elements that contribute to added value, intangible benefits, branding and emotional benefits. The total augmented product relates to everything that is currently being offered, but there is another highly significant layer to consider and that is the potential product. This is everything that could be offered or might be offered in the future. For fashion the future happens very fast and designers spend most of their time working on potential product. They must innovate and update, moving product design forward each season with new design ideas, fabrics and technologies. The concept of potential product is therefore of vital importance.

Levitt's model highlights another important point. "Consumers don't buy products or product attributes. They purchase benefits and emotional meaning." This means that potential product must also be about identifying innovative ways to deliver extra value and benefits to the customer.

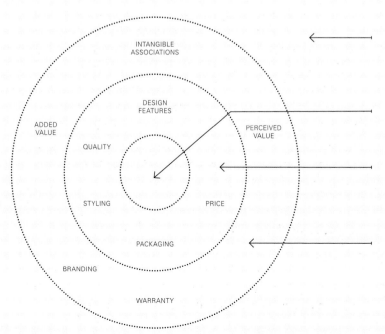

THE TOTAL PRODUCT CONCEPT

THE POTENTIAL PRODUCT
This represents the potential features not yet offered. It is also about innovation and concerns what the product could be in the future.

THE GENERIC PRODUCT
This is the core product, such as a coat, a jumper, a dress.

THE ACTUAL OR EXPECTED PRODUCT
The real product is a combination of the generic product plus the tangible attributes. This represents the customer's basic minimum expectation or requirement.

THE TOTAL PRODUCT
This is what Levitt calls the augmented product. It represents everything the customer receives. Generic product + the tangible attributes + intangible attributes. The total product represents the added value, that is, all extras added to elevate the product and make it different from product offered by competitors.

Synthesizing the practical with the emotional

A waterproof coat

A waterproof coat or jacket is a good example of a garment that can be designed with many practical features and tangible attributes. A coat made of a fully waterproof material has the obvious benefit of keeping the wearer dry in the rain. For someone who wanted a coat to protect them during outdoor or country pursuits, a loose-cut practical waxed jacket might provide the benefits they require. If in addition it had a detachable inner lining, then the benefits of flexibility and keeping warm could be added to the list. At an emotional level, a consumer might choose a waxed Barbour country jacket, not only because of the durability, warmth and protection it offered, but because emotionally, the wearer connected to the heritage and values of the Barbour brand. The wearer might feel 'earthy' or 'connected to the land' when they wore it. They may appreciate quality and tradition and practicality. A different consumer, on the other hand, who wanted to feel 'active and alive' or 'daring and adventurous' might purchase a lightweight waterproof with high-performance features, even if they wore it in an urban setting or to go to the shops. The wonderful benefits of a high-performance or practical country jacket are likely to be of no interest to someone who wanted to feel alluring, fashionable and chic while they kept dry. For this consumer the silhouette or shape of the coat may be of major importance, along with the fashion status of a brand name. They may desire a designer label raincoat with a belt so that they can cinch in their waist and show off their figure to best advantage.

Each of the garments described provides the functional benefits necessary for specific uses or activities. But clothing provides more than the merely functional. The clue to understanding this is to view attributes from the consumer perspective and try and determine what consumers might feel, desire or aspire to when they purchase fashion product. Each attribute will generate a set of emotional meanings that augment the tangible or physical benefits. This is why fashion in general and branding in particular can be so powerful – they have a unique ability to confer the intangible and create a short-cut straight to the emotional.

Left
American actress Maggie Gyllenhaal looks sophisticated and urban in a belted trenchcoat.

Below
French actress Fanny Ardant makes a simple, classic raincoat look alluring and desirable.

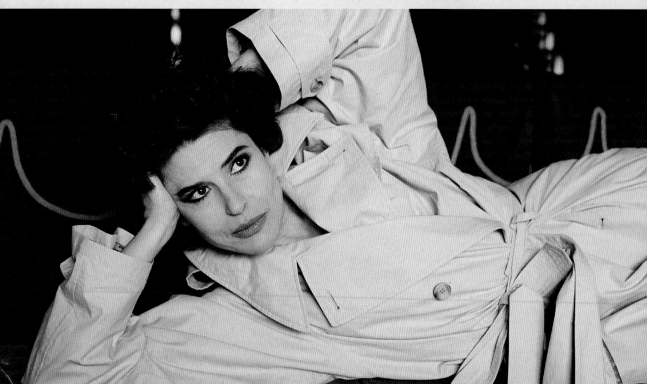

Price

In this context price means manufacturing costs, wholesale and retail prices, discounted prices and of course margin and profit. For marketing purposes it is possible to view pricing from two perspectives; one is from the point of view of cost, what an item actually costs either to produce or for a buyer to purchase. It considers tangible expenditure so that a cost price can be calculated. The second standpoint, selling price, looks at the situation from the customer or end-consumer's perspective. It considers what might be a realistic selling price and factors in issues such as affordability and perceived value. Perceived value reflects the apparent worth of a product; this may not directly relate to the actual cost of production or wholesale purchase price. An understanding of customers' perceptions of value is therefore very important, as is knowledge of competitor pricing within the marketplace.

Research is an essential element in understanding pricing both from a customer or end-consumer perspective and in terms of what the competition is up to. And of course, prices change frequently so research helps gain insight into:

» How customers perceive price

» What customers consider good value

» How much customers are willing to pay for specific products

» What customers will pay more for

» How much competitors are charging

Above

The display in the John Varvatos Malibu store features a range of products including jeans, shoes and accessories. The product mix offers customers an opportunity to buy into the Varvatos collection at a variety of price points.

It is rarely only one item that will need to be priced. A well-balanced selection of product will need to be constructed and a coherent pricing strategy devised not only for each individual item but for the entire offering.

Price architecture

A pricing structure will have to be planned or built up from the lowest-cost items right up to the most expensive. This is known as the **price architecture**. Within the price architecture there should be products offered at:

» Introductory or low price points

» Medium prices

» High price points

PRICE ARCHITECTURE

Price architecture is dependent on the type of market, the market level and the product concerned. The proportion of styles and the stock volumes within each of the tiers is adjusted so that the business can satisfy the greatest number of customers and generate the highest potential sales margin and profit.

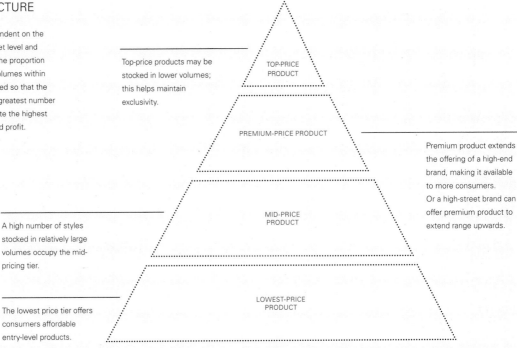

Top-price products may be stocked in lower volumes; this helps maintain exclusivity.

TOP-PRICE PRODUCT

PREMIUM-PRICE PRODUCT

Premium product extends the offering of a high-end brand, making it available to more consumers. Or a high-street brand can offer premium product to extend range upwards.

MID-PRICE PRODUCT

A high number of styles stocked in relatively large volumes occupy the mid-pricing tier.

LOWEST-PRICE PRODUCT

The lowest price tier offers consumers affordable entry-level products.

It is customary to create a price band for each of these tiers. For example, a high-street retailer might set their lowest price band at £15–49, the mid-price band at £50–99 and the top band at £100–200.

Each retail price band can then be further subdivided with specific price points. The top price band might, for example, have only four price points, £115, £125, £150 and £200. The lowest pricing tier might have something in the region of eight to 12 separate price points. Skilful setting of price points and consideration of the number of styles offered at each price within a pricing band are essential elements to the planning of a balanced range. It may not be possible to achieve the desired profit margin on every style but judicious flexing of prices should help to increase margin on enough product so that a workable margin is achieved overall.

Place

In essence, place is about getting the right product to the right place at the right time and in the right amount. It concerns logistics and the various methods of transporting, storing and distributing merchandise and the means by which a company's products reach their target customer; termed as 'route to market' this relates to **distribution** and **sales channels**. The key sales channels by which apparel product reaches the end-consumer are:

Above
Stella McCartney talking to customers
at a trunk show in the Chicago store of
Barneys New York.

» Direct routes via online shopping or by purchasing
on the telephone

» Service-orientated channels; in other words a retail store,
or what is termed as **bricks and mortar retail**

» Catalogues – some companies start by producing a
catalogue. They may then expand to open stores or
operate a **concession** within another store. Most printed
catalogues will operate a second channel online

» Public events such as sports or fashion events, or craft
or country fairs

» **Trunk shows**, **online trunk shows** or preview events

A trunk show is a special preview event where a designer will show
off their latest collection to a select group of invited guests and
customers. Usually guests will be able to purchase or order items
during the event. Trunk shows are commonly held in a boutique or
in the designer section of a department store and are excellent for
marketing as they allow a designer to reach an audience that would
not normally attend catwalk shows. They also provide an excellent
opportunity for the designer and retailers to obtain vital pre-season
information on which styles will be successful.

Trade fairs and exhibitions

Timberland takes a stand

Industry trade fairs provide an important opportunity for companies to showcase their new product ranges and sell to retail buyers from around the globe. The advantage of a trade fair or exhibition is that buyers can view and compare a variety of brands all showing at the same event. Shows will be sector specific; Première Vision in Paris for fabric or Pitti Filati in Florence for yarn spinners, CPD in Düsseldorf for womenswear and accessories, or Bread & Butter in Berlin for street and urban wear, for example. Thousands of trade buyers typically visit these fairs; 33,500 visitors from over 59 countries attended the Igedo fashion fairs in February 2008. Exhibiting companies invest heavily in creating show stands that represent their brand and their products to best advantage.

The Timberland trade-show stand for its Outdoor Performance range is created using re-purposed industrial objects and natural recycled materials. Shipping containers have been redeployed to create selling booths where clients can view the Timberland product range and place orders. The innovative trade-show stand, designed by Minnesota-based design firm JGA, reflects Timberland's commitment to environmental sustainability. The highly distinctive design is constructed from 98 per cent 'earth conscious' materials (53 per cent re-used, 18 per cent renewable, 27 per cent recycled), and 88 per cent of the stand can be recycled at the end of its use.

Timberland trade-show stand for their Outdoor Performance range (above). Graphics set the mood in the central 'meet and greet' space where trade buyers are welcomed onto the stand by Timberland sales representatives to view the products and place orders.

JGA also designed the stand for the Timberland Pro series (below). The highly flexible build is designed to accommodate different trade-show footprints. Sales rooms display the Pro Series products and provide worktable seating for 8–10 people.

Moda Operandi is a members-only e-commerce website, or **pretailer**, that enables users to purchase straight from the runway through online designer trunk shows. This approach means that members can obtain pieces as seen on the runway, rather than purchasing later in the season when looks may be edited for mainstream retail.

Design houses are also using the digital trunk format so that customers can browse and pre-order new collections before they hit the stores. Italian brand Salvatore Ferragamo's micro-website trunkshow.ferragamo.com makes the Ferragamo ready-to-wear collection available for pre-order via an interactive digital trunk show. Shoppers can see catwalk videos, view the lookbook and experiment with a 'style yourself' feature. Any digital platform such as this must be viewable on a variety of devices.

Customer requirements or purchasing patterns are likely to vary between different national or international locations. A store in Germany might carry a different selection of styles and colours compared to one in southern Spain for example, and the size range of garments may need to be adjusted to take into account variations in physique prevalent within different cultures. The merchandise offer will also be determined by factors such as the dimensions or layout of the retail space. Not every location will be able to display the same volume of stock, so the selection will need to be modified to suit the practicalities of each specific store.

For fashion trade, routes to market can be via the following channels:

» Trade fairs

» Agent's showroom

» Company-owned showrooms either at head office or located in key global locations

» Digital and online platforms

» Via a sales team

» Direct from manufacturer

» Via an agent

» Trunk shows

Promotion

Promotion is about communicating with customers and includes all the tools available for marketing, communicating and promoting a company and its products and services. The combination of promotional activities, such as advertising, sales promotion, public relations, personal selling or direct marketing, is known as the **promotional mix**. The idea behind this is similar to the marketing mix and relates to the mixture of promotional tools that can be employed to achieve a company's promotion objectives. Some of the most recognized promotional vehicles for fashion are the advertising in high-profile fashion magazines like *Vogue*, *Harper's Bazaar* or *Elle*; catwalk shows that gain extensive media and public interest; and the PR and razzmatazz that surrounds celebrities and their endorsement of designer fashion. There are, however, many innovative and creative ways to promote fashion, particularly using the ever-growing capabilities of digital and social media. These will be discussed further along with other promotional ideas and campaigns in Chapter 6.

Below
Massey & Rogers produce beautiful printed items such as bags, brooches, tea towels and greetings cards. They take great care with presentation – their set of three bird-print tea towels are packaged with cotton tape and branded with a simple swing ticket.

Physical evidence

Consumers increasingly demand more in terms of value, experience or extra service, and as the ability of fashion retailers to match each other's product offer rises, so the criterion of physical evidence plays an ever more important role in differentiating one retailer from another. Physical evidence relates to packaging, brochures, business cards, carrier bags, staff uniforms, in-store décor, ambience, facilities, retail fixtures, store windows and signage and the design, content and usage of digital media and e-commerce platforms.

The fashion experience is about so much more than just the clothes or accessories themselves, it's all the little extras that make a difference. The label in the garment embroidered with the designer name, the well-designed and beautifully crafted swing ticket, the carrier bag so special that it is kept as a treasured souvenir, or stunning windows and store displays that capture the imagination and make a shopping trip feel thrilling. All these extras are vitally important aspects of the marketing mix. They are persuasive factors that add value, enhance customer perception of a retailer or fashion brand and elevate one company above another in the hearts and minds of consumers.

Process

Process describes the customer's experience of the brand or service from first point of contact onwards. It considers the experiences and procedures they may have to go through in order to make a purchase either in-store or online, and includes issues such as information flow, ordering, payment, delivery, service and return of products. In the modern marketing climate, with increased reliance on e-commerce and marketing via digital media, process is a potent tool, especially for businesses wishing to build customer loyalty and ensure customer retention. Whatever the exact nature of a business, it is always worthwhile to take time to review the processes customers must go through and consider each step of the journey from the customer perspective rather than just what might be efficient for the company.

A customer purchasing a wedding dress will go through a series of steps from first consideration to final purchase and ultimately wearing the dress on her wedding day. The first step may be looking at wedding magazines and doing online research to find suitable ideas, designers or retailers. Next, there could be telephone conversations or emails to gather further information or book an appointment to view a collection, sessions to select fabric and develop a personal design, followed by several fittings, the final fitting, taking delivery of the dress and then the wedding itself. Each step in the process is a moment where the consumer and company providing the service interact. Every interaction provides an opportunity for the business to differentiate itself from competitors, create value and ensure a positive experience for the customer. With social media at their fingertips, it is worth remembering that consumers have the power to broadcast their views and opinions of your brand, whether positive or negative.

Bear in mind that the criterion of process expands the marketing viewpoint beyond the product itself and recognizes the value of smooth interactions and good service. In combination with great product, process builds trust, loyalty and repeat custom. Hopefully, a wedding dress will be a one-off, once-in-a-lifetime purchase, so positive customer experience is less likely to result in a repeat purchase but it will certainly contribute towards an enhanced reputation and customer recommendations. Conversely, customer irritation with any part of the process could lead to a lost sale, deterioration in trust and erosion of customer goodwill or loyalty. In the case of a wedding dress there may be other people to please along the way – the bride's mother or a best friend or bridesmaid. Process may appear to relate to systems and organization but in reality it is all about people and their potential.

People

'People' in this instance does not just refer to consumers, it has much wider implications and opens up the scope to include all those who add value to the development and delivery of a product or service. People can therefore include employees, partners, stakeholders, collaborators, producers and suppliers. It can be a trap to consider fashion as only a product-based industry; it is just as important to view it as retail and a service experience. People add value along the entire length of the supply chain and are, of course, integral to the service provided by any company. People should therefore be considered as a vital part of the marketing mix.

Changing the Ps to Cs

The most up-to-date marketing theories, such as **relationship marketing**, recognize the importance of building relationships between a business and its customers or social media followers. The aim is to develop brand loyalty and foster a sense of engagement. A model devised by Professor Robert Lauterborn

Top to bottom:
Dutch fashion label Laundry Industry sold their promotional material in-store. This branded View-Master came in a presentation box with two reels, one showing images of a previous collection and the other with information on the history of the brand.

Kate Spade purse and packaging, which comes in a range of joyful colours to complement the product.

A Tracey Neuls shoebox is wrapped in a publicity poster and transformed into a bag with the addition of plastic handles.

Creating an inviting retail space

Alice + Olivia

Fashion brands must offer beautiful and inviting physical environments in which to sell their products. The New York-based brand Alice + Olivia by Stacey Bendet opened its first standalone store in the International Finance Centre (IFC) mall in the Central district of Hong Kong. The 74-sq-m (800-sq-ft) boutique, nicknamed 'the jewel box', has a vibrant colour scheme. The black and white chequerboard floor stretches outside the store and into the mall; this connects the store to its environment and draws customers in. The fun, fresh and eclectic style of the Alice + Olivia brand is reflected in the décor. The Hong Kong store, the first to open as part of an expansion programme in a partnership venture with ImagineX, a leading distribution and brand management company in Asia, allowed the Alice + Olivia brand to extend its global reach far beyond the US.

The Alice + Olivia Hong Kong store, nicknamed the jewel box.

reframes the marketing mix. By changing the Ps into Cs, Lauterborn shifts the emphasis away from product, price, place and promotion onto the customer.

The Lauterborn model may not have been created with fashion specifically in mind, but it is possible to consider its implications. What, for example, might it cost consumers in real terms to satisfy their needs or fashion passions? Is their enthusiasm for fashion limited to product alone, or does it include pursuing a deeper level of satisfaction by engaging with fashion via digital and social media content? Factors such as time and convenience also have to be integrated into the framework of marketing. Data from iResearch showed that apparel e-commerce constituted nearly 13 per cent of online retail sales in 2013. However, shopping can also be viewed as a social or leisure activity, an experience often shared with friends. A morning perusing the high street or mall or searching online might be perceived as time well spent, even if very little was actually purchased. Many women and occasionally some men buy clothing and fashion completely spontaneously, having had no original intention to purchase anything that day. Some consumers could be described as fashion addicts. For them, convenience is not an issue; they might be willing to make special trips or even pilgrimages to ensure they fulfil their fashion dreams or requirements. Others may spend hours monitoring an online auction to ensure that they are the ultimate victor in a bidding war for an exclusive fashion item. There are also, of course, customers with limited interest in fashion and little inclination to spend their time trawling the shops or browsing the Web, who nevertheless need to buy clothing for themselves or their family members.

Think
OUTSIDE IN!

In other words imagine being the customer. What kind of service do they require? How can you improve the processes they go through to purchase your products? How can you make the process smoother, more exciting, more engaging, more efficient and memorable for the right reasons?

Now think
INSIDE OUT.

Have you made internal processes smooth and efficient? Will internal processes support customer experience – even if employees don't deal directly with customers their internal or interdepartmental processes may cause glitches that indirectly affect results.

MARKETING MIX – Ps	LAUTERBORN MODEL – Cs
PRODUCT	CUSTOMER NEEDS AND WANTS
PRICE	COST TO THE CONSUMER
PLACE	CONVENIENCE
PROMOTION	COMMUNICATION

Valuing people

Earnest Sewn jeans

Earnest Sewn is an American denim brand founded by Scott Morrison in Los Angeles. The name is central to the brand concept – literally translating as 'product sewn in earnest'. The denim label is underpinned by fundamental core values of quality, integrity and authenticity and the Japanese concept of Wabi-Sabi, an aesthetic system honouring the traditional beauty of imperfection. Traditional Wabi-Sabi products are produced by hand and weathered by time. For these values to have any significant worth or real meaning they must be utilized by Earnest Sewn and be embedded into the company's design and manufacturing processes and integrated into the marketing strategy. In order to achieve this Earnest Sewn abandoned the normal assembly line approach to production. Wherever possible one person carries out the majority of the sewing for each garment; in this way the company endeavours to manifest the ideals by which it stands. Each maker is able to focus on an individual pair of jeans, increasing the opportunity for subtle inconsistencies, imperfection and the irregularity of things made by hand. Typically, three people oversee and monitor the jeans' progress from design through to shipping. When the jeans are complete, those involved in their production put their name to their work by signing the pocket lining. This validates the authenticity of the jeans and signals the integrity of the manufacture. The signed pocket lining communicates that the jeans are indeed, 'product sewn in earnest'.

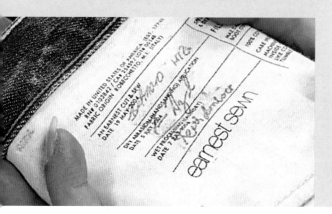

This pair of Earnest Sewn jeans carries the signatures of the three people responsible for creating them from design through to shipping. One person carries out the majority of the sewing on each pair of jeans. This innovative approach changes the dynamic of the manufacture from 'production line' to something closer to 'hand-made'.

Consumer psychology and communication are the unifying principles that tie this new set of criteria together. There is a need to understand the psychological impulses behind consumer fashion choices and recognize sensitivities to time, costs, value and convenience. By viewing marketing from the consumer's perspective, far more must now be achieved than just delivering the right products at the right price. The way consumers value fashion, style, self-expression and identity should naturally be viewed as part of the marketing equation.

STP marketing strategy

It is an extremely tough challenge for a fashion manufacturer, supplier, designer brand or retailer to appeal equally to all customers or consumers. It makes sense therefore for a business to concentrate its resources and activities and focus on a specific area of the market, fine-tuning or 'positioning' the brand, product offer, service and digital content so that they appeal more directly to a specified and well-defined target audience. This is the fundamental principle underpinning **STP** (segmentation, targeting and positioning) **marketing strategy**.

Segmentation and targeting

Market segmentation is a key function of marketing; its purpose is to divide a market into smaller, more focused sectors. The fashion market can be segmented in several ways, for example by product type or market level. There is a market for couture, the luxury designer market, the accessory market and branded sportswear. The process of segmentation can also be used to cluster consumers into groups that share similar characteristics.

Customer segmentation is the research and analysis technique used to define these groups. It categorizes consumers in terms of their age, attitudes, behaviours or by the type of products and services they might need. (This is described in greater depth in Chapter 4.) Segmentation is a means to an end; the tool that facilitates the next step in the process is targeting. This is the practice of developing products or services specifically aimed to appeal to a particular customer segment. Companies that offer petite ranges, for example, are targeting smaller-sized customers. A fashion brand targeting older female customers might design and cut garments to flatter the figure of the older woman.

Positioning

Having segmented the market and selected which sector and consumers to target, a company must now position its brand within the market, so that it will appeal directly to the target market. This is an approach taken by the Arcadia Group, the UK's largest privately owned clothing retailer. The Group operates nine well-known

"Retail is a people business. For sure, customers pay their money for whatever it is that you, the retailer, sell to them, but there's so much more to the relationship than this exchange."

Martin Butler

RELATIONSHIPS IN THE SUPPLY CHAIN

The framework of the marketing mix and the overall business and marketing processes can be applied to any business throughout the fashion and textile supply chain. Each interaction along the chain should be viewed as a business relationship; this is why it is important to include the criterion of 'people' within the marketing mix. This diagram represents a simplified version of the supply chain but it could be expanded to take into account other businesses, such as agents and distributors.

PEOPLE... PRODUCT... PRICE... PLACE... PHYSICAL EVIDENCE... PROMOTION

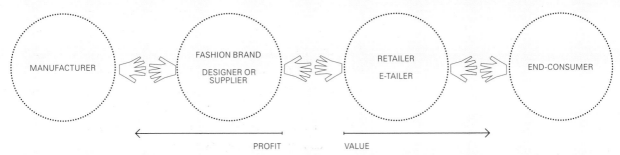

high-street retail brands, each positioned to attract a particular type of fashion consumer. Topshop, one of Arcadia's most famous brands, targets young girls and women aged 13–25 and positions itself as a brand offering 'cutting-edge fashion at affordable prices'. Dorothy Perkins (DP) is aimed at a broader range of women aged 25–45. The average DP customer is in her thirties and is a busy mum or working woman; the core value at Dorothy Perkins is 'value for money'.

Positioning, however, is a slightly complicated issue, because it is really a matter of perception. It is about the position a brand occupies in the mind of a consumer or potential consumer. Furthermore, this position is relative. Positioning is about where a brand or product is perceived to be within the marketplace relative to the other brands or products operating within the same sector. So, for example, consumers may feel that a Prada handbag is inherently more desirable than a bag sold by another luxury brand which they might perceive to be more traditional or staid, or they may consider the garments made by one sports brand to be of a higher quality than another, when in reality both use the same factory to manufacture their apparel.

In order to position itself, its brands or its products effectively a business must develop a positioning strategy. The strategy will be dependent on where competitors position themselves and how the business wants its brands or products to compete. So, taking the example of a luxury accessory brand viewed by consumers as more traditional and less cutting-edge than Prada; this brand could decide to strategically position itself close to Prada – to compete head-to-head and try and beat the competitor brand at its own game. If this were the strategy, then the brand would offer similar products or services at comparable prices. It is, of course, high risk and costly to compete aggressively with a market leader and there may be no real advantage for consumers in having two virtually identical brands. Another option would be to position the brand within the same market but to offer something distinctly different, or provide extra benefits.

When working on a positioning strategy it is helpful to create a **positioning map**. This can be used to pinpoint the desired position for a brand and give a visual overview of this position relative to that of competitor brands within a market. Given that positioning is actually dependent on the perception of consumers, the company must also attain knowledge of how consumers perceive their brand within the market. Once research has been carried out, a **perceptual map** can be produced. This is very similar to a positioning map but is based solely upon consumers' perceptions of

"Positioning is not what you do to a product. Positioning is what you do to the mind of the prospect."

Ries & Trout

the brand rather than where the company wishes to position it. The map will indicate the consumer perceptions of the brand's current position and identify where shifts are required to align them with the company's desired position. This pursuit of alignment is called repositioning, the process of redefining the identity of an existing brand or product in order to shift the position it holds in consumers' minds relative to that of competitors.

So to summarize the positioning process:

» Define the market in which the brand or product will compete

» Decide where to position within the market

» Determine whether to compete directly against a
   competitor or how to differentiate and compete
   by being different

» Understand how consumers perceive the current position

» Determine if repositioning is necessary

Once a clear position for the brand or product has been established, the next step is to ensure that it is communicated to consumers. All facets of the brand, its image, products, packaging, retail environment, promotion, advertising, website and social media strategy should convey this position and it is therefore vital that every aspect is congruent and supports the desired strategy. Positioning and repositioning are costly exercises; moving a brand's position is not a tactic to be carried out repeatedly. The aim is to establish a strong and recognizable position that is consistent over time and to make sure products and brands are clearly different from those offered by competitors. This is the principle of **differentiation**. Closely allied to the concept of positioning, it is the next strategic tool to be discussed.

POSITIONING OR PERCEPTUAL MAP

A positioning or perceptual map plots the relative positions of brands or products. Two key criteria are chosen, one for each axis. The polarities of each criterion are positioned at the end of the axis: this example shows pricing ranging from prestige to more affordable levels.

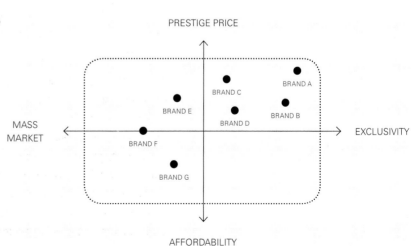

Differentiation

Differentiation is the concept of developing and marketing products or services so that they are different and hopefully superior to those offered by competitors within the same marketplace. It is a fundamental strategic approach that ensures products and services are distinctive and stand out from the crowd.

The ultimate aim of differentiation is to achieve what is known as a competitive advantage. A company achieves an advantage if it is able to provide products or services of greater value to consumers than those offered by competitors. As mentioned earlier in the chapter, value is not just an issue of price. Customers might value premium service or luxury quality or the high status of a particular fashion label and they may indeed be willing to pay more for it. Alternatively it might be street credibility that gives a brand a competitive edge or the fact that a world-famous celebrity endorses the brand. These extra elements augment the basic product, add value and help achieve competitive advantage.

Opportunity to differentiate exists at every stage of the marketing process. Differentiation and competitive advantage can be achieved through design and technology innovation, by strategic management of the supply chain or in the way a brand or product is retailed, distributed or promoted. The Potential for Differentiation table shown opposite uses the 7P marketing mix as a framework for exploring possible areas for differentiation and competitive advantage. Once relevant areas for differentiation have been identified, then practical steps can be planned and strategic actions put into place so as to achieve the desired outcome. The chosen tactics must also contribute towards creating a competitive advantage for the company and, of course, offer clear value and benefit for the consumer.

Competitive advantage

The Potential for Differentiation table should highlight some of the ways a business might differentiate itself and achieve an advantage over competitors. One obvious way to compete in a marketplace is to be the cheapest and gain a cost advantage. In this case the design or quality of products might be comparable but the competitor that offers them at the lowest price might gain the advantage. However, this is likely to be a short-lived victory. The problem with this approach is that it soon becomes unsustainable. Competitors will usually reduce prices to match and a vicious cycle of cost reductions will eventually lead to erosion of profits for all concerned. Cost alone no longer provides a strong enough advantage; it needs to be aligned with other beneficial factors

POTENTIAL FOR DIFFERENTIATION TABLE

MARKETING MIX VARIABLES	POTENTIAL AREAS FOR DIFFERENTIATION	TACTICS TO ACHIEVE DIFFEREN-TIATION	COMPETITIVE ADVANTAGE	VALUE FOR CONSUMERS
PRODUCT	» Design and construction of products » Quality of products, fabrics and components » Range of products on offer » Fashion level of merchandise			
PRICE	» Prices in comparison to competitors » Pricing structure and price architecture of a range			
PLACE	» Routes to market » Locations of stores » E-commerce platforms			
PROMOTION	» Designer collaboration » Advertising » Celebrity endorsement » Sales promotions » Limited editions			
PHYSICAL EVIDENCE	» In-store environment – signage, seating, changing rooms etc. » Website and content such as blog and social media » Marketing extras – swing ticket and labelling, carrier bag, brochure, in-store magazine			
PROCESS	» In-store and customer service » Website and e-commerce design and ease of use » Aftercare, return of products			
PEOPLE	» Structure of company » Opportunities for staff » Ethics of garment production » Collaboration and co-creation with consumers and social media followers			

such as speed and what is known in the trade as **fashionability**. In other words, companies that manage to get reasonably priced catwalk-inspired styles or the right trends into the market faster than rivals have not only managed to achieve a cost advantage but also a speed advantage and what could be termed a fashion advantage; this of course is the operating principle behind the concept of fast fashion. Zara, one of the brands owned by the Spanish Inditex Group, has consistently been able to offer reasonably priced stylish interpretations of catwalk trends at exceptional speed. A tightly controlled production system allows Zara to move swiftly from a design drawing to a finished garment delivered to store in a period of between two to three weeks. The international retailer achieves its speed advantage because the Inditex Group possesses its own manufacturing and distribution capabilities and operates what is termed a **vertical supply chain**. The company is well known for perfecting its highly integrated production and distribution model. It is Zara's legendary lead-time (the time between placing an order and the stock arriving in-store) that gives it its competitive advantage.

ASOS illustrates the next development in the competitive platform. The company that started life as 'As Seen On Screen' was established in June 2000. In 2013 ASOS had five million users globally, delivered to over 200 countries and became one of the most visited fashion sites in the world. The e-tailer stole the advantage by bringing must-have fashion ideas direct to the consumer. ASOS gained a competitive advantage by adding new dimensions to the cost, speed and fashionability dynamic, namely convenience, interactivity and connectivity. Suddenly, Zara's vertically integrated production model and speed to market became old news; ASOS extended the parameters of fashion beyond retail into a new realm of interactive consumer engagement.

The Zara and ASOS examples illustrate what have now become standard criteria for competitiveness within a fast-fashion market:

> » Cost
> » Speed
> » Fashionability
> » Convenience
> » Interactivity
> » Connectivity

When a fashion brand competing in this market achieves these measures of competitiveness, it raises the bar for others to match or surpass and eventually new platforms for differentiation and advantage emerge. Companies or brands that find the differentiating element above and beyond the standard will steal the advantage.

ASOS recognized the need to play at an emotive level and tap into the desires of a new breed of consumer. Capitalizing on emerging technologies and a growing consumer appetite for engaging directly with brands, it published an online fashion magazine, generated its own content, integrated social media into its strategic arsenal and harnessed the potential of e-commerce technology with features such as Scan to Shop, mobile phone apps, and shoppable videos.

Competitive strategies

One competitive platform to consider is sustainability. Demand is growing for ethically sourced fashion and sustainable production methods. Levi Strauss & Co. produces its sustainable line, Dockers Wellthread, as part of their Dockers brand. The challenge for the design, production and marketing team is not only to ensure the best possible sustainable practices but also to market the collection effectively. Sustainable production can be expensive, and consumers are not always willing to pay a premium. By limiting the number of fabrics used and shifting the dyeing process from mill to factory where garments can be processed to order, Levi's are able to reduce fabric wastage and manage costs. The sustainable approach provides a business advantage and with careful control of the supply chain the savings can be passed on to the consumer.

Unique selling proposition

ASOS has set itself apart, not only because it was one of the first companies in the UK to make the Internet a viable fashion retail destination but also because it provides a unique 'As Seen On Screen' ideology. This is what gives the Internet brand its distinctive emotional pull and provides its **unique selling proposition (USP)** or unique selling point. A USP represents the fundamental distinguishing proposition being offered to the customer. It is the synthesis of a brand's positioning and differentiation and should encapsulate its overall competitive advantage. The unique selling proposition is a marketing tool that can be used to emphasize and articulate specific points of difference that make a particular product, service or brand unique and therefore distinctive in the marketplace.

Signature style

For many designers or fashion brands it is their unique signature style that helps define their USP. A signature style is a look that is so clear and distinctive that it can easily be attributed to the designer or brand in question. It is also possible for an individual to have a signature style. Karl Lagerfeld, for example, has an instantly

recognizable and clearly defined personal style, as has the designer Vivienne Westwood.

For a fashion designer, developing an individual signature style or being able to interpret the style of an existing fashion brand is an advantageous and important skill. It is usual for designers to work for several different fashion companies during their career and with each move to a new design label, they will be expected to adapt quickly and produce designs that fit the signature style of the design label or brand. Marco Zanini, for example, was at Dolce & Gabbana and Versace before taking on the role of Creative Director at Halston in 2007, Rochas in 2009 and Schiaparelli in 2013. Many designers use their time working for others to hone their skills and experiment with a variety of styles until their own distinctive style emerges and they feel ready to go it alone and launch their own collection.

Creating a strategic planning document

The culmination of the strategic planning process is to write a marketing plan for achieving the company's marketing goals. The plan should review and explain the existing circumstances of both the business and the market, set out key marketing objectives and strategies, and detail the actions an organization intends to take over a specified time-frame. Although the marketing plan is a separate entity to the business plan, they are linked – the marketing plan will ultimately become a key component of the total business plan.

The first step in creating a marketing plan involves an internal marketing audit and a review of the external market situation. This is known as **situation analysis**. In order to move forward a company must first establish where it stands now, and determine what strategies have worked effectively so far and what has been less successful. This is covered by an internal audit used to examine the strengths and weaknesses of the organization and assess the efficacy of its current marketing strategy. The audit should include a review of the company's utilization of the key marketing tools described so far in this chapter, namely:

>> Marketing mix
>> Target customers
>> Positioning strategy
>> Differentiation strategy and USP
>> Competitive advantage

Situation analysis also includes an investigation of the current state of the relevant market sector, and should cover the following:

A timeless signature style

Coco Chanel

Coco Chanel was renowned for her signature personal style, often challenging the dress conventions of her day; she wore black, for example, a colour more traditionally associated with mourning. Accessorizing her quintessential look with copious oversized strings of pearls, Chanel created quite a stir with her dramatic costume-style jewellery in an era when the wearing of 'fake' jewels would have been a novelty. The custom at the time would be to embellish outfits with precious or heirloom jewellery so as to indicate wealth and status. Key elements of her signature style are the little black dress, the classic Chanel suit with gilt buttons, costume jewellery and the quilted handbag. These emblems have become the established signifiers of the brand. They are so powerful that they are reinterpreted and used season after season, and not only for the clothes, but also on the sets of Chanel ready-to-wear catwalk shows in Paris.

Above
Chanel wearing her signature pearls, photographed by Boris Lipnitzki in 1936.

Centre
A colossal Chanel quilted bag adorns the carousel-style catwalk.

Below
Models on the carousel decorated with giant versions of the Chanel signature emblems at the Autumn/Winter 2008/9 ready-to-wear show in Paris.

THE FLOW OF
MARKETING STRATEGY

This diagram shows the steps involved when applying an STP marketing strategy. The first step is to analyse the market and divide it up into smaller, more focused sectors. This is known as segmentation. This process enables a company to better understand the specifics of a market so that they can develop appropriate product targeted to appeal to a particular group of customers. The next step is to analyse competitors so that the brand or product can be positioned within the market and can be differentiated in some way so that it is clearly distinctive from other brands. The ultimate aim when applying an STP marketing strategy is for a brand to achieve a competitive advantage within the marketplace.

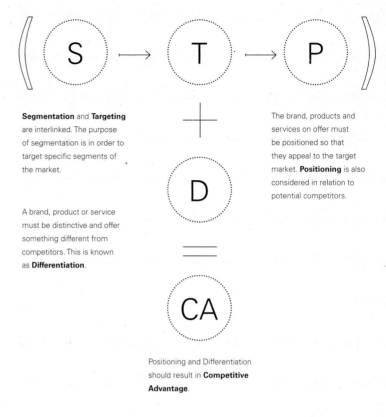

Segmentation and **Targeting** are interlinked. The purpose of segmentation is in order to target specific segments of the market.

A brand, product or service must be distinctive and offer something different from competitors. This is known as **Differentiation**.

The brand, products and services on offer must be positioned so that they appeal to the target market. **Positioning** is also considered in relation to potential competitors.

Positioning and Differentiation should result in **Competitive Advantage**.

Market data – information on the size of the market and its current state. For example, is it a growing market? What market opportunities have been identified?

Customers – who are the existing and potential customers of your business? From which brands do they currently buy and why? Why would they purchase from you?

Competitors – what brands are in direct competition with your business? What products and services do they offer and at what price? Where are they positioned in the market compared to your own brand? What is their USP? What customers are they targeting and how do they do this?

So in order to write the plan, it is essential to carry out detailed research. In the following chapter, the scope of marketing research will be explained and information given on how to conduct this research, carry out the internal audit, analyse the findings and complete the marketing plan.

3

Research and Planning

"If you knew everything about tomorrow, what would you do differently today?" *Faith Popcorn*

To be effective, marketing needs to be planned consciously, managed strategically, researched continuously and reviewed consistently. This ongoing cycle of endeavour is vital in a highly competitive, fast-paced industry such as fashion. This chapter highlights the importance of research as an adjunct to the business, marketing and planning process and outlines key areas of investigation to consider when carrying out marketing research investigations. Fundamental research and analytical tools, including **PEST** and **SWOT analysis**, Porter's five forces analysis and Ansoff's Matrix, will be explained to show how key marketing and strategic tools are utilized within the planning process. The value of both primary and secondary research will be highlighted and helpful tips on how to carry out simple but effective primary research and observation of the marketplace are given. The chapter will conclude with information on how to utilize this research so that you can now write a marketing plan.

Above
An Indian worker processes raw cotton at the Cotton Corporation of India in Warangal District, 150 km (90 miles) from Hyderabad.

Competition exists at all levels of the supply chain. India is the world's third-largest cotton producer after China and the US. Cotton is India's largest crop, with 5.3 million tonnes harvested in the crop year to September 2008. India competes with the other cotton-producing countries to sell its raw material. Buyers research the market to determine the best cotton source in terms of quality, price and delivery.

Marketing research

Marketing research is a vital component of both business and marketing. For a fashion company to be able to determine its future business direction and marketing strategy, it will need to continuously gather, analyse and integrate information obtained from a diverse range of business, fashion and market sources. You can see that the criteria of the 7P marketing mix – product, price, place, promotion, physical evidence, process and people – are all valid topics for marketing research. Kotler defines marketing research as:

> *"Systematic problem analysis, model-building and fact-finding for the purpose of improved decision-making and control in the marketing of goods and services."*

Marketing research may take place in order to analyse and resolve a specific problem but it can also take place in order to keep up to date, assess the state of the market, stay proactive in a declining market, anticipate future trends, pursue opportunity or to develop and expand a business.

Research is an essential activity because it can help to eradicate false assumptions, expose potential risks and ensure that decisions are underpinned by relevant and current data. Research needs to be systematic and carefully planned, but it can be a creative and insightful exercise. Getting to know one's subject in depth and investigating a broad spectrum of relevant issues can be a stimulating experience that provides useful insight. The aim of research is not only to find reliable, unbiased answers to questions about the market, substantiate plans, determine production sources, reveal risk factors and decide strategy but also to seek ideas and direction, draw inspiration and foster innovation.

It is important to define the difference between marketing research and **market research**. Market research forms a subset of marketing research and refers specifically to investigations of the market itself, comprising the marketplace, competitors and consumers. Marketing research relates to a much wider-ranging set of concerns, which include business, politics, economics, cultural and social trends, fashion trends, developing technologies, logistics, promotion and product research.

The macro marketing environment

The macro marketing environment refers to the wider situation impacting on all businesses. The macro environment is outside a

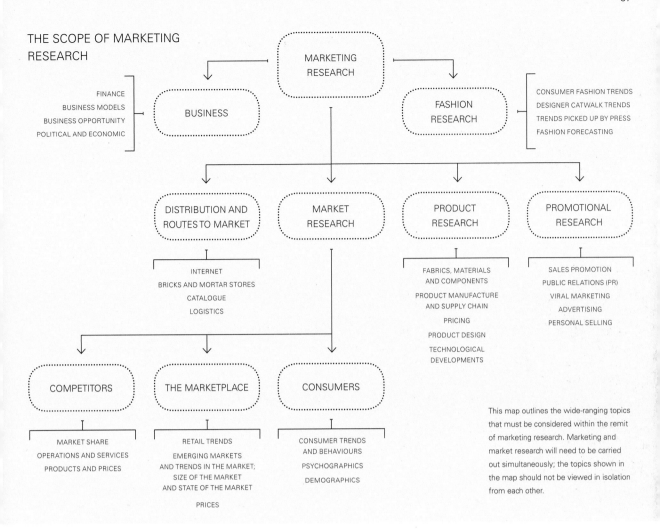

THE SCOPE OF MARKETING RESEARCH

MARKETING RESEARCH

FINANCE
BUSINESS MODELS
BUSINESS OPPORTUNITY
POLITICAL AND ECONOMIC

BUSINESS

FASHION RESEARCH

CONSUMER FASHION TRENDS
DESIGNER CATWALK TRENDS
TRENDS PICKED UP BY PRESS
FASHION FORECASTING

DISTRIBUTION AND ROUTES TO MARKET

MARKET RESEARCH

PRODUCT RESEARCH

PROMOTIONAL RESEARCH

INTERNET
BRICKS AND MORTAR STORES
CATALOGUE
LOGISTICS

FABRICS, MATERIALS AND COMPONENTS
PRODUCT MANUFACTURE AND SUPPLY CHAIN
PRICING
PRODUCT DESIGN
TECHNOLOGICAL DEVELOPMENTS

SALES PROMOTION
PUBLIC RELATIONS (PR)
VIRAL MARKETING
ADVERTISING
PERSONAL SELLING

COMPETITORS

THE MARKETPLACE

CONSUMERS

MARKET SHARE
OPERATIONS AND SERVICES
PRODUCTS AND PRICES

RETAIL TRENDS
EMERGING MARKETS AND TRENDS IN THE MARKET;
SIZE OF THE MARKET AND STATE OF THE MARKET
PRICES

CONSUMER TRENDS AND BEHAVIOURS
PSYCHOGRAPHICS
DEMOGRAPHICS

This map outlines the wide-ranging topics that must be considered within the remit of marketing research. Marketing and market research will need to be carried out simultaneously; the topics shown in the map should not be viewed in isolation from each other.

company's direct control and comprises a complex set of variables that can be simplified into four key areas: **P**olitical and legal factors; **E**conomic factors; **S**ocial and cultural factors; **T**echnological factors.

Research and analysis of these factors is known as a **PEST analysis**, an essential element of marketing research. PEST analysis ensures an organization is responsive to the political, legal, economic, social, cultural and technological situation at any given time.

Political and legal factors These play a significant role in the regulation of business. A company must be conscious of the prevailing political and economic situation at home and abroad (if trading overseas) and keep up to date with relevant legislation, taxation and trade tariffs. They must understand the implications of interest rates, rates of inflation, employment levels, currency exchange rates and fluctuations in prices of raw materials, goods and services. Although the example that follows happened a considerable time ago, it illustrates how trade tariffs can affect the supply chain. In 1999, the cashmere industry was threatened by

The marketing environment

Marketing research takes place within the **marketing environment**. The modern marketing environment is heavily influenced by an increasing array of factors within what is now a global marketplace. To be fully effective, a business must understand and recognize the impact of these factors at a local, national and possibly multinational market level. The marketing environment is subdivided into three perspectives, the macro marketing environment, micro marketing environment and internal marketing environment. Each of these three areas needs to be explored in turn.

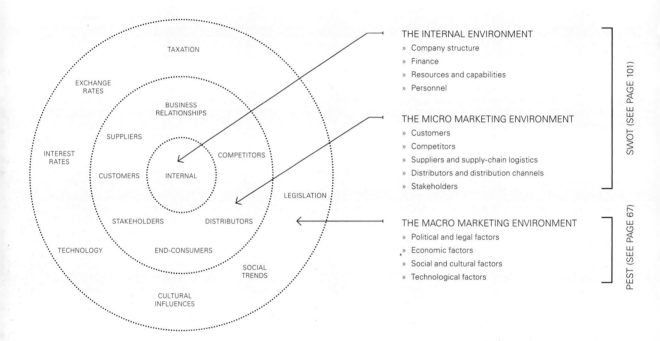

THE INTERNAL ENVIRONMENT
» Company structure
» Finance
» Resources and capabilities
» Personnel

THE MICRO MARKETING ENVIRONMENT
» Customers
» Competitors
» Suppliers and supply-chain logistics
» Distributors and distribution channels
» Stakeholders

THE MACRO MARKETING ENVIRONMENT
» Political and legal factors
» Economic factors
» Social and cultural factors
» Technological factors

SWOT (SEE PAGE 101)

PEST (SEE PAGE 67)

a tit-for-tat trade dispute between the US and Europe over banana imports. The US, angered by the European Union imposing high tariffs on bananas produced by Latin American growers, announced that it would fight back and levy 100 per cent import tariffs on certain European imported goods, including cashmere. The knock-on effects of the 'Banana Wars' were potentially disastrous; the livelihoods of Mongolian goat herders were threatened and thousands of jobs in the Scottish and Italian cashmere garment manufacturing industry were put in jeopardy. Luckily, in an eleventh-hour reprieve, cashmere was spared and the US government agreed not to carry out its threat. In 2013 the EU increased its import tariff on American-made premium jeans, which accounted for 75 per cent of the world's designer jeans market at that time. The top five US premium denim brands exporting to Western Europe were 7 For All Mankind, J Brand, Levi's, True Religion and Lee. These businesses had to decide whether to absorb the cost of the extra tax or move manufacturing out of the US to countries like Mexico or Asia. However, moving production offshore would impact the value of the brand and desirability of their products, if they could not be marketed as 'made in USA' or 'made in LA' premium denim.

Economic factors The economic climate has significant influence on markets and affects consumer confidence and spending power. The number of clothing, fashion and cosmetic retailers going into administration in the UK rose 21 per cent in the first half of 2008. During the recession of 2008–2009, consumers cut back on discretionary spending, saving their money to combat rising fuel and food costs. Economic factors, such as the weakness of sterling against the dollar, affected many fashion retailers and wholesalers, as raw material and manufacturing purchase prices are usually quoted in US$. The economic downturn did have a positive effect for some high-street fashion brands at the time. The Swedish retailer H&M and its rival Zara both managed to stave off the worst by providing spot-on fashion at prices customers could afford.

Social and cultural factors As demonstrated above, it is not only economics that make an impact, but also social and cultural trends. Changes in consumer attitudes and purchasing behaviour in response to political or economic events must be considered but film, television, music and art can have a significant impact too. The HBO *Sex and the City* (SATC) television series and movies, for example, were influential in bringing high fashion and designer brands to the attention of a new generation of young women who fell in love with the SATC girls' fashion style. AMC's *Mad Men* had a major effect on fashion, particularly the trend of younger men wearing a classic slim-cut suit, white shirt and narrow tie. Other social and cultural factors to research include shifts in the demographic of the population, developing lifestyle trends and leisure activities, as well as changes in consumer attitudes and purchasing behaviour. These will be discussed in Chapter 4.

Technological factors Technology has a tremendous importance within the fashion and retail industry. Issues to consider are wide-ranging, including EDI (electronic data interchange) and just-in-time product replenishment technologies for stock management. Computer-aided design (CAD) offers designers the opportunity to develop an entire fashion product range on screen. Sophisticated computer software allows greater flexibility for experimentation without having to cut the cloth or waste money sampling products in the early stages of development. 3D printing for fashion and accessories is becoming ever more accessible and technologies for e-commerce are developing and improving at an astounding rate.

Below
Retailers devise promotional strategies in direct response to economic and consumer trends. They may have to react quickly to capitalize on a short-term trend. Jos. A. Bank Clothiers in Chicago launched the 'Risk Free Suit' promotion to drive sales during the recession back in March 2009. The business promised both to refund the price of the suit and let the purchaser keep it, if he lost his job.

Sales of men's pinstripe suits in the City of London were affected during the financial crisis. Bankers, too ashamed to be associated with a profession that was receiving bad press at the time, opted to wear more discreet suit styles.

Above

André Courrèges and Mary Quant revolutionized womenswear in the early 1960s. Both designers are reputed to be the inventor of the miniskirt. Here, models showcase the Courrèges collection of minis worn with thick white tights in 1968. Tights were a relatively new innovation, made possible by the invention of Lycra® in 1958.

Innovation and technological advances in fabric and materials must also be researched. The implications of innovation can be quite dramatic. Take, for example, the invention of nylon in 1935 and the subsequent development of Lycra® by DuPont™ in 1958. These two innovations were utilized in the first tights, or 'pantyhose' as they were known when they were created by Allen Gant Senior. This ground-breaking hosiery development paved the way for the 1960s miniskirt revolution, a fashion trend that would never have taken off without the benefit of tights. Smart textiles and wearable technology are in the process of evolving but are set to revolutionize the traditional apparel market as computer technologists and researchers experiment with the integration of electronics and textiles.

The micro marketing environment

The micro marketing environment refers to factors that impact more directly on an organization and affect its ability to operate within its specific market. Factors to consider are:

» Customers
» Competitors
» Suppliers and supply-chain logistics
» Distributors and distribution channels
» Stakeholder and partner relationships

Unlike the macro marketing environment, which affects a wide scope of businesses whatever their nature, the micro marketing environment will be determined by the market sector in question and will be unique to each company. The main thrust of the marketing environment is one of impact; the rationale is to investigate and understand factors that might have significant impact on a business or organization, particularly those that influence the relationships a company has with customers, suppliers, distributors, partners and stakeholders.

PORTER'S FIVE FORCES

Porter's five forces model highlights key areas of investigation that must be carried out in order to understand the specific nature of the pressures impacting on a business.

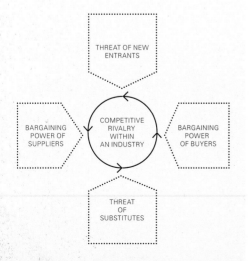

Porter's five forces analysis

This is a tool that can be used to assess pressures within a competitive business environment. Porter's model identifies five forces that impact the competitive power and profitability of a business within a particular industry:

» 1. The bargaining power of suppliers
» 2. The bargaining power of buyers
» 3. Rivalry between competitors in the market
» 4. Threat of new entrants to the market
» 5. Threat of substitute products or services

From screen to catwalk

Downton Abbey and *The Great Gatsby*

The television series *Downton Abbey*, aired in over 100 countries, inspired a rash of designer fashion collections, a phenomenon known as 'The Downton Effect'. Prada, Louis Vuitton, Burberry and Ralph Lauren all looked to Downton for inspiration for Autumn/Winter 2012. Cloche hats, tweed caps, jackets with bellows pockets, plus fours and Fair Isle knits all made an appearance on the catwalk. Men fell under the turn-of-the-century spell too. Double-breasted suits and waistcoats featured in the menswear shows. Two-button and three-button jackets were included in collections by Rag & Bone and Burberry, while Thom Browne, Paul Smith and J. Crew had round-collar shirts. Traditional men's outfitters and tailors on Savile Row in London reported a boom in trade fuelled mainly by interest from American clients. As the television story rolled into the 1920s, the fashion world kept pace; dropped-waist dresses and 1920s-style evening gowns emerged as the next wave of the Downton trend. The 1920s theme gained further momentum with the launch of *The Great Gatsby* film in 2013.

> "The Downton Effect for us is a global appreciation of fine English tailoring, with British milled cloth as the gold standard of understated elegance."
>
> Douglas Cordeaux
> Managing Director, Fox Brothers & Co

Below
The Gentleman Blogger, Matthew Zorpas, wears a Gucci suit in a 1920s setting inspired by the Gatsby era.

Right
Inspired by The Downton Effect, designers looked to the past for Autumn/Winter 2012. Ralph Lauren showed tweed, cloche hats and Fair Isle knits.

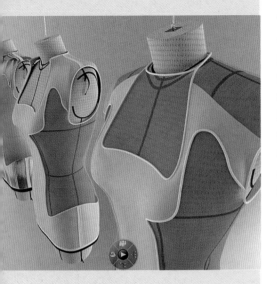

Cutting-edge couture

FashionLab by Dassault Systèmes

French designer Julien Fournié has revolutionized the processes of design and sampling with the help of a 3D computer-modelling program developed by the French company Dassault Systèmes, initially created for aircraft design. Now Dassault has set up FashionLab as a technology incubator dedicated to assist fashion designers to test virtually the limits of material and form. Fournié describes haute couture as a research laboratory where he can push boundaries and revolutionize technical processes and finishes. FashionLab's unique 3D modelling technology allows Fournié to sketch silhouettes, test fabrics and simulate fabric behaviour on the computer. By using this advanced technology Fournié has been able to combine perforated neoprene rubber with classic silk organza fused on top of a layer of Bakelite plastic and resolve the detailed stitching required to work a metallic chrome weave fabric into a stunning couture garment.

Digital rendering of garment designs by Julien Fournié.

The bargaining power of suppliers A supplier or manufacturer will have a strong bargaining position if they provide a unique product or a necessary service. If a particular fashion trend takes off, perhaps one featuring lace or hand embroidery, then a manufacturer in India or China with capability to produce delicate handwork may find that they have a stronger bargaining position on price. Suppliers that have built up a strong relationship with their customers will also be in a stronger position as it can be costly for customers to switch to a new supplier or manufacturer, especially if considerable money, time and energy have gone into product development, creating samples and working on product fittings and specifications. Each season, suppliers and manufacturers put pressure on their business customers by attempting to put their prices up; if customers have driven a hard bargain the previous season, a supplier is likely to try to claw back lost revenue. If a supplier understands that a particular style is on-trend and that there is great demand from end-consumers, then the balance will be tipped in their favour, particularly if they can offer a fast lead-time and deliver quickly. In this case the supplier will have stronger bargaining power and may be able to demand a higher price knowing that the buyer needs the stock urgently.

The bargaining power of buyers On the other side of the equation, buyers will naturally want to purchase products or services at the best possible price as well as profitable trading terms and agreements, so that they can ensure they are competitive in the marketplace. Suppliers need to keep their order books filled, so they will be under pressure to meet buyers' demands, particularly in difficult economic times, or if the market is strong and there are lots of companies competing for the same business. Buyers from the large retail chains will not only bargain for low prices but will also demand favourable discount terms and usually require suppliers to contribute to markdown costs on stock that does not sell at full price. Fashion designers and retailers that produce their own collections will gain the upper hand in negotiations with manufacturers if they place high-volume orders.

Rivalry between competitors in the market Competitive rivalry has been touched upon earlier in this book in the section on differentiation and competitive advantage (*see* page 58). Apparel retailing is awash with a myriad of available brands and fashion labels, all competing with one another for the end-consumer's custom. Retailers will compete with each other to have exclusivity on certain brands. It is standard practice for a boutique to refuse to carry a particular brand or label if it is stocked by a rival shop in the locality; and suppliers will be competing to ensure they are stocked in the most prestigious stores. Rivalry between competitors does

Sustainable pioneers

The North Face

Technological advances in sustainable design have made a
significant contribution to the development of new fashion
products and retail stores. This issue is of particular relevance
to high-performance outdoor sports apparel brands. The North
Face, for example, is committed to pushing the boundaries
of innovation and the company continually explores ways to
minimize their impact on the environment. Many of their high-
performance outdoor garments are designed using recycled
materials such as PrimaLoft Eco insulation, made from a
combination of post-consumer products and post-industrial
plastic waste. The North Face also uses innovative sustainable
technology when designing and building their retail stores.

The brand's 805-sq-m (8,665-sq-ft) store in Boise, Idaho, was
accomplished using the talents of Minnesota-based design
firm JGA, a leader in retail architecture. A wide range of high-
efficiency and energy-conserving technologies was utilized
throughout the building for lighting, heating and air-filtering
systems. Materials were recycled, kept to a minimum and
chosen for optimum energy use. Exciting new organic and
sustainable materials such as Plyboo renewable bamboo
plywood and SkyBlend, a wood particleboard material
manufactured from 100 per cent pre-consumer recycled wood
fibre, were used for store fixtures and the cashwrap counter.

The overall objective for the project was to create an exciting
retail environment that was both sustainable and commercial;
this has been achieved to stunning effect. The sustainable
makeover incorporates signature North Face elements including
large graphics, wooden surfaces, and red accents.

The North Face sustainably designed
store in Boise, Idaho. Dramatic graphics
are used to set the scene for their
outdoor performance gear. Photographic
images of mountain climbers make a
dynamic backdrop for the mannequins
in the foreground.

not only relate to retail, it will also be an issue further back along the supply chain. Textile suppliers will compete to gain fabric orders, while manufacturers within a particular country or region are in competition with each other to gain an order from foreign buyers, and will compete on price, quality, lead-time or extra services such as design capability, warehousing and other logistics.

Threat of new entrants to the market New entrants to a market can threaten companies already operating within it. In fashion, it is costly and time-consuming to design, develop, produce and sell a collection or product range, so new start-ups may not pose an enormous threat in the first instance. However, an established brand diversifying into a new market could constitute a severe threat. A brand with loyal customers and a solid business might capitalize on their existing resources to extend their operation into a new sector of the fashion market; a successful womenswear retailer deciding to develop a range for men, for example. For retailers there is a constant threat that competitors or new companies will establish their stores just across the road. While this poses a threat, it can also increase footfall, raising the number of customers visiting the area and encouraging healthy competition.

Threat of substitute products or services If customers can find an alternative product or service, they may switch their custom, thus weakening the power of a business to succeed. The threat of substitution applies equally to the end-consumer who may choose from several retailers offering similar fashion styles at comparable prices, and to business customers who could decide to purchase from a competitor if they offer a replacement product or service that could reasonably substitute for the original.

Internal environment

The internal or organizational environment refers to factors inside a company that affect the way it carries out its business and marketing function. These include:

> » Company and departmental structure
> » Personnel
> » Finance
> » Resources
> » Internal systems
> » Technological capabilities

The internal structure and culture of a business organization will impact on the way it operates. In Chapter 1 Seth Godin was quoted as having said that marketing is not a "last minute add-on". To be really effective, marketing should be integrated throughout a business. If this is so, then it follows that marketing will be affected by the allocation of resources, the extent to which responsibility for marketing is shared throughout an organization, and the way internal processes and procedures are set up. A key stage in the process of creating a marketing plan is to carry out an internal audit. The audit provides a company with an opportunity to review its internal procedures, capabilities, resources and marketing strategies.

Market research

So far we have outlined the wider scope of marketing research; now we come to the vitally important subsection of market research. The fashion market is a challenging arena. Designers must come up with fresh new ideas every season and thousands of products must be pumped out from factory to store on a regular basis. At the same time, retailers need to understand current and developing consumer trends so that they can purchase and sell the right products at the right price. It is crucial therefore that organizations, whether large or small, carry out market research investigations to gain an in-depth understanding of the market situation, assess shifts in trends, understand competitors and gain knowledge of consumers and their requirements. The market research process involves gathering, analysing and interpreting information, data and statistics on:

> » Market size
> » Market trends
> » Competitors and their market share
> » Consumers

Once research information has been gathered then its relevance can be assessed and the data analysed. The aim is to establish facts that can help with business and marketing decisions. Research data obtained by first-hand investigation is termed **primary research**. New data is gathered to address a specific question, using direct methods such as interviews, or indirect methods such as observation. Information gathered by reading reports and surveys compiled by someone else is called **secondary research**. This involves the collation and analysis of found data to explore the question to be addressed.

In addition, research can either be qualitative or quantitative.

Qualitative research Qualitative research investigates the quality of something and provides evidence about how and why the market is the way it is. Qualitative research is exploratory in nature and is useful for gathering facts on what consumers think or feel about particular issues relevant to the investigation. It can

THE MARKET RESEARCH PROCESS

```
┌─────────────────────────────┐
│                             │
│             1.              │
│   DEFINING THE PROBLEM      │
│   AND SETTING OBJECTIVES    │
│                             │
└─────────────────────────────┘
              ↓
┌─────────────────────────────┐
│                             │
│             2.              │
│   PLANNING THE RESEARCH     │
│   AND SETTING TIMESCALE     │
│                             │
└─────────────────────────────┘
              ↓
┌─────────────────────────────┐
│                             │
│             3.              │
│      GATHERING THE          │
│   INFORMATION AND DATA      │
│                             │
└─────────────────────────────┘
              ↓
┌─────────────────────────────┐
│                             │
│             4.              │
│      ANALYSING THE          │
│      INFORMATION            │
│                             │
└─────────────────────────────┘
              ↓
┌─────────────────────────────┐
│                             │
│             5.              │
│   WRITING THE REPORT AND    │
│   PRESENTING FINDINGS       │
│                             │
└─────────────────────────────┘
```

be carried out on its own or used as a forerunner to quantitative study. It helps form an overview of a market and assess the need for more in-depth quantitative investigations. Qualitative consumer research usually takes place face-to-face in small focus groups or individual interviews. Many fashion retailers or design companies invite a selection of consumers to preview a product range and try on garments prior to the seasonal launch in-store. This helps the company gauge the likely response to the range and to specific products, packaging and marketing materials. Feedback is very useful in working out what could potentially be the best sellers. Buyers can have a better chance to determine appropriate quantities for the buy and work out the ratio of various styles and colours if they receive pre-season information of this nature. Social media is a great tool in the first instance as it can provide a starting point for identifying trends and gaining consumer insight. Facebook and Twitter can assist the researcher in identifying suitable respondents to invite for face-to-face interviews or to join focus groups.

Quantitative research This type of research is numerically orientated. It quantifies the market, and can be used to calculate market share and provide detailed statistics on consumers. Market research surveys that gather data from a large sample of respondents are quantitative in nature. They can be conducted face-to-face either in the street or home, via online questionnaires, by post or via telephone.

Primary research or field research Primary research is the collection of original data gathered directly by going out into the field. Market research surveys, questionnaires, **focus groups** and individual interviews are examples of primary research. Primary research can also be used to collect data on products in the market and to investigate competitors. Field research does not have to be complicated – visits to the high street or mall, recording information on product, styles, colours, prices, special offers and markdown and generally keeping an eye on fashion, all constitute primary, or field, research. Research excursions to the high street are relatively quick and provide a simple way to gather current information first-hand. If research is conducted on a regular basis then it should be possible to notice both subtle and dramatic changes that occur in the marketplace over time.

Secondary research or desk research Secondary research investigates and reviews existing data published either on the Internet, in books, magazines, trade journals or via academic, government or industry sources. This kind of research is used to determine the size and make-up of a particular market sector and get background information and more detailed financial data. Much

Real-time market research

Stylitics

Setting up and running a focus group can be costly, particularly as it is likely to gather information from a limited number of consumers. However, market research companies can use digital technology to gather data from hundreds of thousands of consumers across the globe. Stylitics, founded by Rohan Deuskar and Zach Davis, is a New York-based technology company whose innovative approach allows them to translate consumer passion for fashion into real-time data on what styles are trending worldwide. The Stylitics app allows consumers to create a virtual wardrobe, keep track of the brands, styles and colours they wear and monitor how much money they spend on clothes. But this is only part of the story. Stylitics also provides market and trend data to clothing brands and retailers looking for consumer insight and behavioural data. In return for allowing Stylitics to use this data, consumers are rewarded with discounts and freebies from brands.

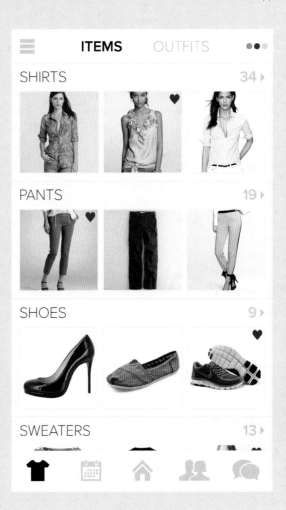

The Stylitics virtual closet, fashion planner and style chat app.

Left

Topshop in New York. It is vital for fashion designers or buyers to get out into the field to visit fashion stores and carry out primary research of the market. It is worth taking a small notebook with you when you go so that you can take note of important information and pricing details.

Above

Trend and forecasting companies usually use freelance trend scouts to take photos and report on street fashions in cities around the world. Trend forecasting company Stylesight, for example, have reporters around the globe feeding ideas back on emerging trends. Now it is easier than ever to track street style and culture using apps such as Pose or Fashism.

of this type of information will be available for free from libraries, but some sources require payment for access to their material. Companies that supply industry information as a commercial venture usually charge quite substantial sums, but the cost is likely to be considerably less than those incurred if hiring a market research company to conduct extensive primary research.

Market research methods

The approach to primary market research investigations will be dependent on the exact nature of the project and why the research has been commissioned. Before research gets underway, first determine the aims and objectives of the study. Marketing and market research should be considered when:

» Starting a new business
» Entering a new market
» Launching a new product or product range
» Creating a brand identity or brand redesign
» Adding a new service
» Targeting a new customer segment
» Developing a major promotional campaign
» Reviewing progress or resetting targets
» Researching how to compete in a market
» Investigating issues of underperformance

Once the purpose of the research is clear and the exact aims have been clarified then the next step is to determine who might be most suitable to carry out the research, analyse the findings and produce a final report. Large-scale market research projects are usually carried out by consultancies or agencies, but it may be possible to farm out some aspects of the project to a number of different specialist companies or carry out parts of the project in-house. A full-service market research agency will be able to help determine the scope of the research and assist with the development of a customized project. They will be able to carry out quantitative research and provide personnel to design and conduct market research surveys, questionnaires and interviews. They will also be able to analyse and evaluate data.

Another option could be to use a trend and market consultancy. They usually concentrate on qualitative research and provide information on consumer types, lifestyle trends and market trends. Condé Nast, for example, the publisher of *Vogue* magazine, commissioned The Future Laboratory to carry out consumer research so that they could learn more about the motivations and needs of the modern fashion magazine reader. Consultancy companies are practised in conducting focus groups and running interview panels. They may have viewing facilities where interviews and discussions can be watched or recorded. (It is important to stress that market research is subject to guidelines and laws regarding data protection.) Trend consultancies may use the services of a network of freelance **trend scouts** located in major fashion and trend hot spots across the globe. Consultancies will also commission people to go out into the marketplace as a **mystery shopper** or to carry out an investigative procedure called **comparative shopping**. Consultancies of this type may be able to provide additional quantitative research; they may subcontract this element out to a field-work and tabulation agency specializing in data collection and survey analysis.

Another possible option would be to conduct market investigations in-house or commission one company to carry out field-work and then engage a data preparation and analysis agency to analyse the results; these agencies will have sophisticated software programs suitable for in-depth data analysis. If the plan is to employ an outside agency to conduct research or analysis then it is important to define the task and brief the consultancy or agency. A brief should contain:

>> Information on the company and its current market
>> The background for the research
>> The issues the research should address
>> What the research should achieve
>> Detailed time-frame for the project
>> Deadline for submission of the report
>> Available budget and resources

Even if a company wishes to carry out all or part of the investigations themselves, it is important that they are clear on the above points before they get underway with the project. The next section will take you through basic primary research methods. While professional market researchers will be able to carry these out in great depth, students, designers, buyers or individuals running a small business enterprise can also use most of the methods outlined just as effectively.

Observation

A great deal of practical and easy research can be carried out simply and at little cost. One of the most beneficial market research methods for anyone working within the industry is observation of the market. It is fascinating how much valuable knowledge can be gathered first-hand by watching people in the street, perusing the shops and studying consumer behaviour as they browse and shop in-store. Constant observation of street fashion and scrutiny of the fashion retail environment is routine within the industry. Designers, buyers and marketers visit key fashion cities regularly, and check out activity in their local fashion stores as part of their working routine. Manufacturing companies and suppliers will also send their personnel out into the marketplace to monitor what is going on. This practice is known as comparative shopping or the comp shop.

Comparative shopping

It is very important to visit the stores of key competitors and monitor what they are up to and review their product offer. Comparative shopping is a simple process that involves observing and recording information on the composition of fashion ranges, colours, fabrics, price points, promotional activity and visual merchandising in competitors' stores. Comp shops are a form of primary research. The usual procedure is to visit the stores and look directly at the products, but a great deal of comparative information can also be garnered using the Internet. Websites and social media platforms can themselves be the subject of a comparative exercise; they can be compared in terms of ease of use, technology, service, content, extra offers or discounts and consumer engagement.

Below
Luisa Via Roma is a must for any fashionista visiting the historic Italian city of Florence. The store houses an extensive selection of international luxury and contemporary fashion brands. The Rick Owens collection is given a prominent position within the store and promoted using a large-scale photographic backdrop.

Bottom
Colette is the number one fashion destination to visit when in Paris. This cutting-edge concept store offers a whole universe of fashion, art and design.

Like-for-like product comparison

The **like-for-like (LFL) product comparison** is a more detailed investigation into a specific product. This is carried out when a company wishes to investigate in depth how a particular product they currently produce or are planning to develop compares with similar items offered by competitors in the market. LFL comparisons are generally carried out to compare core products or basics. The usual procedure will be to purchase the item from several retailers. So take, for example, a retailer such as Gap wanting to compare their men's basic white T-shirt with those offered by competitors within the market. They may go and purchase similar product from Uniqlo, American Apparel, Marks & Spencer and Calvin Klein. The garments will be compared in terms of price, fabric and make quality, design details and fit, wash care and performance. It would be normal to send the garments to a testing laboratory to check on issues such as piling, spirality and shrinkage. Obviously purchasing garments and sending them to a lab for testing will incur some costs, but it is possible to carry out LFL comparisons without purchasing garments. In this case comparisons will be mainly for price, styling, fabric compositions and available colour options.

Mystery shopping

Many market research companies employ researchers who are tasked to enter shops in the role of a potential customer. As an undercover observer they are then able to monitor and report back on their experience of customer service and other retail activities. Retailers may commission mystery shopping as part of their overall market research so that they can analyse and compare the service offered by competitors. In light of the growing relevance of 'process' (*see* page 50) as part of the marketing mix and the increasing need for retailers to provide an exciting and engaging shopping experience, mystery shopping should be viewed as a worthy investigative method.

Focus groups

Focus groups and discussion groups run by experienced market researchers help provide information concerning consumer opinions, attitudes and purchase behaviour. Fashion companies often use these groups to gauge reaction to new marketing campaigns or product ranges prior to their launch. A selection of consumers will be invited to view the collection and give their feedback. This information can be extremely helpful for

Above
Mannequins in Barneys New York display the Stella McCartney collection. It is common industry practice for designers and fashion buyers to travel to cities such as New York, Paris, London and Milan as part of their fashion research and market observation. It is not ethical to use a camera while you are in a store but comp shopping and fashion research can be a fun way to test your memory! A good tip is to take a small pocket notebook with you and record your findings as quickly as you can before you forget the details.

LIKE-FOR-LIKE COMPARISON CHART

PRODUCT MEN'S FIVE POCKET JEANS	PRICE	FABRICATION » FIBRE COMPOSITION » FABRIC WEIGHT » FABRIC FINISH OR WASH	STYLING DETAILS	WASH CARE INSTRUCTIONS AND AFTERCARE » GARMENT LABELLING	ADDED VALUE (DETAILS OR SPECIAL OFFERS THAT ADD VALUE)
COMPANY A					
COMPANY B					
COMPANY C					
COMPANY D					

A simple table can be used as a framework for a LFL product comparison. The criteria along the top should contain price, fabrication, design details, wash care instructions and additional labelling or product information. A column can also be added to indicate how many colour options the item comes in. Products can also be compared with regards to details that might achieve added value – this could be a unique technology utilized to enhance the product or promotional campaign with a special offer.

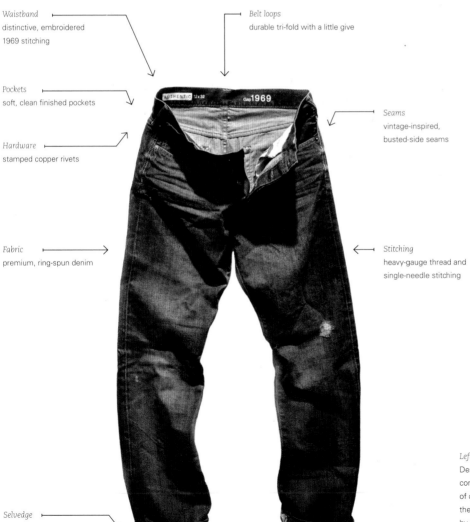

Waistband
distinctive, embroidered
1969 stitching

Belt loops
durable tri-fold with a little give

Pockets
soft, clean finished pockets

Seams
vintage-inspired,
busted-side seams

Hardware
stamped copper rivets

Fabric
premium, ring-spun denim

Stitching
heavy-gauge thread and
single-needle stitching

Selvedge
authentic red selvedge

Left
Designers doing a product LFL comparison will scrutinize every detail of competitors' product. Gap promotes their 1969 premium jeans collection by highlighting all the authentic design features that make the style a classic.

designers, buyers and merchandisers who can use the data to determine which styles and colours will be popular. The downside to research of this nature is that a small sample group may not be representative of consumers as a whole. There can also be a risk of the results being skewed if one person in the group becomes too dominant and sways the opinions and responses of other participants. However, if the sample consumer group is selected by a reputable consultancy and the session steered by a professional moderator, then focus groups can provide insights into consumer attitudes and help negate any assumptions that might have been held by a retailer about the customer or the product.

Interviews

Face-to-face interviews are useful for gathering more in-depth consumer information. They can be used to expand on data from questionnaires and to gather qualitative data. Interviews can be run as a semi-structured discussion where respondents can share their opinions and views. This type of interview allows researchers to gather customers' feedback on a particular brand under investigation and on competing products and services. Generally an interview lasts 10–30 minutes and can be conducted on any number of selected individuals within the target market. Interviews can be carried out over the telephone but face-to-face is better for more lengthy discussions, or if the research requires the interviewee to look at products. The biggest drawback can be the time it might take to carry out the interview, particularly if it is taking place on the street. Busy people do not always want to be stopped or devote time to lengthy questions.

Questionnaires

Questionnaires are extremely helpful for collecting quantitative information from a large number of people. It is essential to ensure that questions are not leading or biased in any way and that they are designed to obtain accurate and relevant information. Questionnaires must also be designed so that the data can be analysed systematically once it has been gathered.

It is important to make sure the questionnaire looks professional but also simple and user-friendly; this helps to maximize the response rate. Try to ensure that a questionnaire will not take too long to complete. A short statement explaining the purpose of the study should be included at the beginning – you want to establish a rapport with respondents and engage them with the project. Sometimes the company that commissions the research offers

Top
The Zacarias Bilbao bag designed by Rita Nazareno; the unique shape is inspired by Frank Gehry's Guggenheim Museum in Bilbao.

Above
A small focus group meets in Manila in the Philippines to preview cutting-edge bags designed by Rita Nazareno for the new brand, Zacarias, manufactured by S.C. Vizcarra. The focus group allowed Nazareno to gather important consumer feedback on the prototype designs.

a prize to those that complete the survey. When designing the questions, think carefully about the objective of the survey, what it is you want to know and why. Make sure to:

» Keep questions short and simple
» Make questions precise
» Avoid ambiguity
» Avoid negatives

Open-ended questions allow respondents to formulate their own answers. Closed-format questions force respondents to choose between several prescribed options. It is possible to use a mixture of these two formats but it is best to keep open-ended questions to a minimum, as they are much harder to analyse than closed-format questions. The **Likert scale** can be used to gather consumer attitudes to particular statements. For example, "sustainable fashion should be fashionable as well as ethical". The scale offers five positions, set out below:

» 1. Disagree strongly
» 2. Disagree
» 3. Neither agree nor disagree
» 4. Agree
» 5. Agree strongly

Responses to questions using the Likert scale can be easily analysed by using a numerical system that equates to each position, so for example, agree strongly = 5, agree = 4, and so on. The format of questions using a five-point system can be adapted, so for example you could ask 'How important is price to you when you shop for clothes?'

» 1. Of no importance
» 2. Not very important
» 3. No opinion
» 4. Fairly important
» 5. Very important

It is, however, not good practice to design a questionnaire using this system alone. Respondents can have a tendency to choose one or two of the five positions and tick them consistently. Another option is to use questions that offer a checklist from which respondents can choose. So a questionnaire designed to find out if respondents owned clothing made from sustainable fabrics might offer the following tick list. Respondents are asked to mark as many options as applicable:

» Garments made from hemp
» Garments made from organic cotton

Ethical fashion exhibition and questionnaire

What's your e-motive?

When the London College of Fashion ran its first sustainability week they invited industry professionals, lecturers and students to attend seminars, debates and conferences to discuss issues surrounding sustainable and ethical fashion. An exhibition and interactive data-gathering exercise entitled, 'What's your e-motive?' was held as part of the activities. The exhibition aimed to raise awareness and inform on sustainable and ethical fashion, engage the audience with the debate and encourage them to share their views. The overall objective was to capture consumer views and understand consumer purchasing decisions and behaviour when it comes to sustainable fashion.

The interactive exhibit showcased garments and products from a broad selection of fashion designers and companies. Adili, Amazon Life, Blackspot Shoes, Del Forte jeans, howies, Simple Shoes and Terra Plana were some of the companies whose product was featured. Research was inherent to the exhibition; an online 'eco-wardrobe audit' questionnaire was posted on the university website and computers were situated within the gallery so that visitors could answer the audit. The combined results of the interactive exhibition questions and online eco-wardrobe audit provided the London College of Fashion with over 400 individual responses and almost 200 people answered the questionnaire. This revealed that 97 per cent of respondents were interested in purchasing and wearing garments that they believed to be ethical and sustainably produced, but that only a third claimed to actually own a garment that was fairly traded or made from sustainable materials.

Respondents were asked the importance of the following criteria when making purchasing decisions about clothing.

> » Fashion and style
> » Price
> » Fabric
> » Ethics behind the production of the garment

Sixty-three per cent said that fashion and style was very important when choosing clothes, while the ethics behind the production of garments was judged by 55.6 per cent to be only fairly important. Interestingly 56.3 per cent of people said that anti-sweatshop was very important in a separate question that asked respondents to compare the importance of:

> » Anti-sweatshop
> » Fair-trade
> » Sustainable fabrics such as organic cotton
> » Recycling and re-using garments

This result highlights the importance of language and context. The emotive and more specific term, 'anti-sweatshop', may have been easier for people to grasp than the idea of ethics.

'What's your e-motive?' An exhibition of ethical fashion at the London College of Fashion. The exhibit provided an opportunity to collect data on consumer attitudes to ethical fashion.

Consumer questionnaire: fashion shopping habits

1. How much do you spend on average each month for clothing?

☐ £20–50 ☐ £51–80 ☐ £81–100 ☐ £101–200 ☐ Over £200

2. Where do you shop for clothes?

☐ High street ☐ Independent boutiques ☐ Department stores
☐ Vintage stalls ☐ Street markets ☐ Supermarkets ☐ Online

3. What fashion labels or brands are you wearing right now?

4. How often do you normally shop for clothing or accessories?

☐ Every week ☐ Twice a month ☐ Every month

☐ 4–6 times a year ☐ 2–3 times a year ☐ Only when there is a sale on

5. Which sentence most represents when / how you shop?

☐ Only when I need something specific

☐ Whenever I fancy something new

☐ Whenever I go shopping with friends

☐ As soon as the new fashion season hits the shops

☐ It's always spontaneous, when something catches my eye

6. Are you ever influenced by what celebrities are wearing?

☐ Yes ☐ No ☐ Sometimes

7. Age: 8. Gender:

9. Occupation: 10. Salary:

» Garments made from bamboo fabric
» Garments made from any other sustainable fabric
» Don't know

Ranking is another option that can be used. Respondents are asked to rank a list of criteria in order of importance or relevance.

"Please rank the following as to how relevant you consider them to be to ethical fashion." (1 = most relevant – 5 = least relevant)

» Fair-trade
» Anti-sweatshop
» Low carbon footprint
» Ethical production
» Sustainable design
» Recycling and re-using

When setting out the order for your questions it is best to start with more general questions about the topic under investigation. Start with the easiest and simplest questions and work through to those that are most particular or complex. If you are going to have a mixture of closed-format and open-ended questions, then start with the closed-format questions.

The questionnaire should conclude with questions designed to collect demographic data. You will want to know the age bracket, sex, profession and status of respondents. Think about these questions logically. If you are only asking young women to respond to the questionnaire then it is not necessary to include a tick box for male or female. It is vital to preserve confidentiality and to abide by data protection laws. Make sure it is clear who is carrying out the research and for what purpose.

It is a sensible idea to pre-test or pilot a draft survey on a small sample of respondents before it 'goes live' to a large sample of people. This helps refine questions so they are not leading in any way, eliminate any ambiguity and iron out any other teething problems. A well-designed questionnaire should be easy for respondents to answer by themselves either online, via email, in response to a survey in a magazine or if sent in the post. Questionnaire results should be presented in a report that outlines the purpose of the study, explains the methodology employed to gather data, includes a summary of results and provides conclusions and recommendations based on the analysis. The main body of the report will analyse the data and illustrate results with detailed charts and tables.

Monitoring the market

Now that we have looked at some fundamental market research methods, the next step is to review the purpose of market research and outline the aspects of the market that should be monitored. Market research and analysis should be used to:

» Define the size and composition of a market sector
» Determine the state of the market
» Assess trends within the market
» Establish which competitors operate in the market
» Analyse competitor strengths and weaknesses
» Research consumers and understand their requirements

The following section will explain the key aspects of researching and analysing market size, market trends, competitors and market share. Consumer research will be discussed in more detail in Chapter 4.

Market size

The size of a market can be determined in terms of numbers of consumers purchasing within a specific market, or more commonly, as a financial figure expressing the value of a particular market. For example, the global apparel market was valued at US$1.7 trillion in 2012, the Brazilian fashion market at US$63 billion and kidswear in Brazil worth approximately US$8 billion. The first figure indicates the size of the global market; the second piece of data shows the size of a specific geographic market relative to the global market; and the final figure gives the size of a specific market sector in that region. The fashion and apparel market can be broken down and categorized in a number of ways. Data can be compiled on any of the following:

» **Location of market:** global, international, national

» **Product category:** accessories, apparel, lingerie, perfume, homeware

» **Who the product is for:** women, men, tween market, children and baby

» **Product type:** pro-sport, active wear, sport-luxe, casual wear, denim, formal wear, evening wear

» **Market level:** couture, premium, mid-market, value or commodity market

Once the size of a particular market has been established, the next important issue to determine is the direction and trend within the market under investigation.

Market trends

Even though information on the size of a market at a specific point in time is extremely helpful, it is even more useful to track market data over a longer time-frame. This helps to reveal prevailing trends, indicating if the market is expanding, stagnant or contracting. If a market is experiencing a period of growth then there is opportunity for those already operating within the market to increase their business. But market potential may also encourage new entrants. This means that even in good times, existing players cannot get complacent – they still need to be competitive or they may lose business to newer market participants. If a market is static or contracting (this could be due to cultural, social or demographic changes or as a result of an economic downturn), operators in the market will be fighting to ensure they do not lose business or go out of business altogether. However, even in a recession or challenging market situation, opportunity exists for businesses to grow. Examples include luxury fashion brands expanding into emerging global markets, the rise of the premium denim market and the growing market for e-commerce.

Emerging global markets During the economic slowdown in Europe and the US, which began with the global recession in 2008, multinational luxury brands such as Chanel, Louis Vuitton, Marc Jacobs, Prada and Salvatore Ferragamo recognized the potential of emerging global markets such as the BRIC countries (*see* page 26), whose economies were growing. The brands expanded into these regions, either through licence partnerships with local companies or by opening a direct-ownership store. Once established brands had made the leap, so others became more willing to test the market.

Premium denim The market for premium denim, fashionable jeans with superlative fit and specialized wash and fabric finishes, took off at a time when many fashion consumers were price-conscious and reluctant to spend. Premium jeans were viewed as a second skin that could be worn almost anywhere, and therefore worth investing in.

E-commerce An article on *Business of Fashion* in June 2013 claimed that apparel is the fastest-growing e-commerce category in the US. In China three-quarters of all online sales are in apparel. With this rise in online and multi-channel sales, new businesses have entered the market. Farfetch is a fashion marketplace and community that unites independent boutiques around the world with consumers. The online shop posted a sales figure of US$129 million in 2012, a rise of 145 per cent on the previous year. The Farfetch business model reduces risk by not carrying stock. Instead they co-ordinate the purchasing process between consumers and

After-sales service has become a distinguishing factor for fashion brands and retailers to consider. Premium denim brand Nudie Jeans (top) offer a free in-store repair service to their customers. Alternatively, the Nudie Jeans Repair Kit containing thread, denim patches and a thimble can be sent to customers. The Japanese retailer Uniqlo (above) offers an alteration service and will hem jeans for free.

boutiques, with just one checkout procedure irrespective of how many boutiques the consumer buys from. Orders are then sent out directly from the boutiques. Another fashion e-commerce site started in London is NOT JUST A LABEL (NJAL), which connects emerging designers directly with consumers.

Fashion forecasting and market intelligence

An essential element of monitoring the market is keeping abreast of changing fashion trends. A watchful eye on developments in global fashion culture, catwalk trends, street style and the market in general is vital. But it is not just about monitoring the present or analysing the recent past; the trick with fashion is to try to predict the future. Designers start planning their collections up to a year in advance of when they will sell in-store. Fabric mills develop their ranges at least two years in advance, and fibre manufacturers and colour prediction agencies work even further ahead of the season. This is why fashion can be such a risky business and why so much research must be undertaken. Fashion forecasting, market intelligence and trend reporting are indispensable constituents of the apparel and accessory industry. Retailers, design houses and manufacturers will use market intelligence and forecasting information to help them with important product and strategy decisions. The trend forecasting industry was reported to be worth US$36 billion in 2011 with a significant number of companies worldwide providing forecasting and market intelligence services. Agencies' services range from specialist consultancy, tailored to meet the specific requirements of the commissioning company, to off-the-peg forecasting, styling and market intelligence reports that can be purchased by fashion industry professionals. US companies WGSN and Stylesight, Trendstop in the UK, and French companies Trend Union, Promostyl and Peclers are among the best known. Many of these agencies operate an online subscription service with updates daily, weekly and monthly.

Most fashion forecasting and intelligence agencies will supply:

>> Market intelligence
>> Consumer insight
>> Information on emerging global trends
>> Reports on street style
>> Catwalk reports
>> Key styles and design ideas
>> Colour forecasting
>> Fabric trend information
>> Information on print and graphic trends

For a larger fashion business, a subscription or bespoke package with a trend forecasting agency will be affordable, but for an individual or small business the expense may not be viable. It is possible to access relevant information on trends, colour and street style at little or no cost through primary research and observation. Social media and photo-sharing services such as Instagram, Tumblr and Pinterest make it easy to monitor trends.

Fashion designers, manufacturers, retail buyers, merchandisers and brand managers will all use a mélange of market and trend information as a basis to predict the future direction for their businesses. Sales forecasting is a key part of the research and analysis process carried out by buyers, merchandisers and product managers. This type of forecasting uses data on historical sales patterns to gauge potential sales for the coming season. This background data must be used in conjunction with trend forecasting information so that a design and buying team can have the best chance of 'getting it right' when stock finally hits the shops. In fashion retail, sales data is usually reviewed on a daily basis and analysed in more depth every week. Major assessment of sales, consumer purchasing patterns and product performance will take place at the end of each season for both retail and wholesale businesses. Designers and product developers will build on this information with research into colour, fabric, design and technical trends so that they can develop appropriate products for the coming seasons.

Life cycle of a fashion trend

An important point about markets and fashion trends is that they change over time; this is why research should be an ongoing discipline.

A fad A **fad** is short-lived and usually difficult to predict. A fashion fad can be an individual item, look or style that becomes intensely popular almost overnight and then dies out as suddenly as it came

Below
Thousands of international buyers and designers visit Première Vision in Paris each season. Around 700 textile suppliers from approximately 28 countries exhibit their fabric collections and innovations. Fashion industry professionals use the fair as an opportunity to preview up-and-coming trends and colours, and to place orders for sample fabrics so they can begin the design and development process for the next season.

LIFE CYCLE OF A FASHION TREND

The first stage of the trend life cycle is the introduction stage. The next is growth, then comes the maturity stage, and finally the decline, which may tail off to nothing, or remain low and constant in the case of a fashion classic. Sales of a fashion fad might take off suddenly. Growth might be rapid, reach a peak and then drop quickly; the fad will die out once everyone who wants the particular fashion has it. Fashion buyers need to be sharp when it comes to fads – while they obviously have great potential if you get it right, there is a risk of getting on the bandwagon too late and being caught with stock no one wants. When a fashion trend reaches maturity, sales will flatten out. This is the indication that the market is saturated and sales will start to go into decline. Declining sales for a specific retailer or supplier could also result when a trend is established, and other competitors offer something similar that consumers prefer.

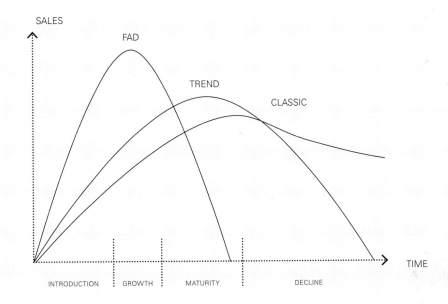

in. A fad might be in fashion for one season only and then next season be most definitely out of fashion. A fad generally lasts for a year or less.

A trend The main difference between a fad and a trend is duration. A fashion trend may start slowly with low acceptance in the early stages and then build momentum over time. It will peak and then taper off, either disappearing altogether or flattening out and remaining in fashion long enough to be reclassified as a classic. The women's trouser suit has become a classic. The seed of this trend was sewn in 1966 when Yves Saint Laurent introduced 'Le Smoking', a tuxedo trouser suit for women. This illustrates how a trend may be initiated at couture or designer level and then work its way down through the market levels to be sold in high-street stores; this is known as the trickle-down effect. Trends can also move in the other direction, they can start on the street and bubble up through the fashion hierarchy to be reinterpreted by designers on the catwalks of Paris, London, Milan and New York.

Megatrend A megatrend is a large social, cultural, economic, political or technological change that is slow to form but will influence a market over an extended time-frame. Denim jeans could be described as a megatrend.

Opposite
Three Norwegian friends came up with the idea of sewing their sweatpants to their hoodies and introducing a long zip for easy access. Thus the OnePiece label was born and the trend took off. Celebrities and pop stars wore them, causing a spike in sales during Christmas in 2012.

Balancing instinct and data

Trend forecaster Geraldine Wharry

Geraldine Wharry is a trend-forecasting consultant with clients including Samsung, WGSN and the British Library. As a forecaster, Wharry uses a mixture of intuition and research to summarize information and develop an actual forecast. It is important to remain objective and not let personal preferences get in the way of trends you are forecasting; instinct needs to be counterbalanced with solid information, data and facts.

> "I work in both a very organized and organic way. At the beginning of the creative process I may get inspired by a socio-economic or science article as much as something I saw on a street wall or in an art book or on a catwalk. Then I gather all these images, articles and data and from this a story or concept comes to life. I have a process I call hunting and gathering."

Hunt – Trend experts search and document trends as they surface. New developments in fashion, design, arts and culture, colour, consumer behaviour, architecture and materials are monitored, as well as the latest in politics, business and technology.

Identify – After all the research is identified and edited, key themes are carefully analysed. From this analysis aesthetic macro trends emerge, and from these future product trends can be identified. Macro trends are the drivers that will influence design businesses one to two years in advance.

Gather – Once the key macro trends have been identified, the next step is to show how they might apply to the design of product collections for the womenswear, menswear, childrenswear, sports and accessory markets, with detailed direction on colour, styling for key product items, textile trends and graphics.

Trend forecasters are often asked how they source up-and-coming trends. Wharry explains that it depends if you're looking to communicate the latest trends or working on more long-range macro trends. Working on latest trends is termed trend analysis. In this case, editorials, catwalk shows, street fashion, entertainment, celebrities and exhibitions, as well as retail trends, will be analysed so that information on existing key trends can be collated. For anticipating future macro trends you also have to stay abreast of advances in areas such as science, technology or craft. Wharry monitors online sources such as the TED Talks on www.ted.com that interview thinkers and influencers. She researches social, cultural, scientific, technological and political data as well as checking out innovative fashion labels or even fashion students. Everything experimental and different is considered.

Do forecasters create trends, or are they just reporting on developing trends? Wharry explains,

> "I don't think we create trends out of the blue. We act more as a sponge. We keep our antennae alert; we study, edit and select what is important, then curate the message. Trend forecasters give a voice to specific trends, thereby amplifying their visibility to a captive audience."

Trend forecasting performs a vital role within the fashion industry. Many companies, from raw material producers to manufacturers and retailers, value trend information, not only for the creative stimulation but to stay competitive in an increasingly complex world of fashion. Trend forecasters enable businesses to make the right strategic and design decisions so they can make relevant products in a fast-changing world.

Pop-up stores

Pop-up stores and guerrilla projects are now an established trend within fashion retail. This particular development really hits the spot in terms of satisfying customers' appetite for the buzz of newness while at the same time protecting businesses from the costs of long-term investment. Pop-ups allow a business to test the market and bolster the high street by ensuring empty properties are rented in the short term. The benefits of opening for a limited time are increasing consumer interest and desire, as they know the project will only last a short while; and giving consumers an element of insider knowledge, which is de rigueur in the information age. In 2013, Rebecca Minkoff opened a Holiday Pop-up store in New York. Consumers were enticed by good discounts, available for just one weekend, a Benefit makeover and beauty gift with purchases, and hair styling by TRESemmé. Visitors could take photos of their new look at a 'selfie station'. The aim of such promotions is to make a shopping trip into an experience that is then shared online.

Identifying competitors

It is important for a business to monitor its competitors, keep an eye on what they are up to and scrutinize the products and services they offer. The first step is to identify competitors and determine which ones to research. This is not always straightforward. A twenty-year-old Japanese fashion consumer may choose to purchase in Uniqlo and Louis Vuitton. A forty-five-year-old woman with an artistic sensibility and creative sense of style may purchase designer labels such as Crea Concept, Shirin Guild, Eileen Fisher or Oska but may also shop in high-street stores such as Marks & Spencer, Zara, Uniqlo and Gap. Within the manufacturing market, an apparel manufacturer in China might find that they are in competition not only with other Chinese manufacturers but also with countries in the Asia region such as Vietnam that may have lower labour costs, or other global producers in Turkey or Eastern Europe that are closer to the European fashion markets.

The most basic way of categorizing competitors is to define those that offer and supply similar types of products and services at the same level of the market. So one could say that Gucci and Prada, or Nike and adidas, are brands that are in direct competition. But this is a very simplistic way to view the competitive landscape, especially for fashion.

Competition is not so much an issue of brand against brand; it is more a case of:

Top
The SuperPier in New York City transformed the old Marine & Aviation Pier into a vibrant cultural hub re-using 460 shipping containers as retail units. During development it offered pop-up opportunities for fashion and film events.

Above
BOXPARK in London's Shoreditch is a semi-permanent pop-up mall made of old shipping containers. BOXPARK is home to a mix of well-known and indie fashion and lifestyle brands, galleries and restaurants.

Opposite
SPINEXPO™ Trend moodboards created by Sophie Steller Studio. SPINEXPO™ is an international trade fair specializing in fibres, yarns and technical textiles. Each season SPINEXPO™ publishes information on key trends, colours, yarn developments and fabric concepts in collaboration with trend forecasting consultancy Sophie Steller Studio. The studio has worked with brands and retailers including Polo Ralph Lauren, H&M and Gap.

» Product type and usage
» Consumer psychology
» Product and brand positioning
» Shopping location

....

COMPETING FOR RETAIL SPACE

*Product stocked in a boutique or department
store is not just competing for the end-
consumer's custom but also the store buyer's.
Labels that perform well are more likely to be
bought season after season by the buyer and
may be given more floor space and a better
profile within the store. Brands that don't
sell so well risk being positioned in a less
prominent location, having their floor space
diminished or being dropped by the buyer.*

....

Above
In the Zen Plaza department store in Ho
Chi Minh City, Vietnam, young Vietnamese
fashion designers have set up a shop
with their exclusive work. Here they are
competing directly with one another for
the customers' attention. In Vietnam there
is a growing middle class and a demand
for younger, trendier fashion.

Let's take a man who wants to buy a well-made classic but
contemporary suit from an upmarket designer brand. He wants
to purchase a respected label because he feels that a designer
suit will last, be well tailored and of *good quality*. This shopper
lives out of town but plans a trip into the city to look for the suit.
Prior to the visit, he goes online to gather information, compare
prices and check store locations. Once in town he starts with a
visit to Armani. He likes the brand's *classic simplicity* and knows
it has a great reputation for men's tailoring. On the basis of classic
simplicity, Calvin Klein might be considered a direct competitor, so
our potential customer heads for a department store to continue his
search. Once there he notices a suit by Paul Smith and is intrigued
by the fusion of *classic style* with quirky designer details; the suit
most certainly is contemporary. So now this brand also enters his
consideration. This short scenario should help to illustrate how
competition is dependent upon the interplay of several factors:
the type of product, the positioning of brands under consideration,
the requirements, needs and psychology of the consumer as well
as the options actually available to our potential purchaser in the
locale at the time of his shopping expedition. Throughout this
description certain words have been highlighted in italics. They have
been used to indicate the qualities the man expects; he wants a
suit that is classic yet contemporary, simple yet stylish and good
quality. Also of importance is that it should be a designer brand.
However, he may not adhere to these particular criteria for other
products. Imagine he also wishes to purchase two or three basic
white cotton shirts and some T-shirts to wear with the suit. He
might not consider Armani, Paul Smith or Calvin Klein for these but
head straight to Gap, Uniqlo or Zara to buy what he considers a
commodity product at a more reasonable price.

Pushing the idea further, if a consumer goes to a shopping centre
with the aim of purchasing, then any one of the shops in the mall or
brands in a department store housed in the mall has the potential
to be in competition for the shopper's custom on that particular
shopping trip. This leads us to the concept of indirect competition.
The best way to view this is to think of it as everything that might
compete for a consumer's discretionary expenditure. A woman
who wants to splash out and treat herself may decide to spend her
money on make-up or beauty products rather than fashion, or she
may purchase a new iPod or iPhone rather than an item of clothing
or fashion accessory. The trick in determining who competitors

could be is to try to consider the topic from the consumer's perspective. This is why understanding the consumer is so important. Constant monitoring of the market will also help to reveal what is going on and ascertain which competitors to examine.

Competitor analysis

Once competitors have been identified, the next step is to analyse their business. The aim is to evaluate how they are performing and investigate their operation in terms of size, **market share**, capabilities and resources, product offer, services, routes to market and number of retail outlets, if this is applicable. The purpose is to assess their strengths and weaknesses and determine how best to compete. Analysing a competitor is the first step to creating a competitive advantage. Monitoring competitors also allows a competing company to react quickly to economical or strategic changes made by competitors. Background research using published industry and trade data should help to reveal the competitor's overall financial situation, share of the market and operational activities. Market share is expressed as a percentage. It can be calculated by dividing the total market value by the sales revenue of each business operating in the market, or by dividing the total volume of units sold in the overall market by the number of units sold by each market participant. It is possible for a market leader to maintain a steady market share over a long period, but their share may not necessarily remain stable, so it is important to monitor the market and market share over time. Market share is used to indicate the composition of the market and highlight the value of key competitors relative to each other, thus helping to gauge their importance and power. This links to Porter's five forces, as powerful companies may have a stronger negotiating position with suppliers.

Utilizing marketing research

Market research must be used in combination with more extensive marketing research to monitor the state of the market, gauge the viability of projects, assess their feasibility, work out how to implement projects and support the writing of business and **marketing plans**. Wide-ranging research is crucial for those planning to start a venture, introduce new product lines, or enter a new market. Research may also be needed so as to re-confirm existing plans and direction, respond to changing situations within the market, or address issues surrounding underperformance of a business or product. In order to determine the remit for a research project and navigate through the research process, it can help if you

Above
The 2007 Fendi fashion show on the
Great Wall of China. The extraordinary
catwalk extravaganza showcased the
Spring/Summer 2008 collection as well
as an additional mini-collection created
specifically for the occasion. The entire
production was said to have cost in the
region of US$10 million. This enormous
investment gives a clear indication of
the importance of the Chinese market
for luxury brands, particularly during the
recession in Europe and the US.

ask questions about what it is you need to know. To review this and look at how market and marketing research blend together, let's take a luxury fashion brand planning to expand into the Brazilian market. In order for the company to invest in such an initiative and follow through with their plans, they would need to carry out wide-ranging research to assess the potential for retailing foreign luxury goods in Brazil. So the following questions need to be asked:

What size is the Brazilian market and is there potential for expansion into this market?

What other foreign brands have already moved into this market?

What is the local fashion market like and who are the key players?

To answer these questions, investigations will need to review market trends and data from the recent past and gauge the current market situation. In addition, forecasting and analysis will need to be employed to determine and predict the future potential of the market. Brazil has a growing market for luxury goods, driven by an expanding middle class and an increasing number of multi-millionaires with an appetite for brands such as Chanel, Dior, Louis Vuitton, Gucci, Missoni, Burberry and Armani. All these brands have stores in the main cities of São Paulo, Rio de Janeiro and Brasilia. High-street giants Gap, H&M and Zara have also extended their operations into the region. Added to this, Brazil has a notable domestic fashion industry. The boost to the Brazilian economy due to the 2014 FIFA World Cup and 2016 Olympics must also be factored into the expansion of the fashion and sportswear markets.

Market research into the size and trends within a market does not provide enough information on which to base decisions. Broader marketing research should also be carried out to assess how best to operate in a new geographic market. The process of importing, distributing and selling European manufactured luxury goods in Brazil is challenging; information on local taxes, import duties and supply-chain logistics will need to be researched. Import duties into Brazil are extremely high, making luxury goods much more costly for Brazilian consumers than if they are purchased abroad, and government procedures are complicated. When extending a business into new territories there will be political, economic, cultural, technological and logistical implications to consider, so PEST analysis will be required (*see* page 67). The next question should therefore be:

What issues will the PEST analysis reveal, what resources will be needed and are there local business partners or agencies that could help?

It will be necessary to establish and understand the impact of cultural differences, both in the way business is conducted and as reflected in consumer preferences and purchasing behaviour. The luxury brand will require this information so they can determine how they might adapt their operation or modify their product offer to ensure it is suitable for the Brazilian market. There may be subtle differences from one city to the next. This cropped up when the British chain-store brand Marks & Spencer entered the Chinese market, opening a store in Shanghai back in 2008. The company made assumptions based on their understanding of the Hong Kong market, where they already had ten stores. Unfortunately this did not equate to the realities of mainland China, where different consumer behaviour and needs applied. One of the problems was that Marks & Spencer had miscalculated the correct sizing for their clothes ranges – all the smaller sizes rapidly sold out. Sir Stuart Rose, CEO at the time, stated in an interview with the *Financial Times*, "We need to get the A to Z of sizing right and we need better market research."

There are market research companies that specialize in providing intelligence on different sectors of the global market and there are also many auxiliary businesses set up to aid businesses that wish to expand into new markets, such as trading agents, **sourcing** agents and supply-chain and logistic experts. These companies understand the intricacies of the local market and can help foreign companies wishing to navigate these complexities. For example, the Hong Kong sourcing giant Li & Fung Limited manages the sourcing and supply-chain logistics for global fashion brands including Kate Spade, Juicy Couture, Lucky Brand and Isaac Mizrahi. Many of the major foreign luxury brands now trading in China and Asia have formed similar alliances, negotiated business partnerships or entered into **licensing** deals with local Hong Kong and Chinese trading companies.

Planning and strategy

Analysis of data and information gathered from marketing research is essential in underpinning the planning process and for the creation of a marketing plan. In essence the planning process aims to clarify an organization's current marketing position, define what the business is aiming to achieve and determine the most effective strategies to use. Strategic planning makes use of the key marketing and strategic tools discussed in the previous chapter, namely, the marketing mix, segmentation, targeting, positioning and differentiation. Now with these tools in place it is possible develop and write a marketing plan.

RESEARCH QUESTIONS
Posing a question helps focus the direction for research and makes it easier to determine where to look for answers.

What is the purpose of the research? Who is the current customer? Is there a new customer to target? What potential is there to expand into a new market? Do customers like our products? Is there a new service we could provide?

Below
The Marc by Marc Jacobs diffusion line helps increase the sales of Marc Jacobs branded fashion by offering a more affordable collection to a wider audience.

Eugenialejos, the label created
by Spanish designer Eugenia
Alejos, is promoted and sold
on NOT JUST A LABEL.
Eugenia has a reputation for
creating futuristic pieces for
advertising, artists, catwalk
and film.

Fashion direct from the studio

NOT JUST A LABEL (NJAL)

Aspiring fashion designers and entrepreneurs can face
difficulties finding outlets to sell their work. Stefan Siegel
recognized that this presented a business opportunity, so
he set up NOT JUST A LABEL as a free showroom where
designers could gain exposure, market and sell their products.
NJAL receives a commission from the retail price for all sales
made through its platform, but it offers substantial benefits
in return. NJAL takes on responsibility for administration,
payment security and customer care. This frees up the
designers to concentrate on what they do best and showcase
their work to the site's global audience of media, stylists,
celebrities, individual purchasers and industry buyers. NOT
JUST A LABEL is not just a commercial selling site but also
a community, creative hub and networking forum offering
marketing and business support in brand development, digital
promotion, mentoring, legal advice and PR.

The marketing plan

The marketing plan is where the two indispensable disciplines of research and analysis come into play. The purpose of the plan is to review and assess the existing circumstances of both the business and the market, to determine marketing objectives and strategies, and establish the actions an organization intends to take in order to achieve its marketing and business goals. The marketing plan is of ultimate use as a document that represents the results of systematic research and planning. It should contain the following elements:

» **Situation analysis**
Where are we now?
What is the current state of the market?
Utilizes SWOT and PEST analysis

» **Objectives**
Where do we want to go?
What are the market opportunities?

» **Strategy and tactics**
How do we get there?
What actions do we need to take?
Who will carry them out?

» **Sales forecasts, predicted costs and budgets**
How much will it cost?
What is the predicted return on investment?

The first step for undertaking the situation analysis is to carry out a SWOT analysis.

SWOT analysis

The SWOT analysis provides a framework to collate and review investigative information. It is used to audit the internal strengths and weaknesses of a business enterprise and identify external factors that might provide potential opportunities within the marketplace and business environment. A SWOT is also used to determine and assess external issues that could pose threats to the enterprise or its brands. Once the strengths, weaknesses, opportunities and threats have been established they can be presented in a simple overview table. It is important to stress that the SWOT analysis is not merely a list or the chart itself but an analytical tool that corresponds to four key strategic positions detailed below.

SWOT ANALYSIS

A summary of the results of a SWOT analysis can be recorded in a simple table. The example here gives an overview of the possible issues to consider for each area of investigation.

Internal

STRENGTHS	WEAKNESSES

External

OPPORTUNITIES	THREATS

STRENGTHS

» The reputation of the company, brand or fashion label

» Distinctive signature style and USP

» Expertise of staff

» Strong relationship with suppliers

» Loyal customer base

WEAKNESSES

» Undifferentiated products with no clear USP

» Lack of skilled staff or support

» Weak relationship with suppliers

» Cash flow or financing problems

OPPORTUNITIES

» Strategic alliance or opportunity to partner with others

» New market identified

» New fabric or manufacturing technology

» New supply source available

» Government trade incentives

THREATS

» Changes to fashion trends, signature look goes out of style

» New competitor enters market

» Changes in import or export duties affect pricing or supply

» Rising operational costs

» Key buyer drops the label

» **1. Strength + Opportunity**

Utilizes internal strengths to capitalize on external opportunity and potential

» **2. Strength + Threat**

Utilizes internal strengths to overcome external threats

» **3. Weakness + Opportunity**

Works to address or minimize internal weaknesses to ensure opportunity is not jeopardized

» **4. Weakness + Threat**

In this position a company is exposed and at risk. The strategy would be to mitigate weakness and ward off threats

The real purpose of the SWOT is to use the information to determine how to capitalize upon a company's internal strengths, using them to create opportunity and potential or to determine how strengths could be best employed in order to overcome threats in the market. It is not always easy to assess internal weakness but facing up to issues that might be holding a business back is vitally important. Again the idea is to address weaknesses in order to ensure that opportunity is not being missed.

Market opportunity – Ansoff's Matrix

Ansoff's Matrix is a tool that offers four potential scenarios for opportunity that could be used by a company that has an objective to achieve growth.

» 1. Market penetration

» 2. Market development

» 3. Product development

» 4. Diversification

Market penetration means continuing to sell existing product within an existing market with the aim of capitalizing and improving upon the profitability of the current market proposition. Essentially this presents several key strategies:

» Increase number of customers

» Increase average spend

» Increase margin (raise prices and
   buy in at lower cost price)

» Improve product mix and range plan

ANSOFF'S MATRIX

	EXISTING PRODUCTS	NEW PRODUCTS
EXISTING MARKETS	CONSOLIDATION OR MARKET PENETRATION	PRODUCT DEVELOPMENT
NEW MARKETS	MARKET DEVELOPMENT	DIVERSIFICATION

This first scenario equates to the general situation within fashion. Although fashion product could be considered new each season, many designers and retailers producing their own collections stick to a recognized formula and it is usual for ranges to include signature or carry-over styles that customers have come to expect.

Market development is the second proposition for achieving growth. This is also common within fashion when brands expand their business by taking an existing product to a new market. Topshop did this by expanding into the US market when they opened a 2,790-sq-m (30,000-sq-ft) flagship store in New York. Versace has invested more than US$56 million in developing its Asian market, and opening several stores across the region.

Product development, the third option for opportunity, relates to developing new product for an existing market. This allows for growth by capitalizing on a brand name to launch a new individual product or branded product range such as a diffusion line.

Diversification means developing new product for a completely new market, such as homeware or fragrance. This is the most risky of the four options. It usually requires solid strategic partnerships and is most likely to be achieved by licensing the brand name. Licensing is discussed further in Chapter 5.

The planning process

Once the current market situation has been established and an internal audit carried out, the next step is to use the information in order to set marketing objectives and strategy. The Potential for Differentiation table shown in Chapter 2 (*see* page 59) can be used as a framework to set objectives and determine necessary strategies and tactics. The key is to ensure that objectives are SMART, in other words: **S**pecific, **M**easurable, **A**chievable, **R**ealistic, **T**ime-based.

It is important to establish how each objective will be achieved, who will carry it out, and to set a planned schedule for key activities with interim staging posts for monitoring and review. The key to creating a plan is to keep it simple and realistic; the overall vision should be easily understood by everyone engaged in bringing the plan to fruition. Expenditure will need to be carefully researched and calculated; the proposed strategies and tactics will all have a cost. It is important to set a budget and determine time-frames to ensure the best use of resources. However, even with a solid plan in place, it is unlikely that everything will go according to plan. It is not always possible to predict with accuracy how markets will behave, what customers want or what competitors will do.

If things do not go to plan, it may not be the strategy that needs amending but how it is achieved; tactics might need to be reassessed and budgets trimmed. It is always useful to consider, 'could we do more with less?'!

Structure of a marketing plan

A clear, well-written marketing plan helps communicate the company vision and objectives to internal staff as well as strategic partners, investors and stakeholders. It is useful to have a plan so that progress can be monitored and results gauged against targets. The basic structure of the plan should include:

» A cover page with overall title, date, name of author
  or company

» A contents page listing sections covered with relevant
  page numbers

THE PLANNING PROCESS

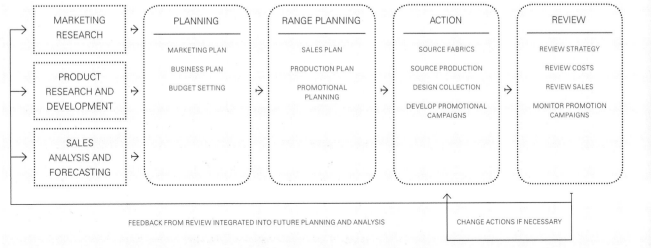

MARKETING RESEARCH	PLANNING	RANGE PLANNING	ACTION	REVIEW
	MARKETING PLAN	SALES PLAN	SOURCE FABRICS	REVIEW STRATEGY
PRODUCT RESEARCH AND DEVELOPMENT	BUSINESS PLAN	PRODUCTION PLAN	SOURCE PRODUCTION	REVIEW COSTS
	BUDGET SETTING	PROMOTIONAL PLANNING	DESIGN COLLECTION	REVIEW SALES
SALES ANALYSIS AND FORECASTING			DEVELOP PROMOTIONAL CAMPAIGNS	MONITOR PROMOTION CAMPAIGNS

FEEDBACK FROM REVIEW INTEGRATED INTO FUTURE PLANNING AND ANALYSIS   CHANGE ACTIONS IF NECESSARY

» A brief introduction setting the context and purpose of the plan. For example, it might be part of an overall business and marketing planning process, or required because of a new venture, brand repositioning exercise or to resolve a current marketing problem

» A one-page executive summary that summarizes key points from the overall document, gives key financial data and an overview of objectives, strategy and recommendations

» The main marketing plan

» Relevant references and appendices

The main body of the marketing plan brings everything together. The actual structure for the main body is open to interpretation; it should be tailored so it is relevant to the type and size of business concerned. The key is to analyse and utilize the marketing research and internal audit information to produce a cohesive document that outlines the following:

» The market sector – giving figures to show size and financial trends

» PEST analysis

» Information on the company's current position within the market

» Information on targeted customers

» Internal audit including SWOT analysis

» Current products, services and USP

» Current marketing mix including routes to market, distribution and promotion

» Current positioning, differentiation and competitive advantage

» Information on key competitors

» Conclusions and recommendations

» Key marketing objectives, proposed strategies, actions and anticipated outcome

» Timescales, costs, budget and anticipated return on investment

» Resources, strategic partners and stakeholders, relevant staff skills and capabilities

4

Understanding the Customer

"I dress everyone from students to superstars.

The end user is what I am, what I do." *John Rocha*

Researching and understanding the customer is central to marketing and promotion. Indeed, recognizing the requirements and needs of the customer is essential for those tasked with creating, selling and promoting fashion products. This issue concerns business at every point in the supply chain from manufacturer to retailer – without customers there is no business, so detailed knowledge of their preferences, motivations and purchasing behaviour is crucial. This knowledge better equips designers, manufacturers, retailers and fashion promotion professionals to design, produce, sell and promote products and services that fulfil or exceed consumer requirements.

Defining the consumer

Not all consumers are the same – each individual will have their own complex set of motivations and shopping behaviour. However, it is possible to group consumers into clusters of broadly similar characteristics, needs or fashion traits. This process is known as **customer segmentation** and is a key feature of STP (segmentation, targeting and positioning) marketing strategy (*see* page 54). Basic customer analysis can be carried out effectively by a small business or individual designer with a limited budget; an example appears later in the chapter showing the type of research carried out by someone setting up their own fashion boutique. A national brand wishing to expand into a new global market may require more in-depth and detailed analysis; for this the services of a professional market research consultancy may be necessary. This chapter explains the basics behind consumer research and analysis and explains the various criteria, or **segmentation variables**, used to classify and profile existing or potential new fashion consumers. The process of creating a **consumer profile** will be explained with details on how to write a customer pen portrait. The chapter concludes with information on simple ways to analyse business customers.

UNDERSTANDING CUSTOMERS

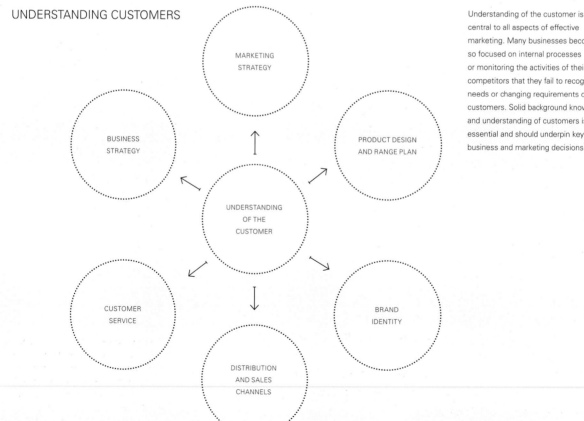

Understanding of the customer is central to all aspects of effective marketing. Many businesses become so focused on internal processes or monitoring the activities of their competitors that they fail to recognize the needs or changing requirements of their customers. Solid background knowledge and understanding of customers is essential and should underpin key business and marketing decisions.

Before going any further, it is important to establish the difference between the often interchangeable terms of consumer and customer. The consumer, or **end-consumer**, is the eventual wearer of the product and will generally be the customer who purchases the garment or accessory. However in the case of a baby or small child, while they would be the end-consumer, they would not be the purchasing customer. In this case, the retailer needs to understand not only the special requirements of a baby or child but also the motivations and expectations of the person who purchases the clothes, most generally the mother.

'Customer' is a broader term. It can be used to refer to the end-consumer who will be a customer of a particular fashion retailer or it can be used to describe a business customer, which could be a business or organization operating within the fashion supply chain. In the first instance the relationship described is **B2C (business-to-consumer)**. When a business is the customer of another business, it is termed as **B2B (business-to-business)**. A boutique owner, for example, who purchases collections from a wholesale design company is a B2B customer. Companies supplying this boutique must not only have a good knowledge and understanding of the boutique owner as their business customer but also a thorough understanding of the end-consumers or customers who purchase from the boutique.

Customer segmentation

Customer segmentation is one of the key functions of marketing. It aims to divide a large customer base into smaller subgroups that share similar needs and characteristics. Typical criteria for classification are age, gender, occupation, financial situation, lifestyle, life stage, residential location, purchasing behaviour and spending habits. Segmentation helps enhance a company's understanding of its customers so that it can position its brand and offer products and services designed to appeal to the targeted customers. Lifestyle plays a crucial role in segmenting fashion consumers; clothing needs and style preferences will be highly influenced by a person's type of work, peer group, and their sporting or leisure activities. Attitudes and opinions on a variety of issues, such as politics, art and culture or environmental issues, might also affect someone's choice of clothing. When analysing a consumer's lifestyle and determining what type of customer they might be, the aim is to gain insight about what they buy, why they buy, which companies they purchase from, and how and when they purchase.

Above
Fashion customers will have a variety of clothing needs dependent on their lifestyle and personality. The person illustrated here may be required to wear a traditional suit to work. Outside the workplace they might wish to dress less formally and adopt a more flamboyant or relaxed style.

Segmentation variables

At the beginning of any consumer analysis it is important to determine the segmentation variables that will be used to classify and characterize consumers. It is normal to use a combination of criteria; the exact mix will be dependent on the objectives of the research project and the specifics of the company and its market. Traditional segmentation falls into the following main categories. **Demographic**, geographic, and a combination of the two known as **geo-demographic**, all focus on identifying who customers are and where they live. Behavioural and **psychographic segmentation** look at the psychology behind consumer purchasing behaviour. Here the idea is to decipher what consumers think, how they behave, why they purchase and what product benefits they require.

SEGMENTATION VARIABLES

DEMOGRAPHIC VARIABLES

» Gender

» Age

» Generation

» Ethnicity

» Marital status

» Life stage

» Occupation

» Education

» Income

» Social grade classification

PSYCHOGRAPHIC AND BEHAVIOURAL VARIABLES

» Lifestyle

» Social aspirations

» Self-image

» Value perceptions

» Purchasing motives and behaviour

» Interests and hobbies

» Attitude and opinions

GEOGRAPHIC VARIABLES

» Region

» Urban / suburban / rural

» Residential location

» Housing type

» Size of city or town

» Climate

USAGE AND BENEFIT VARIABLES

» Benefits sought from products

» Usage rates

» Volume of purchases

» Price sensitivity

» Brand loyalty

» End-use of product

Demographic segmentation

Demographic segmentation is one of the most widely used methods of classification. It uses key variables such as age, gender, generation, occupation, income, life stage and socio-economic status. Each of these factors is extremely important, but they should not be considered in isolation – for example, age. A woman may spend heavily on lounge-wear or exercise clothing for yoga or Pilates; she may work from home and require only casual clothing. Another woman of exactly the same age and stage in her life might be employed in a professional office and need an extensive wardrobe suitable for work. In general men spend less on fashion than women but this is not always the case. Male consumers can be extremely fashion-conscious and spend a significant proportion of their disposable income on clothing or accessories. Some young male consumers are addicted to purchasing branded sportswear, trainers or jeans. An article in *The Times* newspaper on trainer and sportswear addicts by Laura Lovett describes a twenty-one-year-old male who gains kudos by wearing Y-3, the fashion/sportswear fusion brand created by Yohji Yamamoto in collaboration with adidas. This customer explains that while some people collect stamps, he collects Y-3. Gooey Wooey, an avid trainer collector living in southwest England, has a collection of nearly 200 pairs. Gooey trades trainers online, often buying a pair a week or selling some of his prized limited-edition retro sneakers to other enthusiasts.

Demographics also consider the life stage of a consumer; they may still be living with their parents or be single, in a partnership or married, with or without children, or they could have children who have left home. As a person passes through the various phases of life, their priorities are likely to shift and their income and discretionary spend will also be affected. Key stages in the life cycle are:

» **Dependent** – children living at home, dependent on parents

» **Pre-family** – independent adults who don't yet have children

» **Family** – adults with children

» **Late stage or empty nesters** – parents with children who have left home, or older people with no children

Market research companies often attribute names or acronyms to different consumer groups as a way to signify stage in life. Examples of this are:

Top
Nike sneakers on display at the Niketown store in New York.

Above
Gooey Wooey shows off one of his most expensive acquisitions, a pair of Nike Dunk Low Pro SB 'Paris' sneakers featuring artwork by Bernard Buffet. Only 202 pairs of this limited edition were produced, so they exchange hands for prices in the region of US$4,000.

"I don't have an ideal, just someone who genuinely likes my clothes, between 18 and 81."

Erdem Moralioglu

DINKYs – Double Income No Kids Yet

HEIDIs – Highly Educated Independent Individuals

SINDIs – Single Independent Newly Divorced Individuals

NEETs – Not in Employment, Education or Training

YADS – Young And Determined Savers

TIREDs – Thirty-something Independent Radical Educated Dropouts

KIPPERS – Kids In Parents' Pockets Eroding Retirement Savings

NETTELs – Not Enough Time To Enjoy Life

Soccer mom – Spends time transporting kids to sports events

School run mum – Mothers who make an effort to look stylish even for the school run

Consumer generations

Another form of demographic segmentation is to classify consumers by generation. This considers the effect of the existing political, economic, social and cultural situation someone is born into. More specifically, it takes into account the period when a consumer comes of age as a teenager or young adult, as this will play an important part in shaping their opinions and attitudes on fashion, style, consumerism, branding, advertising and technology. Generational traits can impact the way consumers shop, how they spend money, the types of items on which they spend it and their allegiance and loyalty to certain brands. The following section provides a snapshot of the key consumer generations from baby boomers to Generation Z.

Below

The demarcation between one cohort in the Generation Timeline and the next is not always straightforward and in some cases they overlap or there is a gap. This is partly because the exact dates for the generations differ according to various social commentators or census authorities. Over time, experts analysing demographics and social behaviour are also able to refine their knowledge and attribute more concise date brackets to emerging generations.

GENERATION TIMETABLE

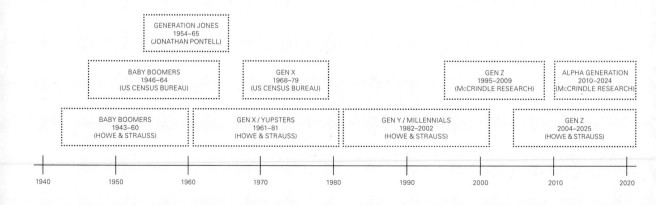

Leading edge baby boomers

Baby boomers were originally defined as those born between 1946 and 1964. However, this 20-year generation span was later broken down into two groups – leading edge baby boomers (1946–1954) and trailing edge baby boomers (1954–1965). The name 'boomer' alludes to the birth rate explosion that occurred during the period of economic stability following the Second World War. As they came of age, baby boomers challenged traditions and adopted styles of dress guaranteed to upset the Establishment – long hair for men, the shortest of miniskirts for women. Ironically, baby boomers are now part of the Establishment and relatively wealthy in comparison to other generations. However, they are increasingly being left out in the cold by fashion companies keen to reposition their brands in order to attract young professionals or the youth market. The boomer generation should not be forgotten – in their heads they are still young, and they still want to look current and fashionable. The trick with this group is to provide good service, better quality and offer stylish clothing with excellent cut and fit.

Trailing edge baby boomers (aka Generation Jones)

The name 'Generation Jones' was coined by American sociologist Jonathan Pontell. Derived from the slang 'jonesin', the name relates to feelings of craving, fuelled by unfulfilled expectations. Pontell identified a generation born in 1954–65 that had mistakenly been lumped in with the boomers, but which was actually a separate group with distinct characteristics.

Above

Each week *The Guardian* newspaper runs an 'All Ages' fashion feature in its Saturday magazine, championing diversity and challenging perceived notions of fashion. Though an important demographic variable, age is not always the best indicator of a consumer's style or what they might purchase. A fashion retailer might stock thousands of units of a particular garment and quite often two women, one thirty-five and another fifty, will purchase the same item. The older customer or 'Forever 40s' is important. She may be in her forties but could also be fifty, sixty or even older. This customer group is connected not by age bracket but by fashion attitude, style and purchasing choices.

Top
Mary Quant stands with models wearing her Viva Viva collection in 1967. Quant opened her boutique, 'Bazaar', on London's King's Road in 1955, selling clothes designed to appeal to the burgeoning youth market.

Douglas Coupland wrote:

> *"Jonathan has it right. My book* Generation X *was about the fringe of Generation Jones which became the mainstream of Generation X. There is a generation between the Boomers and Xers, and 'Generation Jones' – what a great name for it!"*

Generation Jones is a powerful demographic representing 26 per cent of the US population, with almost a third of the spending power, according to the US Department of Commerce's Bureau of the Census. Research carried out by Carat in 2009 identified that they represent 20 per cent of the UK adult population. Barack Obama is Gen Jones and many political commentators believe that it was the Joneser vote that brought him to power (www.huffingtonpost.com 2009). Generation Jones' attitudes and tastes were shaped by the political, social and cultural events of the 1970s and early 1980s. Financially they have been affected by negative equity in the 1990s and the current breakdown of the pension system.

Generation X

Generation X was the title of a book written by journalists Jane Deverson and Charles Hamblett in the 1960s, but the term came to prominence many years later when Douglas Coupland published his novel, *Generation X, Tales for an Accelerated Culture*, in 1991. Described as a lost generation, this demographic came of age in the 1980s and early 1990s, shaped by the Thatcher and Reagan years. Affected by escalating rates of divorce, fear of AIDS, recession, job insecurity and the potential of employment in a menial 'McJob', this disaffected generation, also termed as 'slackers', sought comfort by creating their own self-sufficient culture and alternative tribal family unit of close-knit friends, as illustrated by the television shows *Friends* in the United States and the British drama *This Life*. As Gen X has grown up and matured, they have cast off their more juvenile slacker habits and morphed into 'yupsters', creative urban professionals who endeavour to balance the personal with wider social concerns of family, community and work. Yupsters manage to maintain an intricate set of contradictions; they are corporate but have hip individual fashion style, business minded but independent and entrepreneurial in spirit. They value family time and aim to work smarter not harder.

Generation Y

Generation Y, also known as Millennials, are, according to Howe & Strauss, those born after 1982, although others have classified them as born between the late 1970s and the mid-1990s. This generation are the children of Gen Jones; they have experienced pressure from parents to succeed and overachieve, money has been spent on their education and those with a college education are likely to start their working lives paying off sizeable student loans. For this reason Gen Y have also been given the rather depressing title of the IPOD generation; Insecure, Pressurized, Over-taxed and Debt-ridden, a name coined by Bosanquet & Gibbs in the report *Class of 2005: The IPOD Generation*. This generation also includes the post-1980s children born in China during the one-child policy. Millennials have grown up with technology and increasingly live their lives online; they are plugged-in and globally connected. They understand branding and are media and marketing savvy, they communicate using social media, form online communities and are happy to create their own online content. Conscious consumerism is a label attributed to this cohort. They still like to shop, but if it can be for a cause then so much the better. The environmentally friendly shoe brand TOMS fits this bill. For every pair purchased, the company donates a pair of shoes to a child in need. Gen Y also like to get involved and many are activists at heart; in the US there are over 1,200 university campus clubs raising awareness of TOMS.

Generation Z

There is still much debate as to the dates and characteristics that define this generation. Some say Gen Z consists of those born after the mid-1990s; others such as Howe and Strauss believe it is those born from 2004 onwards. What can be said is that they are the offspring of Gen X and Y and their grandparents are baby boomers or Gen Jones. Gen Z are digital natives. They hop easily between the physical and digital worlds and their online identity is extremely important to them. Research carried out by retail and brand consultancy Fitch discovered that Gen Z have a specific approach to shopping. They like to discover things online by browsing Instagram or Pinterest and are keen to create digital scrapbooks from images taken in-store. They are careful savers, and will track prices before purchase. Uniqlo tapped into this trend with their Lucky Counter campaign. Shoppers visiting their site could choose from a selection of ten garments they would like to see discounted. Clicking on an item produced a pre-written Tweet; the more Tweets generated, the lower the price of the garment would fall. It is worth considering this system of creating discounts by social sharing, because by 2020 Gen Z will account for 40 per cent of consumers in the US, Europe and BRIC countries, according to global management consulting firm Strategy&.

Above

This image photographed by Josh Meister for *Paste* magazine shows the evolution of hipster subculture. From left to right:

The Emo

The Emo Redux

The Ashton

The Scenester

The Twee

The Fauxhemian

The Mountain Man

The Vintage Queen

The Williamsburg

The Meta Nerd

The Alpha generation

Gen Alpha is defined as those born after 2010 and up until 2024. They will be the first full generation to be born this millennium and according to social researcher Mark McCrindle, it could be the largest cohort since the baby boomers.

Geographic segmentation

Geographic segmentation analyses customers by region, continent, state, county or neighbourhood. This type of information is important to consider, particularly as fashion markets become ever more global and retailers and brand managers are required to understand the particular needs of customers in each of the countries or regions where they do business. The product offering, marketing and promotional approach may need to be adjusted in order to address differences of climate, culture or religion. It is also important to consider whether someone lives in a city, large town or the countryside, as this will affect the types of physical shopping experiences accessible to the customer. However, as more and more purchases are made online, geographic location in terms of accessibility may be less important than cultural differences.

TABLE OF 20TH- AND 21ST-CENTURY GENERATIONS

BORN	GENERATION COHORT NAMES	DECADE OF INFLUENCE	AGE IN 2020
1912–27	DEPRESSION ERA AND WORLD WAR II	1930s AND EARLY 1940s	93+
1926–45	THE POST-WAR GENERATION	1950s	75–94
1946–54	LEADING EDGE BABY BOOMERS	1960s	66–74
1954–65	TRAILING EDGE BABY BOOMERS GENERATION JONES	1970s AND EARLY 1980s	55–66
1961–81	GEN X YUPSTERS	1980s AND EARLY 1990s	39–59
1982–2002	GEN Y MILLENNIALS ECHO BOOMERS NET GENERATION IPOD GENERATION	1990s, 2000s, 2010s	18–38
1995–2010	GENERATION Z	2010 AND BEYOND	10–25
2010–2024	THE ALPHA GENERATION	2015 AND BEYOND	UP TO 10

GENERATIONAL COHORT OF FASHION DESIGNERS

GENERATION	FASHION DESIGNERS
DEPRESSION ERA AND WORLD WAR II	PIERRE CARDIN, ANDRÉ COURRÈGES
POST-WAR GENERATION	VIVIENNE WESTWOOD, REI KAWAKUBO, KARL LAGERFELD, YVES SAINT LAURENT, GIORGIO ARMANI, CALVIN KLEIN
BABY BOOMERS	JEAN PAUL GAULTIER, PAUL SMITH, MIUCCIA PRADA, DONNA KARAN
GENERATION JONES	JOHN GALLIANO, MARC JACOBS, TOM FORD, DRIES VAN NOTEN, MARTIN MARGIELA, JOHN ROCHA
GENERATION X	STELLA MCCARTNEY, PHILLIP LIM, NICOLAS GHESQUIÈRE, MARKUS LUPFER
GENERATION Y	CHRISTOPHER KANE, ZAC POSEN, ALEXANDER WANG, SIMONE ROCHA

Geo-demographic segmentation

Geo-demographic segmentation makes use of a combination of geographic and demographic analysis – this can be far more effective for understanding the social, economic and geographic make-up of a population. Geo-demographic analysis divides a country up and then analyses each geographic subdivision demographically. It is particularly useful for helping retailers determine which locations might be the most profitable or how best to adapt stores to fit with the geo-demographic of a location. Research shows that consumers can show strong attachment to their local area, carrying out shopping and leisure activities 5–23 km (3–14 miles) from their home or place of work. Matches is a boutique fashion retailer with a small chain of high-class womenswear and menswear stores situated within London. The owners of Matches recognize that London consists of many small 'villages' and customers prefer to shop close to home or work. Each store has its own fashion profile designed to cater specifically to the unique style characteristics of the local customer. The boutique in Marylebone High Street, central London, is situated in a locale that is both residential and work-based. There are cafés, boutiques and

Above

The table of 20th- and 21st-century generations gives guideline dates for generational cohorts. The table also indicates the decade of influence affecting each cohort as they come of age as teenagers or young adults, which is when they are most likely to form their attitudes, opinions and approach to life.

hip art galleries, so in a bid to attract the art-loving demographic who live and work nearby, the store has been transformed into an innovative retail/gallery space where fashion and art can coexist. The Wimbledon shop, by contrast, has a more intimate style better suited to the village atmosphere of its local residential area.

Geo-demographic analysis and consumer profiling can be carried out using the services of a market research and analysis consultancy, which will have access to sophisticated database profiling systems. However, a small business can carry out simple but effective research using basic census data, free online postcode analysis, statistics from the local council, and fashion industry information on market trends. The example on pages 122–23 describes the basic geo-demographic background research carried out by a boutique owner as she prepared to launch her business.

Geo-demographic analysis tools

There are several proprietary geo-demographic neighbourhood classification systems, such as ACORN (A Classification Of Residential Neighbourhoods), Mosaic and Super Profiles. These database analysis tools use government census data, postcode or zip code analysis and a complicated array of demographic and lifestyle variables to segment populations by neighbourhood and social status. The ACORN Classification Map, created by CACI Ltd, divides the UK population into five categories: Wealthy Achievers, Urban Prosperity, Comfortably Off, Moderate Means and Hard-Pressed. These are then divided into 17 subgroups, some examples being: Affluent Greys, Flourishing Families, Blue-Collar Roots, Settled Suburbia and Aspiring Singles. These groups are then further subdivided into 56 consumer types.

The Mosaic Global system devised by Experian is available in Europe, North America and the Asia-Pacific region. The population is divided into ten neighbourhood types, US examples being Affluent Suburbia, Upscale America, Metro Fringe, Urban Essence or Remote America. These groups are then further broken down into 60 subgroups.

The Super Profiles Geo-demographic Typology was developed by Batey and Brown in 1994 in collaboration with CDMS Ltd, part of the Littlewoods home-shopping organization. The Super Profiles system features three levels. The first has ten lifestyle profiles, some examples being: Affluent Achievers, Thriving Greys, Settled Suburbans, Nest Builders, Hard-Pressed Families and the Have-Nots. This level is divided into 40 target market clusters which are then subdivided into 160 specific profiles.

Psychographic and behavioural segmentation

Psychographic and behavioural segmentation analyses consumers based on their lifestyle and personality type. The purpose is to determine the underlying motivations that drive a person's attitude or behaviour as a consumer. It is possible for consumers to have similar demographic profiles but entirely different attitudes to clothing and appearance. One person, for example, might believe that they must look crisp, smart and well turned-out for all occasions, whereas someone else might choose to wear expensive branded fashion that looks worn and battered even when new, giving the impression they don't care how they look. Psychographic, behavioural and lifestyle studies aim to gain further insight into consumer attitudes, interests and opinions (AIOs) and understand how these influence a person's fashion needs, desires and purchasing choices. This is a complex topic, especially when it comes to attitudes to fashion or to social media. If you remember, the aim of marketing is to satisfy consumer needs and wants and, while it is fair to say that we may want or desire new clothes, most Western consumers certainly do not need more clothes, accessories or shoes. The reality is that many of us have brand new items in our wardrobes that remain unworn; we give copious amounts of unwanted clothes away to charity shops (although the amount has decreased since the recession) and we cast an alarming amount of surplus clothes into landfill. So what is it that motivates us to continue purchasing even if we do not theoretically need any more or can ill afford it? The answer lies in psychology and the theories of human motivation.

Above
Psychographic and behavioural analysis aims to gain insight into consumer attitudes, interests, opinions and purchasing behaviours, which in turn will influence the way a person chooses to dress. A person who believes they must look stylish, appropriate for the occasion and well turned-out may spend a great deal on clothes and take great care with their appearance.

Consumer motivation and behaviour

What motivates us to buy into fashion, what influences our purchasing behaviour, how do our attitudes, interests and opinions affect our purchasing choices? At a simplistic level it could be said that the motivating force to purchase a garment, handbag or pair of shoes is a real physical need; in other words we do not have a receptacle in which to carry our keys, money and mobile phone, or a pair of winter boots to protect us from the cold and wet, so in order to satisfy this need we must purchase the required item.

The reality is that in most cases the motivation is more akin to desire and the need is psychological. Danish brand guru and futurologist Martin Lindstrom argues in his book *Buyology: How Everything We Believe About Why We Buy Is Wrong* that the motivation is neurological and University of New Mexico evolutionary psychologist, Geoffrey Miller, contends in his book *Spent: Sex, Evolution and the Secrets of Consumerism* that evolutionary biology is behind our need to purchase and display conspicuous consumption. Miller's theory of 'display signalling' proposes that we wear certain fashion styles or brands in order to signal specific qualities of character to others. Someone wearing an ethical or eco-fashion brand, for example, is at some level trying to communicate that they are conscientious. A person wearing conspicuously branded designer labels is advertising qualities of wealth and desirability, while someone with an active and sporty style is trying to signal their health and fitness. Now we can post innumerable images of ourselves online and receive responses from a global audience. It could be said that content is the new social currency, and that it has taken precedence over clothing as a method of display signalling.

Consumer purchase decision process

It is evident that fashion purchasing decisions are rarely based on logical criteria alone. The motivations behind our purchasing behaviour are driven by a complex interplay of demographic, geographic, psychological, neurological, economic, social, cultural and personal factors. Research indicates that consumers go through a decision-making process when they purchase a product. The basic steps are as follows:

» Recognition of need

» Information search and identification of options

» Evaluation of options

» Decision

The decision process starts with the recognition that there is a need. This might be a valid physical need; a person may gain or lose a significant amount of weight and need to purchase new clothes to fit. A couple may be planning a traditional wedding and therefore need to purchase or hire appropriate outfits and accessories, or someone might be starting a new job where they are required to dress in a certain way. The need could be cultural – a person travelling to a country where the convention is to dress more modestly may need to acquire a long skirt or a top with sleeves and a high neckline. It is more likely, however, that the need will arise at a subconscious level. If a person thinks, "I'm not wearing the latest trend, I will be judged and no one will find me attractive," deep down they believe they lack something. The belief sets up what could be termed as a false deficit in their mind, the discrepancy between what they believe is lacking and what they desire creates

Below
A highly skilled artisan makes a pair of finely crafted leather shoes for Italian brand Tod's.

the sensation of need; "I need a fresh look. I'd better buy some new clothes." This thought becomes the motivation, leading towards action and a potential decision to purchase.

Once a need has been established, the next stages are to search for information and check out and evaluate options. This usually occurs by going online, reading magazines or gathering opinions from friends, or the person might visit the shops. However, these steps are very much dependent on the situation and the person in question. A 2013 study by luxury media agency Cream reported that UK consumers spending over £100 a month on clothes and accessories accounted for a third of the UK's total £48 billion spend in this sector. These shoppers spent more than twice the national average time browsing online and were 42 per cent more likely to shop online than the national average. On the face of it, research and evaluation are perhaps less relevant for fashion

MASLOW'S HIERARCHY OF NEEDS

Abraham Maslow developed his theory in 1943 and proposed a five-tier hierarchy, starting with basic-level physiological necessities such as food, water and sleep and progressing up through needs of safety, social belonging and esteem, culminating in the highest level of need driven by the motivation for self-actualization, which could also be viewed as self-realization or self-fulfilment. The original premise was that an individual will attempt to meet their needs at the lowest level before advancing to the next level. In reality individuals attempt to meet a variety of needs simultaneously and do not progress up the hierarchy in a prescribed manner. In modern society we do have a basic physiological need for clothing to protect us from the elements, but in most cases consumer motivation regarding fashion need is triggered by a diverse set of desires and stimuli. These might relate to social belonging, gaining approval, affiliation with a group or notions of self-acceptance and esteem. The hierarchical nature of this long-used model has been criticized. Marketers now view consumer needs more holistically with social belonging, esteem and self-actualization linked together by a need for connection, with this need being fulfilled through social media.

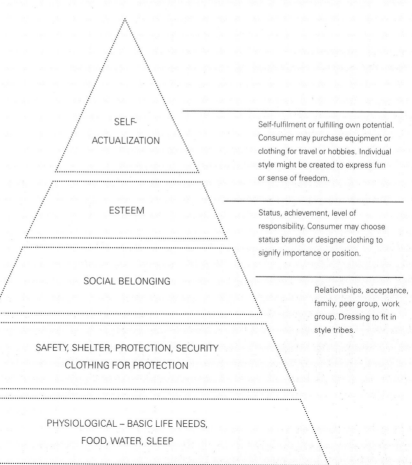

SELF-ACTUALIZATION

Self-fulfilment or fulfilling own potential. Consumer may purchase equipment or clothing for travel or hobbies. Individual style might be created to express fun or sense of freedom.

ESTEEM

Status, achievement, level of responsibility. Consumer may choose status brands or designer clothing to signify importance or position.

SOCIAL BELONGING

Relationships, acceptance, family, peer group, work group. Dressing to fit in style tribes.

SAFETY, SHELTER, PROTECTION, SECURITY
CLOTHING FOR PROTECTION

PHYSIOLOGICAL – BASIC LIFE NEEDS,
FOOD, WATER, SLEEP

Researching your target market

Starburst Boutique

Starburst Boutique is an independent retailer situated in the beautiful and historic coastal town of Dartmouth in southwest England. The boutique offers a unique blend of womenswear and accessories from a host of international designers including Day Birger et Mikkelsen and Rützou from Denmark, Armor Lux and Petit Bateau from France as well as UK labels, Marilyn Moore, Pyrus, Queen and Country and Saltwater. Running alongside the contemporary womenswear collections are one-off vintage pieces, bespoke jewellery and luxurious lifestyle products. The boutique is situated in Dartmouth's most exclusive shopping street and its stylish and relaxed in-store atmosphere is reflective of its coastal setting. It is designed to attract affluent second-home owners, weekenders and tourists, but also to provide local clientele with a chic destination in which to buy exclusive and desirable fashion brands.

Background market research

Starburst Boutique owner and buyer, Hannah Jennings, carried out detailed research in order to set up her business. Investigation of the current status, trends and predicted future of the independent retailing sector and the UK womenswear market was carried out; relevant data was obtained from trade magazines such as *Drapers* and *Retail Week*, industry analysts such as Mintel, WGSN, Fashion Monitor and the British Retail Consortium, as well as a range of relevant websites, magazines and newspaper articles. Information on the demographic of the local area and tourism were sourced from the local and county councils. Jennings also carried out an extensive investigation of existing independent retailers within the locale, including the nearest city, 40 km (25 miles) away. She also travelled to other cities such as London, Edinburgh, Winchester, Bath and Brighton to visit similar stylish independent boutiques.

Research findings and information

Tourism makes a significant contribution to the local economy. Research revealed that Dartmouth attracts 400,000 visitors a year plus an additional 100,000 during a festive regatta week held in August. Sixty per cent of those visiting the area can be economically grouped as ABC1. More UK residents are choosing to take vacations within Great Britain and a resurgence in popularity of seaside towns is highlighted by data released in 2008 that shows footfall in seaside towns grew 4.9 per cent compared to 1.3 per cent in all towns and cities. The local area also boasts the third-highest percentage of second-home owners in the UK, and has experienced a net population increase of 441,000 since 1996 – a result of people migrating to the area in search of a better quality of life. Jennings found market data published in *Drapers* which revealed the UK womenswear market to be worth in excess of £17 billion in 2008, with the independent retailers' market share at just under 7 per cent. Data from a 2007 British Retail Consortium survey identified a growing proportion of UK consumers who preferred not to shop at high-street multiple retailers, and retail expert Mary Portas backed this up with a prediction that customers in their thirties will spend less on fast fashion and transfer their allegiance to local shops where they can invest in quality product and receive a higher quality of personal service. Research also indicates that female shoppers stay 'younger for longer' and that once they have defined their personal style in their thirties they will want to continue purchasing chic, contemporary and stylish clothing through to their sixties and beyond.

Conclusions – the Starburst Boutique customer

Hannah Jennings recognizes how important her background research has been in helping her understand the Starburst Boutique customer and the potential of the market.

> *"The customer profiling I did turned out to be very accurate with regards to my core customers. It is fundamental for my business and I now buy with that segment in mind." Hannah Jennings*

The Starburst Boutique target market can be split into two customer profiles. The first represents the core customer to the business, namely women aged 30–45 who are married with small children. They either have a second home in the area or are weekender or tourist visitors who aspire to coastal living. The second customer profile is represented by slightly older, locally based women, aged 45–60 or over, probably with grown-up children and possibly grandchildren. The 60+ market is important to the boutique as this customer might bring along daughters or even granddaughters. They too may love the chance to shop in the store's chic and laidback environment and snap up something desirable to wear on their holiday or to take back home.

> *"Independent retailers offer a personal service and cultural understanding of the local market."*
>
> Mary Portas

purchases compared to buying a car or expensive piece of furniture. However, it is not surprising that online browsing has become more relevant for fashion; the joy of discovery is an essential element of the process. During research a potential purchaser may decide upon a selection of brands from which to choose; the brands in serious contention for the consumer's purchase are known as the **consideration set**.

Fashion purchases are often unplanned; impulse buys are usually the result of spontaneity combined with opportunity. Impulsive purchasing may occur as a result of a shopper experiencing what could be termed a 'shopping high' or 'buying buzz'. It has been proven that shopping can produce a surge of excitement generated by the brain as it releases dopamine, a chemical involved in the experience of feeling pleasure. Habitual shopping patterns could also be linked to this phenomenon – someone might always go shopping on the day they get their pay cheque, the heady combination of money and shopping producing an elevation in mood.

Other factors may also affect the consumer's choice, such as the country of origin of a product or brand. Consumers may have a positive perception of particular goods from certain countries: Italian leather, French lace, Scottish cashmere and tweed or British tailoring are examples. This is known as the **country of origin effect** (**COO** or **COOE**). It is not only the country of manufacture that can affect perception but also the country of design (COD). In this instance the product may be designed in a country renowned for a particular design skill but manufactured elsewhere – Swedish-designed furniture, for example. There are strict trade laws concerning country of origin so it would be illegal to label garments incorrectly. However it is possible to create and market a brand with an identity that is suggestive of a particular country. The UK fashion brand, Superdry Japan, was set up after an inspirational trip to Japan. Garments are embroidered with Japanese-style writing and given names like the 'Osaka' T-shirt.

Adoption of innovation and trends

Consumers will vary in their response to new trends and ideas. Those who are more conservative or reticent might take some time before they feel ready to buy into a new or developing trend. They might want to feel safe, fit in or not look out of place. Others might feel that a new innovation or style is too expensive. They might wait till the trend hits the mass market and the price comes down; their motivation is to be cautious and spend wisely. There are others who like to be on the cutting edge of style. They may purchase the new season collections at the earliest opportunity; they want to be the first, be noticed or stand out from the crowd. The way in which an innovation, new idea or trend is taken up by consumers and moves through a population can be explained using Everett Rogers' diffusion theory. Rogers identified five types of individual classified by their propensity to adopt innovation.

Innovators – a small percentage of adventurous people who initiate trends or adopt innovations before others. They are risk-takers and visionaries. Designers such as Vivienne Westwood or Mary Katrantzou would fit into this category, along with those that innovate and instigate subculture and street trends.

Early adopters – people who take up a trend in the early stages, often cultural opinion leaders or those that disseminate fashion, style or artistic ideas. This group accepts and embraces change and enjoys new ideas. They will have the confidence to follow

ROGERS' DIFFUSION OF INNOVATIONS

A trend will originate within the innovator group of individuals, adventurous types who are cutting edge in their ideas. As the trend takes hold a **tipping point** will be reached. This is the moment when the trend or idea crosses a significant threshold; the adoption rate increases exponentially and the trend spreads rapidly and reaches the mass market. Eventually the trend will peak and begin its decline. The late majority purchase the trend just as its fashionability and mass-market appeal begin to dwindle. Laggards are those at the tail-end who just manage to cotton on to the idea when it is already too late and the trend is over.

Source: Everett Rogers' Diffusion of Innovations (1995)

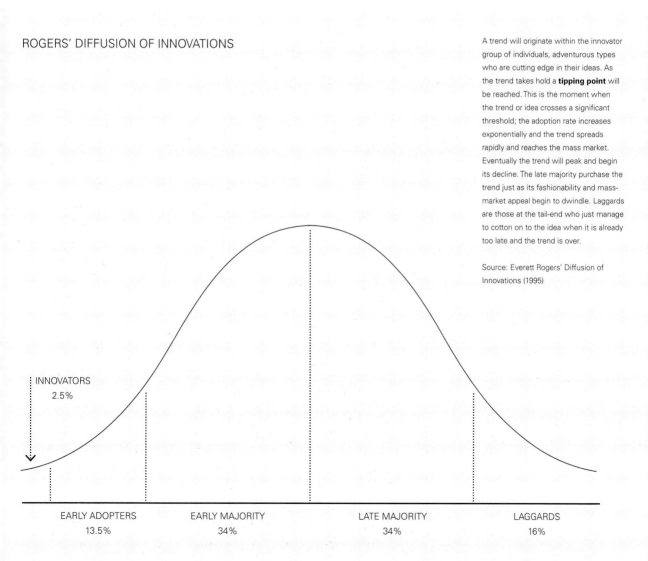

INNOVATORS
2.5%

EARLY ADOPTERS	EARLY MAJORITY	LATE MAJORITY	LAGGARDS
13.5%	34%	34%	16%

CUSTOMER MOTIVATION AND BEHAVIOURS

GETTING A BARGAIN

» Shops in sales

» Attracted to promotional offers

» Buys second-hand or vintage

» Goes to designer outlets, warehouse sales

» Sources vouchers and deals on the Internet

TRYING TO AVOID CLOTHES SHOPPING

» Shops infrequently for clothes

» Purchases mainly for replacement items

» Shops from catalogues or Internet

» Does not browse – heads straight for required item

» Abandons store if queue to pay is too long

STANDING OUT FROM THE CROWD

» Buys from independent stores and boutiques

» Makes an effort to seek out new trends and ideas

» Makes own clothes or customizes

» Shops in street markets

LOOKING LIKE A CELEBRITY

» Avid reader of celebrity gossip magazines

» Attracted to stores and websites that are current with celebrity fashion trends

» Would queue to purchase special celebrity or designer fashion collections

FITTING IN AND BELONGING

» Buys similar style to friends

» Connected to peers via social media

» Shops where friends shop

» Personal style fits with chosen tribe

CARING ABOUT THE ENVIRONMENT

» Tries to buy from ethical fashion brands

» Recycles and upcycles clothing

» Won't buy 'fast fashion'

» Likes smaller local fashion labels

A consumer's attitudes, preferences and motivations will influence their purchasing behaviour. This table presents possible purchasing behaviours associated with a variety of potential motivations. If someone's motivation is to get a bargain, for example, then this will drive certain behaviours, such as shopping during the sales, signing up to a discount website, or scouring vintage stores for that special bargain.

or adapt the trend, mix styles and create the desired look from designer, boutique, high-street and vintage.

Early majority – represents the main bulk of people who adopt a trend as it gathers momentum and begins to penetrate the mass market. This group is likely to take up a trend after they have seen it worn by others or in fashion and gossip magazines or recommended on blogs or websites.

Late majority – those who buy into a trend when it is already very well established and reaching its peak or beginning to decline.

Laggards – these people do not take fashion risks, and are the last people to catch on to a trend, usually when it is already too late.

Rogers also proposed a five-stage model to explain the decision process that an individual follows in order to progress from first knowledge or awareness of a new trend or product innovation through to adoption of the trend or purchase and evaluating their decision.

1. Knowledge – the particular product or trend must come to the attention of the potential consumer. They gain initial knowledge of uses, benefits or key ideas behind an innovation or trend. This could be because they read about it in the press or see others wearing or using the product.

SHOPPING MISSION:
BUYING A PAIR OF JEANS IN GAP

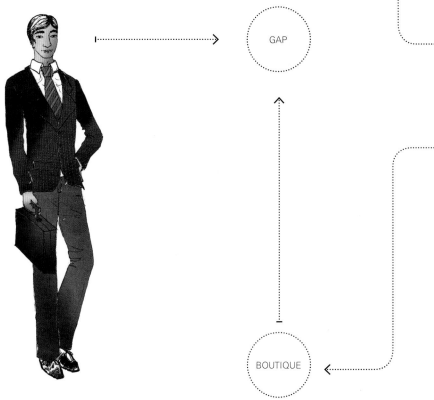
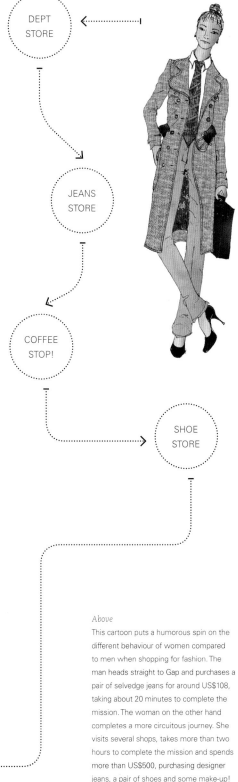

Above

This cartoon puts a humorous spin on the different behaviour of women compared to men when shopping for fashion. The man heads straight to Gap and purchases a pair of selvedge jeans for around US$108, taking about 20 minutes to complete the mission. The woman on the other hand completes a more circuitous journey. She visits several shops, takes more than two hours to complete the mission and spends more than US$500, purchasing designer jeans, a pair of shoes and some make-up! Source: Adapted from Tom Peters (2005)

2. Persuasion – the person forms an opinion about the product. They may be persuaded by the opinions of others. If it is of interest to them, they might begin to desire the product and persuade themselves that it is suitable, useful, a good investment etc.

3. Decision – the person makes a decision to adopt the innovation or trend; in other words they take action and purchase.

4. Implementation – the person uses the product.

5. Confirmation – the person evaluates the results of their decision and compares actual usage of the product with original perceptions.

Another model used to describe the stages from awareness to purchase is AIDA, standing for Awareness, Interest, Desire and Action. These stages are similar to those described above. With the rise of digital technology many marketers believe that these models are now outdated, but it could be said that the AIDA model is still relevant. The awareness (or knowledge) phase and the action step that refers to purchase can now occur online or in-store.

Showrooming is when consumers try products in-store but purchase online, often at a lower price and from another source. In showrooming the persuasion, desire, decision and action stages occur both in-store and online. There is a reverse trend of **webrooming**, when consumers research online and then go to the store to purchase, perhaps because they do not want to pay for shipping or wait at home for deliveries. 'Click and collect' (purchasing online and picking up from the store) could also be considered a type of webrooming.

The process a consumer goes through from first awareness of a product to purchase can be quite convoluted. They may see press articles, traditional advertising or learn about a fashion item or trend online. A report by Kurt Salmon entitled *Putting a Stop to the Showrooming Scare* highlighted several strategies adopted by bricks-and-mortar retailers to ensure they engage with customers and don't lose revenue. US retailer Nordstrom noticed that many younger customers were reticent in approaching sales staff, preferring to use an app, so Nordstrom set up iPads for shoppers to use in the store. Adidas added a virtual footwear wall to their retail environment. The touch-screen wall allows shoppers to view products in 3D, find information on availability and price, see Twitter posts and purchase. Other retailers integrate Quick Response (QR) barcodes into the in-store experience, for example with Spaaza MyPrice (*see* opposite), or Target, which offers rewards when shoppers scan **QR codes** in the store.

Consumer trends

Identifying and understanding consumer trends is a vital element of fashion market research. Observing consumers and gathering information from markets around the globe keeps you up to date. The trick is to keep an eye out for innovators and early adopters; they are likely to be ahead of the curve. Trend watching helps you to develop intuition, spot new ideas and gain inspiration. Trend-forecasting websites such as Faith Popcorn's BrainReserve and Trendwatching.com are excellent sources of information. Remember consumer needs will change in response to political, economic and social change. Trends come and go, but here are some things to think about.

Personalized pricing

Spaaza MyPrice

Fashion retail is now a multi-channel, multi-platform environment, so businesses with retail stores need to find innovative ways to encourage customers to purchase in-store to offset showrooming. Spaaza (in South African slang this means informal shop), co-founded by Dave Sevenoaks and Sam Critchley, aims to bring a little online wizardry to the offline world. Spaaza's mission is to make pricing and rewards more personal; their MyPrice loyalty programme, available to retailers and accessible to customers via smartphone app, offers unique ways to reward shoppers who buy in-store. Trials with Clarks shoes in the Netherlands and Quiksilver in South Africa showed that Spaaza personal pricing accounted for 25 per cent of sales in the first six months with a 40–50 per cent increase in basket size (average spend per customer visit) compared to non-Spaaza baskets. The main benefits of personal pricing are:

» Improves in-store experience for consumers

» Gives the retailer a way to make shoppers happy instantly – no delayed gratification

» Allows the retailer to reduce margin loss through targeted price promotions

» Gives more accurate understanding of shopper behaviour and conversion rates across the shopping journey

Each product in a store where Spaaza MyPrice is in operation has a recommended retail price and a QR code. Discounts can be applied for a number of variables, such as purchasing in-store, consumer loyalty, student discount or as a birthday reward. The nature of the rewards is established between Spaaza and the retailer partner. Customers never pay more than the official recommended retail price, and shoppers get the opportunity to pay a personalized price based on their own purchase history and profile.

Super-cocooning – Faith Popcorn came up with the concept of cocooning in 1981. Now the trend has evolved into what Popcorn calls super-cocooning. Uncertainty and a feeling of vulnerability results in an increase of at-home entertainment with TV and movies on demand. Online communication and shopping mean that it is possible to retreat to the safe environment of the home.

Crowd shaped – Identified by Trendwatching.com. People pool data, profiles and preferences in groups (small and big) to shape new goods and services. 3D printing communities such as Shapeways and the Fab Lab movement are examples, as are clothes swapping, skill sharing, freecycling or random acts of kindness (RAK).

Guilt-free status – People aware of the damage caused by over-consumption look for 'guilt-free' products to indulge their need for status symbols. Swedish jeans brand Nudie, for example, created a range of limited-edition rugs hand-woven from strips of old and worn-out Nudie jeans.

Sellsumers – Consumers no longer just consume, they sell creative output to corporations or fellow consumers. Online democratization means more consumer participation in the world of demand and supply.

Cosy childhood memories – Nostalgic items remind us of childhood days – 1950s florals, tea-time cupcakes, board games, storage tins with 1960s and 1970s branding. Baby boomers and Gen Jones desire to feel cosy and secure in tough times.

The lipstick effect – Tough times mean consumers go for 'trade-down' spending; they forgo extravagant purchases and opt for cheaper feel-good treats like lipstick.

Perfect pieces – Fed up with product overload, consumers want well-considered fashion items. Perfect basics that offer more, beautifully crafted quality pieces designed to last; classic fashion emblems such as the perfect trench, the little black dress, a striped French matelot T-shirt or sweater or Japanese selvedge jeans.

Addicted to niche – Consumers want to find an intricate balance between being one-of-a-kind and fitting in. This is 'niche', just enough to form a tribe but not too many, not a crowd; this is about being one of the few. Niche brands come with a story – niche is knowledge, niche is the kudos of being in the know.

Opposite
Fashion Design graduate Philli Wood won a national design competition run by fashion retailer Warehouse in partnership with the British Fashion Council. The collection features images of cable knits printed onto exaggerated tent-shaped padded parkas, within which the wearer can cocoon themselves and retreat.

Creating a customer profile

Once consumer research and analysis is complete, the next step is to create a consumer profile report to describe the consumer groups being targeted. The report should give background demographic, geo-demographic and psychographic data, information on current or emerging consumer trends, current sales statistics and relevant observational data. It is normal practice for personnel such as buyers, marketing or brand managers, or designers to give presentations summarizing the consumer report to other staff members or to suppliers, partners and stakeholders. A technique used to précis the research and describe the customer is known as a **customer pen portrait**. This written description can be enhanced by the addition of a customer image and lifestyle visual shown on a display board or using PowerPoint or Flash presentation.

Below
Rugs made using Nudie Jeans' recycled denim appeal to the customer seeking a 'guilt-free' treat (*see* page 130).

Writing a customer pen portrait

A pen portrait is a short, written profile that describes the characteristics and traits of a core customer, representative of the target market. The portrait provides a composite picture of the target consumer, which should be built up using information gathered from primary and secondary market research. The portrait should present a realistic and factual description of the consumer demographic, age or age bracket, lifestyle, fashion style, brand preferences, purchasing motivation and attitudes towards purchasing fashion.

Make sure you define their age and gender, describe their lifestyle, social status and stage of life. You can list the clothing brands that they wear or aspire to wear and indicate how much they spend on clothing. The problem with pen portraits is the tendency to describe a fantasy life or the aspirational life of the consumer rather than the reality; it is important therefore to reiterate that the portrait must be based upon researched information and data. Information can be obtained from government demographic statistics, articles in the fashion media, fashion trend publications and websites, blogs and by carrying out a customer questionnaire.

A visual depiction of the customer and their lifestyle is a useful addition to the written portrait. This can be created using a collage of images taken from magazines as well as your own illustrations. Consider magazines that cover interiors, lifestyle, food, gardening, sport, gadgets or technology. When creating a visual profile, it is important to ensure that images reflect the consumer's lifestyle and activities and not just their approach to fashion. Try to use pictures that typify the product or brand choices for that consumer type such as their car, watch, scent, accessories and clothing. The images chosen should reflect accurately the market level and status level of the customer.

Questions for a pen portrait

Try to visualize the person, get inside their head and imagine who they are.

What influences are there in his or her life?

What are their key concerns, opinions or interests?

Think about their routine as they go through the day. Do they have specific clothes or outfits for work, sport or leisure?

What non-clothing brands are important to them and why?

Understanding business customers

Understanding business customers is also extremely important. In B2B situations it is normal procedure for a business to analyse its customer base. This is done for two main reasons – firstly to determine how valuable each customer is to the business, and secondly to understand how best to meet customer needs and service them effectively. In order to fully understand the needs of business customers, it also makes sense to have good knowledge of their end-consumers as well.

Take, for example, an independent designer with their own fashion label who supplies their collection to approximately 40 stores

CONSUMER PROFILE CHART

This chart can be used as a framework to assist in building
a consumer profile. Responses to market research
questionnaires and interviews will provide relevant information.

Interests and opinions

Social media

Fashion needs

Brands they wear

Where and how they shop

Demographic

Magazines and blogs

Emotional motivations

Brands they aspire to wear

Fashion trends they follow

worldwide. They could analyse and classify their customers by country or region, such as Europe, Asia and North America, particularly if end-consumers in each region have differing requirements. The designer may supply independent boutiques that order small quantities from a limited selection of the range, or much larger retailers that take a greater proportion of the collection; so they might want to analyse these customers by the amount they order or by the type of product they order. They may have customers that require little effort to service whereas other customers may have input into the design process, specifying particular colours, styles or fabrics suitable for their end-consumers, and they may require exclusivity, requesting certain styles be made available only to them. These customers might be of great value to the business even though they require a higher level of service.

B2B customers might be assessed by their financial contribution, but there are other assets of value to consider, such as status and reputation of the customer, publicity potential, partnership or networking possibilities, or their ability to provide access to other organizations. In reverse, large high-street retailers usually analyse their supply base so that they can determine which suppliers provide the best service, quality and prices. A large business like a textile manufacturer, for example, might segment its customers by the type of market they represent, separating the companies that purchase for the high-street multiples from other clients who might be at couture or designer level. Below is a summary of criteria to consider when analysing business customers:

» **Location –** local, national, international or global

» **Financial contribution –** how much they contribute to turnover and profit

» **Reputation –** the value attached to their name, type of end-consumer they attract and publicity potential

» **Status –** new start-up or well established, length of business relationship. Loyalty of custom. Financial security

» **Type of company –** department store, independent boutique, e-tailer, retail chain. Or manufacturer, producer or designer

» **Market level –** a fabric supplier, for example, may have customers at couture and designer level, as well as retailers that develop own-brand collections

Building a customer profile

The niche denim market

Sliced Bread is a denim brand created by James Hayes while still a student studying fashion at Plymouth College of Art in the UK. The idea was developed in response to increasing consumer demand for authentic, stylish and nostalgic product. The Sliced Bread concept is simple; to make quality jeans and T-shirts that people will remember. Each piece is hand-made in England using the finest ingredients and production methods. Sliced Bread products are trans-seasonal and 100 per cent fresh!

Researching the customer

James carried out face-to-face, telephone and Internet interviews with young men in their early twenties who might be potential customers for Sliced Bread jeans and T-shirts. He wanted to gather more information on their lifestyles, the type of brands they currently wore and find out more about which brands they aspired to wear. James discovered how much they spent on clothes, what they did for a living and how they spent their leisure time. After conducting a number of interviews, James noticed commonalities in terms of purchasing behaviour, attitudes and brand preferences that appeared to typify the traits of the sample group. James used this information to compile a customer pen portrait for a character he named 'Jason Powell', who would be representative of the target audience for the proposed Sliced Bread brand.

Pen portrait of a Sliced Bread customer

Jason Powell is a twenty-one-year-old student studying architecture at Manchester University. Now in his second year of study, he has rented a student flat with three friends. In the holidays he lives with his parents in Windsor, about 50 km (30 miles) outside London. Jason is entrepreneurial and aspires to set up his own design business. He already communicates online with other young architects and designers around the world and has set up a blog with thoughts, sketches and ideas for his dream city. Jason says that his blog is "Like an ever-changing profile of who I am; it's where people can see what I am like and follow my interests."

AARON WATTS
Age: 20
Student

Wears:
adidas Originals and charity shop
Aspires to wear: None

SAM PHILLIPS
Age: 20
DJ

Wears:
Levi's, adidas, Wood Wood, Religion and Bantum
Aspires to wear: Paul Smith, Diesel Black Gold and Vivienne Westwood

ALEX PUGH
Age: 21
Student

Wears:
Jack Wills, Topman University Gear, Crew Clothing
Aspires to wear: Paul Smith

Opposite
Images of James Hayes' Sliced Bread jeans and T-shirt collection.

Left
Photographs showing three of the young men interviewed by James Hayes during his customer research investigations. James discovered there was a gap between the brands his target group aspired to wear and those that they actually bought. Aspirational brands were Paul Smith, Comme des Garçons, Diesel Black Gold and Dsquared[2]. Labels actually worn were Zara, Primark, charity shop clothes, Topman, Levi's and Jack Wills. It is important to point out that although James focused on young men aged 20 or 21, the potential market for the Sliced Bread concept is likely to extend to customers aged 30, so extra research into customers of this age bracket should also be carried out.

Jason loves T-shirts, particularly those from 5Preview in Italy – "they sell cool, one-off printed Ts, and British brands, To-orist and Tom Wolfe." Jason's passion for architecture translates into a respect for product that is well designed but understated, like a good pair of jeans from Prps, Flat Head, Dr. Denim, Acne or Levi's Red – BUT he can't always afford them unless they are on sale, so sometimes it's down to the charity shop to find something quirky, or a trip to Primark if he is feeling cheap. Jason always pays in cash when he goes shopping for clothes; "If you haven't got it [money], don't buy it." He uses his credit card only when purchasing online. Jason's money goes on his car, rent, going to gigs and clubs, and topping up his mobile phone. At the start of term he spent £180 on a bus pass and £150 on gym membership. Rent is £70 per week and food about £40. Jason spends more on clothes than he used to because now he constantly goes out to clubs in Manchester. "With club culture you have to wear something different every time. I'll go out and spend £300 on clothes in one go and then won't shop again for three months or so – unless something catches my eye."

Knowing your core customers

Dressing the modern Indian woman

Shift by Nimish Shah is a sophisticated and urban label designed primarily for the Indian market. The clothes are made from certified organic cotton and crafted using traditional artisan skills where possible. Fans include celebrities such as actress Kalki Koechlin, who embodies the label's offbeat vibe.

After graduating in Product Design and Development from the London College of Fashion, and work experience at Chloé, Burberry and retailers Browns and Jigsaw in London, Shah returned to Mumbai in 2011 to launch his fashion label. His industry experience informs his designs, and understanding his target customers is an essential part of the process. Shah paints a portrait of his customer with clarity. "Basic staples are important to her: one pair of sunglasses – not three. And sturdy shoes! We design classic items and often rework ideas from previous collections." Shift has gained a following in India, particularly among bloggers, for its relaxed shift dresses.

Shah knows his customers to be confident and sensual women. Shift is not designed for a 'girly girl' but for the woman Shah describes as "hands-on, thinks on her feet and exudes confidence." These women have a strong and powerful body language, but the minute they slip into a dress, there is a ladylike quality to them.

Kalki Koechlin, an Indian actress of French descent, is a fan of Shift and epitomizes its confident yet sensual aesthetic. She is often photographed wearing the label. Above, Nimish with Kalki.

5

Introduction to Branding

"A brand is the sum of the tangible and intangible benefits provided by a product or service and encompasses the entire customer experience."

How Brands Work, Chartered Institute of Marketing

Branding is becoming an ever more important tool for marketing fashion. As companies manage to match each other with their ability to deliver appropriately priced, quality fashionable product, so something extra needs to come into play, something emotional and connecting. This is where the brand comes in. There is no doubt that fashion marketing has evolved. It is no longer just about the products themselves or ensuring that the right products are in the right place at the right time, now it is brand experience that differentiates. Branding is the mechanism by which a company creates and manages a brand and conveys the messages and values that underpin the brand to its customers. Branding is therefore a significant strategic activity for companies wishing to differentiate their products and services. This chapter introduces the key branding concepts, illustrating how these may be viewed within the context of fashion.

Defining a brand

The concrete features of a brand are its logo, strapline, slogan, actual products and physical retail environment. But a brand is more than the sum of its parts – most of what constitutes a brand is intangible. In many ways the brand is a paradox, a composite shaped internally by company strategy and externally by consumer perception and experience. Formed from a unique mix of tangible and intangible elements, a brand is created out of a total package including not only the garments, retail environment, packaging and advertising but also the meanings, values and associations that consumers ascribe to the brand. Walter Landor, a pioneer of branding, famously said, "Products are made in the factory, but brands are created in the mind." Allen Adamson defines a brand as, "something that exists in your head. It's an image or a feeling. It's based on associations that get stirred up when a brand's name is mentioned" (2007). Influential and successful brands manage to engender positive or constructive associations in the minds of consumers, triggering emotions and feelings that can be extremely potent and affirmative. However, each consumer forms their own opinions so there is the possibility that they may develop negative perceptions and beliefs. It is therefore important for those who manage brands to consider carefully the associations that a brand conveys, making sure wherever possible that messages are transmitted by design rather than default. A brand must have clear points of difference, not only in the products and services but also at an experiential level. Consumers need to be aware of the brand's existence, connect with its ethos and value what it has to offer – and of course the brand offering should be relevant to the needs, aspirations and desires of customers.

The values, messages and ideas that underpin a brand will be expressed through:

>> The brand name and logo

>> The product

>> Packaging and display

>> The environment in which it is sold

>> Social media and online content

>> Advertising and promotion

>> Company reputation and behaviour

Below
Flags display the brand names of luxury fashion, accessory and jewellery retailers on London's Old Bond Street. The style and design of a logo and the colour of a flag form a significant manifestation of brand identity.

Bottom
Chanel trademark quilted handbag with iconic interlocking C logo on the clasp.

The brand name and logo

The brand name and logo are tangible features that can be controlled from within the company. The logo provides the most fundamental visible element of the brand; the style of this unique identifier should capture and represent the essence or core idea behind the brand. Intelligent or ingenious use of colour, typeface and symbol can help to achieve a distinguishing logo that hopefully will stand as an iconic and trusted visual agent of the brand. Luxury fashion brands such as Gucci, Prada, Fendi or Chanel use fonts in upper case to create an aura of authority and tradition. Some brands add a crest or cartouche to enhance the logo and bestow an air of grandeur or heritage. Sports brands design their logos with the aim of generating a sensation of movement, speed or direction. Brands that wish to convey elegance or femininity tend to use lower-case script with flourishes and tails. A well-designed and powerfully recognized logo is a great asset to a brand. The logo can be formed using the brand name, i.e. Gucci or Prada; Paul Smith uses his signature as the brand logo. Initials and letters can be exploited to construct a brand name such as DKNY (Donna Karan New York) or used to form a secondary logo, examples being the interlocking letters of Fendi, Chanel or Gucci. There are, of course, legendary brands such as Nike with its iconic Swoosh symbol, so powerful that it instantly identifies the brand without the need for any accompanying name or words. Similarly, the Fred Perry laurel wreath and the Lacoste crocodile also act as iconic emblems for their respective brands.

Trademarks

Brand logos, symbols, slogans and straplines can be registered. It is also possible to register elements of a design that are specific signifiers of a brand. Levi's, for example, has registered the marketing slogan 'Quality never goes out of style'® and the Burberry iconic camel, black and red check became a registered trademark in 1924 when it was used as a lining for the Burberry trenchcoat. A registered **trademark** gives the brand company exclusive rights over usage of the registered article. This helps to protect the brand from piracy or unauthorized use of the trademark. Once a mark is registered it can be identified by the ® or ™ symbol.

A small business intending to trade in their home market can register their mark for exclusive use in their national market. But to ensure more comprehensive protection, it is sensible to be internationally registered.

"Branding is the process by which brand images get inside your head."

Allen Adamson, Landor Associates

CLASSIC LUXURY

Feminine Boutique

modmode

The international sports brand adidas has an instantly recognizable logo, top, featuring its quintessential three-stripes motif. The classic adidas emblem has been modified to create logos for the adidas sub-brands.

When creating logos it is important to consider the underlying message and choose a typeface accordingly. The stretched font and forward direction of the 'Sport Fashion' logo creates a feeling of momentum. An upper-case copperplate Gothic Light typeface communicates the timeless authority of heritage and luxury (Classic Luxury). The italicized Edwardian Script adds a feminine touch to a logo (Feminine Boutique). A contemporary modern look with a retro feel is created using the Bauhaus 93 typeface (Modmode).

Brand canvas

Fashion product provides a fantastic canvas for branding. Logos can be emblazoned boldly on T-shirts or used more subtly in placement embroideries. Denim brands use trademark stitching on back pockets to identify their jeans or use labels, like the iconic Levi's red tab. When designing branded product, think about how to incorporate brand insignia. Clasps, clips, buckles and zips can all be developed so as to include recognizable and identifying symbols or emblems, and fabrics can be woven or printed with trademark stripes, checks and patterns.

The adidas Originals by Originals (ObyO) limited-edition collection created by adidas in collaboration with New York fashion designer Jeremy Scott exemplifies how a logo can be integrated within a garment design to creative effective branding. Scott takes an inventive approach by partly concealing an oversized adidas Originals emblem with layers of fringing.

Below
Burberry's distinctive check is utilized by the brand for many of its products. Here it is used for the menswear collection. The scale of the check has been enlarged significantly but it is still instantly recognizable as a signifier of the brand.

Right
The Fred Perry tennis sweater is branded with an embroidered laurel wreath – the signature trademark of the brand.

Types of brands

Brands exist at every level of the fashion industry. There are branded fibres, branded textiles, sports brands, designer brands such as Armani or Donna Karan, luxury brands like Louis Vuitton or Hermès, iconic couture brands like Dior, fashion retail brands, and even department stores that have achieved brand status. Defining types of brand can be complicated, but they can be categorized as explained below.

Corporate brand This is where an organization has one name and one visual identity across its brands. The corporation is the brand.

The Sri Lankan manufacturing corporation, MAS Holdings, has this kind of structure: MAS Intimates produces lingerie and intimate apparel for global customers such as Marks & Spencer, Gap and Victoria's Secret; MAS Active is a supplier of active sports and casual wear to Nike, adidas, Reebok, Gap and Speedo; and MAS Fabric develops fabrics, elastics, lace and other garment components.

Manufacturer brands These are created and marketed by producer companies who will choose a name for their branded product. **Manufacturer brands** are prevalent within the fibre and textile industry where chemical manufacturers brand their fibres. The science-based company DuPont™, for example, used to manage the well-known fibre brand, Lycra®. Another DuPont™ brand is Kevlar®, utilized in garments worn by workers exposed to a variety of hazards including abrasion and high levels of heat. NatureWorks LLC, a joint venture between Cargill and PTT Global Chemical, produce Ingeo™, a branded fibre made from renewable plant resources derived from corn. The avant-garde French fashion label Marithé + François Girbaud selected Ingeo™ to use in their first eco-inspired designs.

Private brands Private brands are also known as own brands, store brands, retailer brands or **own label**. The US department store, Nordstrom, offers its own brand, Classiques Entier, and Macy's offers a wide portfolio of private label brands, including I.N.C. and Tasso Elba. Private brands raise the profile of a retailer, differentiate its offering and add value for customers. Retailers tend to favour them because they offer opportunity for higher margin than selling designer-branded merchandise.

Endorsed brand An **endorsed brand** is created when a parent brand gives its name to or endorses one of its own sub-brands. The names of the parent and sub-brand are linked. Examples would be Polo by Ralph Lauren or the perfume Obsession by Calvin Klein. The endorsement gives credibility to the sub-brand while also capitalizing on the status and reputation of the existing main brand.

Above
Jeremy Scott's fringed hooded top for the adidas ObyO collection.

"Brands help businesses cross geographic and cultural borders. Global brands are an enormous asset to their home country. They aid exports of products and services to foreign markets."

Clamor Gieske, FutureBrand

Co-brands or partnership brands A **co-brand** is created when two brands join together to develop a new brand. The Japanese designer Yohji Yamamoto a collaborative brand project with adidas, adidas Y-3 (also known as Y-3). Y-3 takes its name from the 'Y' from Yamamoto and the three stripes of the adidas logo.

Brand portfolio When a company has a brand portfolio the aim is to maximize coverage of the market without the individual brands within the portfolio competing with each other. The multiple brands within the company will be designed to address specific needs across different key segments within the market. Kering's brand portfolio includes prestigious and clearly defined luxury brands, including Gucci, Alexander McQueen, Stella McCartney, Balenciaga, Bottega Veneta, Saint Laurent and sports and lifestyle brands Puma and Volcom. The adidas Group has a brand portfolio that includes Reebok, Rockport, the shoe company, and golf brand TaylorMade.

The purpose of branding

The purpose of branding is to establish a clear and distinctive identity for a product, service or organization. The aim is to ensure that the brand offers something distinguishable from competitor brands. Branding should also add value or increase the perceived value of a product, allowing a company to charge a premium for its branded merchandise. On a more complex level, branding works to create emotional connection between customers and the brand. It raises not only the consumer's potential financial outlay but it can also affect their emotional investment in the brand. A pair of Nike trainers, for example, is not just a pair of running shoes but 'my Nikes', imbued with additional associations and meaning. In a pair of Nikes 'I can do it'. This is why a brand can be so powerful and influential – the Nike wearer might feel more committed and better able to get up early and run, they might believe themselves to be more sporty, active and alive when they wear this particular brand. Consumers are therefore more likely to engage constructively with a brand and purchase its products if the brand satisfies several criteria. The brand's products and services must have relevance to their life and needs, the consumer should identify closely with the brand ideology and style, and their association with the brand should trigger positive or affirmative feelings and emotions.

Branding should generate reassurance and a sense of security and trust for customers. If they have connected emotionally with a brand and want what it has to offer then the hope is that they will remain loyal. It is important therefore that the brand remains

The name game – brand identity

Meredith Wendell

Meredith Wendell is a New York-based accessories brand founded in 2008 by husband and wife team, Meredith and Wendell German. Their technicolour bags and accessories are sold in stores and boutiques worldwide including Bloomingdale's, Matches and Scoop NYC. The eye-catching designs and wonderful funky names embody the brand's playful identity.

Bags, left to right:
The Frog, The Green Eye.
Belt: The Fat Skinny Snake.

consistent and continues to deliver the values and promises that customers expect.

The issue of brand continuity is an extremely important factor within the fashion industry. This is because two contrasting factors – newness and consistency – need to be integrated season after season. Customers will naturally demand choice and want to be tempted with fresh merchandise each season, but they also require some sense of stability when engaging with a brand. This presents a challenge to designers who must create and develop new product collections on a regular basis. They must ensure the integrity of the brand remains intact and create the sensation of permanence for customers, even when the products in-store change on a frequent basis. Even though the theme, concepts, colours and fabrics might be different for each seasonal collection, the overarching branding, **brand message** and values need to remain consistent.

Branding is essentially about building a relationship between consumer and brand. This is why a thorough knowledge and understanding of consumers is so vital and why companies invest so much time and money in consumer and market research. The more intimately a company understands its customers, the better able it is to develop products, services, retail environments and marketing strategies that encourage consumer engagement, promote loyalty and foster trust in its brand.

So, to summarize, the aim and purpose of branding is to:

>> Tap into values and beliefs

>> Create connection

>> Generate emotional response

>> Provide reassurance

>> Ensure consistency

>> Build loyalty

>> Add value and charge a premium

An important element of branding is to develop and establish what is known as a **brand identity**. This is one of the foremost tactics for achieving the emotional connection with a target audience that is so vital to the concept of branding.

Brand identity

Brand identity is controlled from within an organization and should relate to how the company wishes consumers to perceive and engage with the brand. People use brands, and fashion in particular, to make statements about themselves – the meanings and associations consumers foster about brands will be closely connected with how they want to feel, how they want to be seen and how they wish to be perceived by others. Consumers are more likely to connect positively with a brand if they associate closely with its overall identity and ethos. It is extremely important therefore for an organization to develop a compelling and engaging identity for its brand. The identity will be built up using the following:

>> The logo

>> The product and services

>> Packaging

>> Retail environment

>> Windows and visual merchandising

>> Promotion, advertising and PR

>> Website, blog and social media

Each outward expression of the brand as listed above will work towards building up the brand identity. One simple way for a fashion designer to strengthen their brand identity and connect with a fashion audience is to bestow garments with names to captivate the imagination. Erdem gives luscious and evocative names to all the garments in his collection. The 'Felicitas' jewelled dress, the 'Invidia' silk blouse and the 'Laverna' skirt, for example. Isaac Mizrahi adds a splash of humour to his collections with colour names such as 'Lorne Green', 'Burlapse' and 'James Brown'. Subtle details such as naming products can set an emotional tone and help make a brand and its products memorable.

It is important to point out, however, that consumers will interpret all of a brand's signifiers and form their own impression of the identity. It is vital, therefore, that each and every manifestation of the brand upholds the identity coherently and consistently. The image of the brand from a consumer perspective is known as the **brand image**.

Brand image

The image of a brand will differ depending on whether it is formed by a brand-user or non-user or someone who has a business association with the brand such as a supplier or stakeholder. Someone who is a devoted customer of a brand would compose his or her image based on actual experience. Take someone who regularly purchases from Ralph Lauren. They may visit the same flagship store frequently, be consistently served by a specific staff member and build up a very personal relationship with the brand and its products. Another person may aspire to the Ralph Lauren lifestyle, but believe the designer clothes to be expensive or extravagant. They might buy into the brand on a rare occasion by purchasing sunglasses, perfume or homeware from a department store such as Bloomingdale's or Selfridges. A fashion-aware non-user would generally construct their brand image from magazines – looking at the adverts, fashion spreads, reading the editorial content – or from social media content such as Twitter posts, Instagram and Pinterest images. The power of a brand rests in its relationship with consumers, so every interaction a customer or potential customer has with a brand is important as it will contribute to their brand experience, either positively or negatively.

The company behind a brand needs to ensure that there is a close match between the identity they control and the brand image as perceived by outsiders and consumers. A large gap between identity and image can result in catastrophic problems for a brand. There have been cases where companies have lost control of their identity. This happened to Burberry when consumers it had not intended to attract started purchasing both legitimate Burberry product and counterfeit products. The skewed image of the brand affected its identity, which no longer related to the strategic intentions within the company.

BRAND IDENTITY AND IMAGE

There is a strong correlation between brand and consumer identity. Consumers are likely to connect with brands that affirm their personal viewpoint and ideals.

CONSUMER IDENTITY

↓

BRAND IMAGE

Consumers will use the external expressions of the brand to form their own perception and opinion of the brand. This is known as the brand image.

↑

LOGO + PRODUCTS + PACKAGING + DISPLAY + PROMOTION + DIGITAL MEDIA AND CONTENT

↑

BRAND IDENTITY

Brand identity is controlled internally from within a company. It is reflected externally through every outward expression of the brand. Each aspect of the brand must be consistent and congruent in order to build a strong and coherent brand identity.

Developing and managing brand identity

Developing and managing the brand identity is an extremely important aspect of **brand management**. A brand is a precious commodity and a valuable asset for a company – a powerful brand name, brand logo and brand identity as well as the accumulated goodwill that exists towards the brand all contribute to the **brand equity** or total worth of the brand as an asset. A brand with high equity and a strong identity can command a price-premium for its product, which is one of the main purposes of branding. Those managing a brand need to ensure that there is a close match between the brand identity created and managed from within the company and the brand image held by consumers and others outside the company. In order to develop and manage an identity effectively it is important to understand that it is formulated from three key constituents:

> » Brand essence
>
> » Brand values
>
> » Brand personality

The brand essence, values and personality govern the overall character and feel of the brand; they give the brand its meaning and uniqueness and serve to differentiate the brand from others in the marketplace. These are vital components of the identity and should be reflected in the outward manifestations of the brand – its symbol or logo, product, packaging, display, promotion and website.

Brand essence

The first step in defining brand identity is to determine and establish the **brand essence**. A brand's essence describes the essential nature or core of a brand. It could be described as the brand's heart, spirit or soul. It is extremely important to understand what lies at the heart of a brand and to be able to articulate it concisely. Edun, for example, launched by Ali Hewson and Bono of U2, describes its mission as "building long-term, sustainable growth opportunities by supporting manufacturers, infrastructure and community-building initiatives in Africa" (www.edun.com). This short statement identifies the fundamental aim of the brand, marks out its central proposition and sums up its essence. Writing a statement such as this is important as a clearly defined essence forms the key building block upon which all other aspects of the brand are built.

Adding the personal touch

The Castlefield Bridal Company

Sophie Taylor's wedding stationery business targets 20–30-year-olds looking for quality and distinction with a personalized touch. Castlefield's brand values include quality, service, communication, distinction and enchantment. While the appearance of the final product is important, Sophie believes that what happens behind the scenes is also a vital part of the brand. "Without a positive relationship with the client, the Castlefield experience would not be complete."

Developing a moodboard

Sophie always starts by making a moodboard and developing a logo. For The Castlefield Bridal Company she researched images of castles, early 20th-century couture, vintage-inspired bridal gowns, royal jewels, vintage perfume bottles, mythical creatures and similar themes. The final logo design with its elegant but clear type, flowing scrolls, and crown fits with the ideal of 'Grandeur and Grace' that Sophie wanted to convey; the warm gold on white keeps the overall look clean with a touch of glamour.

Constructive feedback

Sophie sought feedback during the branding process, speaking with a variety of people of different ages, ethnicities and genders. The most frequent comments were that the name and logo sounded and looked sophisticated, regal with vintage glamour and ideal for a bridal company. Sophie thinks "stylistically the brand appeals to couples who want to feel like royalty on their wedding day as well as those who just want simple elegance."

The finished product

The final brand identity balances grandeur and grace, giving the products a sense of drama and an ornate elegance. Sophie wanted a vein of soft vintage glamour to run through the graphics. She says, "I have always loved the aesthetics of the 1910s, 1920s, 1930s and 1940s, and wanted the branding to reflect a sense of vintage femininity along with a regal touch."

Brand identity and emotion

Davidelfin

The Spanish fashion label Davidelfin was launched in Barcelona in 2002 by a multidisciplinary group of artistic individuals that included a professional model, a journalist, an architect, a film director and musician, and the figurehead, painter David Delfin, who discovered that fashion was his true métier. Davidelfin has become a renowned Spanish fashion brand acknowledged for the quality of its fashion show productions and for the singularity of its fabrics, patterns and tailoring.

In an interview with Mariona Vivar Mompel for cafebabel.com, Delfin commented that young designers starting out face difficulties because the market is at saturation point. "This means that in order to stand out in the fashion industry you need two things: your own identity and ideology." Delfin believes that to succeed it is necessary to be something more than mere fashion designers. "Nowadays you have to be able to awaken emotions." He goes on to say that emotions remain the driving force behind his work.

For his inaugural collection Delfin used second-hand military clothes as the basis for the work. "There was a memory, a fingerprint. Names of the people that inhabited them, grease stains, stitching." The ideology for the collection revolved around the works of the German artist Joseph Beuys, including the left-handed writing that has become a recognizable mark of the Davidelfin brand.

davidelfin
MADRID

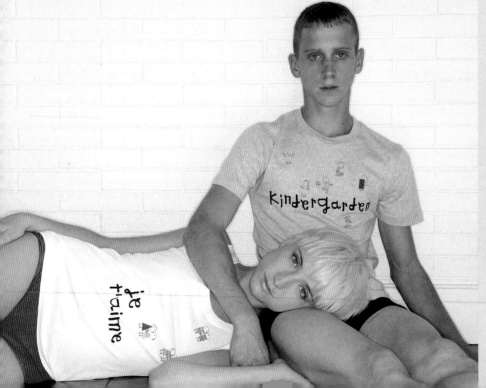

Davidelfin garments printed with text using the same distinctive left-handed script as the brand logo. The felt suit featured on the T-shirt above left is an iconic Beuys work.

Closely allied to the brand essence is the **brand proposition**, which is a succinct expression of what the brand intends to offer or promise its customers. The Edun statement on page 148 clarifies the Edun brand essence but it also explains the Edun brand proposition as shown below.

Edun brand essence – a socially conscious clothing company

Edun brand proposition – to offer beautiful clothing and build sustainable growth opportunities and community initiatives in Africa

As you can see from the example above, the essence and proposition (or promise) explain the raison d'être behind the brand and clarify the motivation for the business. A genuine brand essence in combination with an achievable and deliverable proposition will contribute to creating a well-defined brand identity that in turn can act as a potent force for marketing and set the tone for communication and promotion. If essence is considered to be the heart of a brand then **brand values** (sometimes referred to as core values) are its foundation stones.

BUILDING BRAND LOYALTY

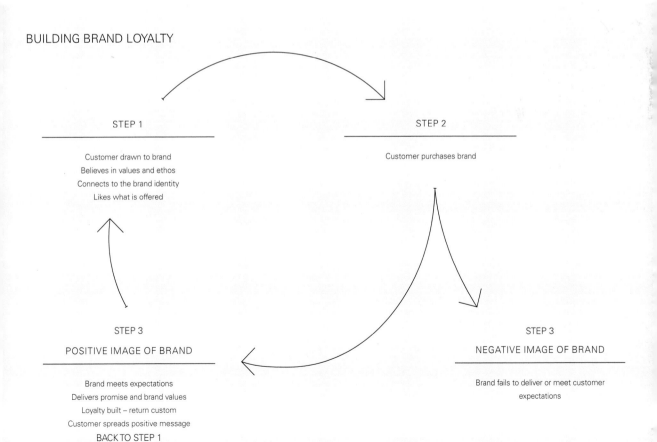

STEP 1

Customer drawn to brand
Believes in values and ethos
Connects to the brand identity
Likes what is offered

STEP 2

Customer purchases brand

STEP 3
POSITIVE IMAGE OF BRAND

Brand meets expectations
Delivers promise and brand values
Loyalty built – return custom
Customer spreads positive message
BACK TO STEP 1

STEP 3
NEGATIVE IMAGE OF BRAND

Brand fails to deliver or meet customer expectations

BRANDING CONNECTS
COMPANY AND CUSTOMER

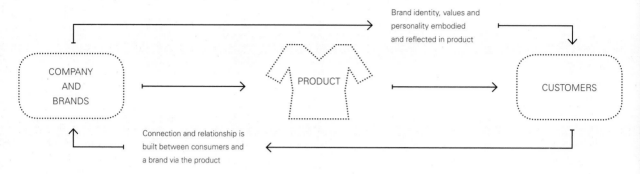

Brand identity, values and personality embodied and reflected in product

Connection and relationship is built between consumers and a brand via the product

Building brand loyalty

Brand identity and the brand values upon which it is built are important tools for establishing **brand loyalty**. Authentic brand values and an engaging brand identity are powerful communication tools, but if consumers engage with a brand because they respect what it stands for they will want to feel confident that the values will be upheld over time. A company managing a brand must ensure that customers' loyalty and trust are honoured and that the brand identity and values are maintained and remain consistent. The diagram on page 151 shows the impact on consumer loyalty of both a positive and negative brand image. If a consumer forms a positive image, they are likely to remain loyal and become advocates of the brand. If the brand fails to deliver, they will be disappointed and form a negative image.

Brand values

Brand values build upon and expand the central theme of the brand essence. They are the core values by which a brand organization operates. The values should inform all aspects of how the company runs its business, designs and develops its products, delivers its services, and markets and promotes its brand (see diagram above). Consumers are more likely to engage with a brand whose values they respect and connect with, as the title of Martin Butler's book, *People Don't Buy What You Sell: They Buy What You Stand For*, testifies.

Honest by (www.honestby.com) is a fashion collection and online store founded in 2012 by Belgian designer Bruno Pieters. The business is underpinned by the value of transparency. Honest by is the first fashion company to make price and manufacturing information on their entire supply chain available to the public. Each product on the website is accompanied by in-depth details on materials, manufacture, how the price is calculated and data on its carbon footprint. The value of transparency is more than just an ideal.

A small clothing company with big brand values

Nau

Nau (pronounced "now") is a US company based in Portland, Oregon that designs and sells its own range of sustainable fashion and performance wear. The team behind the Nau label describe the company as "a small clothing company with big ideas"; they understand the potential of building a brand up from its core values and are committed to the power of business as a force for change. As a business Nau seeks to balance the **triple bottom line**: people, planet and profit. The triple bottom line is an ethical system that measures a company's success in terms of economic, social and environmental criteria. The ethical stance taken by Nau leads the company to pose the question: "Does the world really need another outdoor clothing company?" Only if its products and practices contribute to "positive, lasting and substantive change", they reason.

The Nau website also explains the company design philosophy is: "Built on the balance of three criteria: beauty, performance and sustainability." From this it is possible to extrapolate the Nau core brand values:

> » To contribute to positive, lasting and substantive change

> » To produce and sell clothes that balance beauty, performance and sustainability

Brand values should be more than just a list of impressive-sounding words. They should be a call to action. The idea is to create values that inspire and drive a business forward. The values should be understandable and deliverable; those that manage a brand will need to instigate strategic actions to ensure the values are manifested throughout the company. Valid and authentic brand values strengthen the brand identity, give a business direction and provide motivation for management, stakeholders, partners and employees. Brand values are important not only in terms of their potential for guiding the internal business operation but also for building relationship and communicating with consumers. The key issue is to communicate the philosophy, ethos and values behind the company and detail how they are reflected in the product design and manufacture.

Top
The Profile Fleece jacket made from recycled polyester fabric developed from post-consumer and post-industrial polyester waste.

Above
The Nau team at work. Valid and authentic brand values strengthen the brand identity, give a business direction and provide motivation for the team.

Brand personality

Brand personality works on the premise that brands can have personalities in much the same way as people. Professor Kotler, when describing the differences between the computer brands IBM and Apple, suggested that Apple has the personality of someone in their twenties and that IBM has the character of someone in their sixties!

When related to fashion, the issue of brand personality needs some careful thought. It is all too easy to say that a brand is fashionable, stylish, modern or luxurious. But do those characteristics really capture the flavour of its personality or distinguish the brand clearly from any other? Probably not! The Vivienne Westwood label could be described as British fashion with a twist, so could that of Paul Smith, so it is vital to take some time to delve deeply and define other more descriptive qualities that capture the uniqueness of a brand's persona. Vivienne Westwood is also anarchic, irreverent and perhaps a little subversive, whereas the Paul Smith brand augments its British style with quirky elements of the unexpected.

When a brand is built around the distinctive personality of an individual designer, the brand personality is likely to resemble closely that of the designer in question. New York fashion designer Betsey Johnson has variously been described as exuberant, whimsical, over the top and fearlessly eccentric. Betsey's dramatic personality is

Below

Beauté Prestige International (BPI) creates, develops and markets fragrances for Jean Paul Gaultier, Issey Miyake and Narciso Rodriguez. The Jean Paul Gaultier perfume, Ma Dame, was launched in 2008; BPI worked with branding consultancy Interbrand to define the personality for the perfume, inspired by Gaultier's vision of the perfect woman. Ma Dame's personality is described by Interbrand as a "trendy tomboy with classy sex appeal".

reflected throughout her fashion empire. Her collections are known to be colourful and capricious with sexy silhouettes and whimsical embellished details. The Betsey Johnson retail stores (there are over 50 worldwide) amplify her singular creative vision with an iconic rock 'n' roll meets Victoriana style defined by bright colour, abundant floral wallpapers and bursts of ornamental decoration. As Betsey says on her website:

> "My products wake up and brighten and bring the wearer to life... drawing attention to her beauty and specialness... her moods and movements... her dreams and fantasies."

In comparison to Betsey Johnson it could be said that the Martin Margiela brand sits at the opposite end of the personality spectrum, particularly in terms of colour. Whereas Betsey Johnson draws attention by use of bold bright colour, Margiela creates drama by the use of white. White is the signature for all Margiela boutiques. Sales personnel are styled in lab-assistant white coats – the uniform traditionally worn by workers in a Parisian couture atelier. The signature use of non-colour could be described as self-effacing, like the Belgian designer himself. Famous for keeping a low profile, he has been described by journalist Sarah Mower as "fashion's mystery man". This desire for secrecy exudes from many aspects of the brand personality and identity. A noticeable example of inscrutability is evidenced in the garment label for the women's collection. It is not woven or printed with the Maison Martin Margiela brand name but is left blank. For the other collections, the label is constructed from a simple piece of white cloth printed with a series of numbers 0–23. The specific collection is indicated by encircling the appropriate number on the label. The key to the numbers and the collections is represented below.

0	Garments reworked by hand for women
010	Garments reworked by hand for men
1*	The collection for women
10	The collection for men
4	A wardrobe for women
14	A wardrobe for men
11	A collection of accessories for women and men
22	A collection of shoes for women and men
13	Objects and publications
MM6	Garments for ♀

* The original white label

Basia Szkutnicka is a fashion lecturer and Maison Martin Margiela devotee. She has been wearing and collecting Margiela clothes and accessories since the label launched in 1988. In a conversation

Top
Each Maison Martin Margiela collection is given a number rather than a name. MM6 is a line for women that is more casual and edgy than the main line, MM1.

Centre
Maison Martin Margiela store signage features no name, just the numbers 0–23.

Above
Maison Martin Margiela stores are all decorated in white, the brand signature colour.

with the author in 2009, Basia explained why she connects to the Margiela brand.

> "I love the irreverence and the intelligence... I feel I connect with the ethos of the label... I love the attention to detail, the garments flatter me, they are an extension of me... I love the tradition, craftsmanship and the values of the product. I feel really well dressed – it's like a second skin to me."

This connection to the ethos behind the Margiela brand is mirrored in an interview with a fashion journalist conducted by Mark Tungate. In his book *Fashion Brands* Tungate relates how this well-known journalist had two jackets with them for a trip to the Paris collections; one from Margiela, the other was from Zara. The Margiela jacket cost around five times the price of the Zara garment but the journalist did not mind paying this premium because as they explained,

> "I like what Margiela stands for. I'm paying for the person, not the article." (Tungate, 2005)

This illustrates the potential of brand personality as a tool for building relationships between a brand and its customers. This connection can be achieved more effectively if consumers perceive the product as a visible symbol and physical manifestation of a brand's personality. Social media can play a vital role in this regard. Elizabeth Schofield, founder of Fashion's Collective (www.fashionscollective.com), says, "A living, breathing personality is created on social media and brands must have a content strategy in place to control how people receive the brand personality." If a brand's personality could be described as edgy, modern, intellectual, beautiful, ethically conscientious and socially aware, it is likely to appeal to consumers who connect with these traits; they are likely to be socially aware, ethical customers who wish to feel edgy and intellectual or modern and beautiful.

Carrying the brand

The carrier bag is a highly visual symbol of a brand. This simple item is often overlooked as a marketing tool but just think about it – every time a customer leaves a store carrying their purchases in a distinctive and recognizable carrier bag, they become a walking advertisement for the brand. For many customers, the bag is considered to be an important element of the shopping experience and deemed just as much of a status symbol as the garments or product contained within it. It is an amazingly democratic device, available to all who purchase irrespective of the amount of money they spend.

Below
The carrier bag is often overlooked as a marketing tool.

BRAND TOUCHPOINTS

○ Pre-purchase

◯ Purchase

◌ Post-purchase

There are many touchpoints that affect a consumer when they interact with a fashion brand during the pre-purchase, purchase and post-purchase stages. There can be between 30–100 touchpoints, but it would be impossible for a company to focus on all of these effectively. A limited selection of key touchpoints must be identified. For a retailer with a physical store, the in-store experience and interaction with sales staff will be important touchpoints. For an online retailer, digital content, ease of navigation and effective sales platforms will be key.

Source: Adapted from Davis & Dunn (2002)

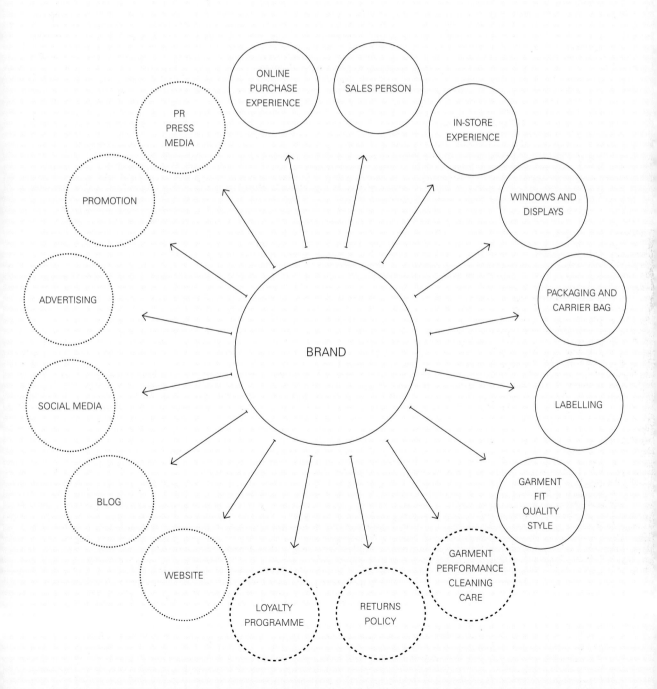

Brand touchpoints

Fashion product is one of the most important vehicles through which a brand transmits its message, values and identity to customers. The product can be described as a **brand touchpoint**, which is a point of interaction between a brand and consumers, employees or stakeholders. The concept of brand touchpoints was first published in 2002 by Davis & Dunn. A brand has between 30 and 100 potential touchpoints and each touchpoint has the potential to make either a positive or negative impression (Davis & Longoria, 2003). Touchpoints affecting consumers can be categorized into those that occur pre-purchase, during purchase and post-purchase. Think about all the possible interactions a consumer could have with a brand. Each touchpoint offers the potential for someone to be converted either for or against the brand. Take, for example, the pre-purchase stage. A person who is not aware of a particular brand or fashion label could see an image on Instagram or receive a tweet relating to the brand and thus become conscious of it. Someone who is already brand-aware may then visit the website or store and take the next step towards actually purchasing. During the purchase stage the potential customer may be converted and make a purchase, or they may be put off in some way by their experience and decide not to buy and not to interact with the brand again.

Creating a brand onion

When analysing a brand and developing a brand onion, it is often easiest to start with the personality layer first. Look at websites, in-store promotional material, carrier bags, labelling, window displays, in-store ambience or advertising – what kind of personality do you think they convey? How do you feel when you connect to the brand or how do you think customers feel when they wear the brand?

Work inwards through the brand onion and determine the brand values and the essence. Finally, don't forget the actions and behaviours section. Try to determine how the brand essence, values and personality are put into action and record findings in the outer ring of the onion.

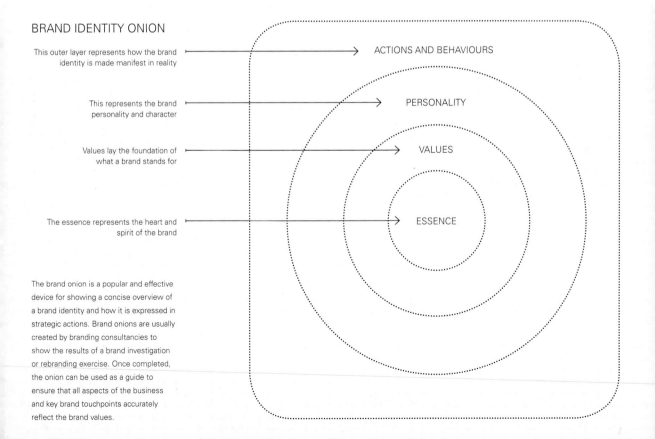

BRAND IDENTITY ONION

This outer layer represents how the brand identity is made manifest in reality → ACTIONS AND BEHAVIOURS

This represents the brand personality and character → PERSONALITY

Values lay the foundation of what a brand stands for → VALUES

The essence represents the heart and spirit of the brand → ESSENCE

The brand onion is a popular and effective device for showing a concise overview of a brand identity and how it is expressed in strategic actions. Brand onions are usually created by branding consultancies to show the results of a brand investigation or rebranding exercise. Once completed, the onion can be used as a guide to ensure that all aspects of the business and key brand touchpoints accurately reflect the brand values.

A new fashion brand and collection

Grandma's Trunk

The brand proposal showcased here forms part of a project undertaken by a student studying fashion at Plymouth College of Art in the UK. The student has set the scene and outlined the concept for the brand, Grandma's Trunk.

Grandma has a hidden trunk full of secret treasures. Dresses, brooches, old ribbons, buttons and scented love letters have remained preserved and undisturbed for decades. It's a girl's dream to rummage through this treasure trove and unearth vintage gems that could inspire new ideas or spark off a trend. Grandma's Trunk transforms faded treasures into delightful, edgy new garments with a surprising, vintage, rock-chic feel. The girl who wears this quirky new brand is adventurous, eclectic and confident. She radiates happiness, is admired as a trendsetter and experiments with creating her own special style by mixing vintage with raw classics.

Below
A brand onion showing how the personality of the Grandma's Trunk brand matches closely the personality of the targeted customer. The brand onion also shows how the potential customers might feel when they connect with its quirky mix of vintage and modern.

Above and right
The concept board for Grandma's Trunk. The imagery gives a visual feel for the brand and the customer.

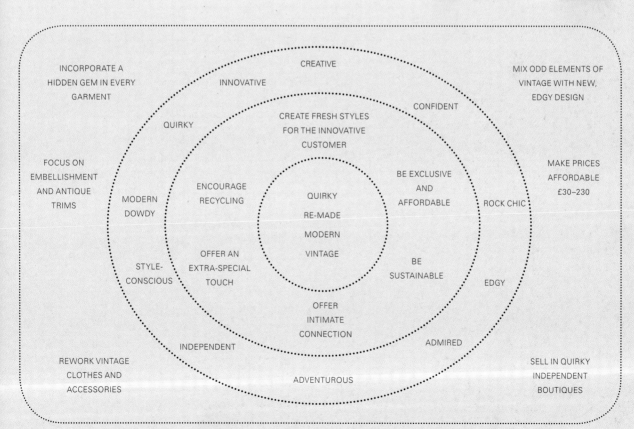

THE BRAND IDENTITY PRISM

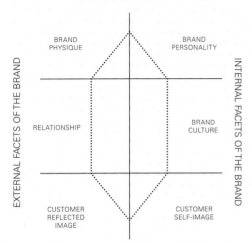

Source: Kapferer and Bastien,
The Luxury Strategy, 2009

Analysing brand identity

Brand touchpoints represent a point of interaction between a consumer or potential consumer and a brand. These touchpoints could also be considered as the brand in action, or in other words, the way in which a brand expresses its ethos and identity in actual strategic actions. This takes us on to a tool used in brand management known as a brand onion.

A brand onion is used to analyse and map the brand identity and show it in diagrammatic form. The brand onion represents the layers of a brand from its inner essence, or core, through to the outer personality layer and brand in action at the surface. The object of the exercise is to summarize the brand identity, capturing the essence, values and personality traits that differentiate the brand from competitors. The real benefit of the tool is its use in establishing how the identity should be made manifest in reality, represented by the 'actions and behaviours' section of the diagram. So, for example, the fashion brand Honest by (*see* page 152) has key values of honesty and transparency. How are these values realized? As we saw earlier, Honest by communicate everything about the materials, the manufacturing methods, and even the pricing strategies of the products stocked on the website. Every part of the process is transparent, including the store mark-up calculations.

The brand identity prism

Another model for analysing brand identity is Jean-Noël Kapferer's Brand Identity Prism, first introduced in 1992. Kapferer's six-sided model aims to capture the complexity of brand identity and the concepts behind it are perhaps harder to pin down than those of the simpler brand onion.

Both systems of analysis attempt to depict the internal and external aspects of brand identity. Kapferer's model does this by dividing the diagram by a vertical axis, whereas in the brand onion the internal elements are placed towards the centre and external aspects, such as 'actions and behaviours', are situated on the outer layer of the onion.

Physique – this equates to the essence of the brand as well as its physical features, symbols and attributes. At a symbolic level Nike is signified by the Swoosh and Levi's by a red tab, while Ralph Lauren is epitomized by Polo. The physical facet also comprises iconic products like Levi's 501 jeans or Yves Saint Laurent's 'Le Smoking' dinner jacket.

Personality – the character, attitude or personality of the brand. Kapferer believes a brand should have a unique personality. In his book, *Strategic Brand Management* (1992), Kapferer modifies the definition of USP, changing it to become 'unique selling personality'.

Culture – a brand has its own distinctive culture and brand values. At Hermès the culture is built around luxury, craftsmanship and exceptional quality; at Ralph Lauren it is formed from a unique blend of preppy American, rugged outdoorsy casual and classic English tweed.

Relationship – this relates to beliefs and associations connected with a brand. What does the brand promise? How is the brand perceived in the outside world? What does wearing a particular brand say about someone? It concerns social communication and the idea of using brands to belong to a style tribe or group.

Reflection – this is the idealized image of the consumer as reflected in brand advertising. Kapferer describes this facet as the 'external mirror' of the brand. In a short film advertising Chanel No 5, Nicole Kidman reflects the allure, sophistication, elegance and mystery of the Chanel brand.

Self-image – corresponds to the mental image consumers have of themselves when wearing the brand. Kapferer refers to this as the consumer's 'internal mirror'. Someone who wears Ralph Lauren might aspire to live the American dream or a person wearing Chanel may wish to feel independent and classy.

Branding: emotion and feeling

Branding aims to create connection by generating an emotional response. Brand personality and brand values are instrumental in achieving this. Teri Agins says in her book, *The End of Fashion*: "Fashion happens to be a relevant and powerful force in our lives. At every level of society, people care greatly about the way they look, which affects both their self-esteem and the way other people interact with them" (Agins, 2000). Kapferer's brand prism takes this into account by including relationship and self-image among its six dimensions, while the brand onion positions the personality layer as the interface between the brand and consumer. Both models can be used to analyse why consumers might connect with a particular brand and how they might feel when they do. Bernd H. Schmitt includes a chapter entitled 'Feel' in his book, *Experiential Marketing*. Schmitt explains that the aim behind the marketing and promotion of fashion and fragrance is to evoke certain types of emotions or feelings likely to make a customer want the brand; this is what Schmitt calls 'sense marketing' (Schmitt, 1999). The naming

"Branding connects corporate strategy with consumer psychology."

Pamela N. Danziger

CORE AND PERIPHERAL
FASHION MARKETS

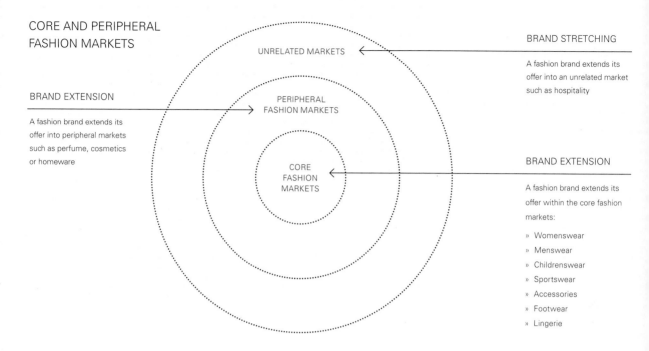

BRAND STRETCHING

A fashion brand extends its
offer into an unrelated market
such as hospitality

UNRELATED MARKETS

PERIPHERAL
FASHION MARKETS

CORE
FASHION
MARKETS

BRAND EXTENSION

A fashion brand extends its
offer into peripheral markets
such as perfume, cosmetics
or homeware

BRAND EXTENSION

A fashion brand extends its
offer within the core fashion
markets:

» Womenswear
» Menswear
» Childrenswear
» Sportswear
» Accessories
» Footwear
» Lingerie

convention for fragrances illustrates this concept; for example, Joy by Patou, Happy by Clinique, Pretty by Elizabeth Arden or Beautiful by Estée Lauder.

Brand strategy and management

Establishing a brand is a long-term and costly process and companies do not take on this risky task lightly. Creating a brand with a clear identity takes time – it usually takes several years or decades to achieve brand status. Orla Kiely, for example, started her business in a small way working from home. It took approximately ten years for the company to expand and morph into the modern fashion and lifestyle brand so loved today. Luxury brands like Fendi, Gucci and Prada started out as small family businesses. Fendi was a furrier, Gucci a handbag manufacturer and Prada designed and sold handbags, shoes and luggage. It was not until Mario Prada's granddaughter Miuccia took the helm in 1978 that Prada started its journey to becoming a global fashion brand. Once a brand is recognized and valued by consumers then opportunity arises to capitalize on the power of the brand name and leverage the brand identity in order to take the brand forward. While it could be argued that a brand is formed in the minds and hearts of consumers, it is a valuable business asset that must be managed effectively from within the brand organization. Two of the most widely used strategies utilized in brand management are **brand extension** and **brand licensing**.

Brand extension and stretching

Brand extension and brand stretching relate to Ansoff's Matrix for growth discussed in Chapter 3 (*see* pages 103–4). Brand extension allows a brand company to capitalize on the power of an existing brand's equity and value to launch new products in a broadly similar market. This relates to product development in Ansoff's Matrix. Brand extension exploits a brand's identity, associating the meanings and values behind it with new products. So an apparel supplier who manufactures a branded range of men's performance and outdoor apparel would be extending their brand into another area of the apparel market if they launched a similarly branded womenswear collection. The benefit of brand extension in this case is that distributors and buyers are likely to perceive less risk when taking on the women's version of the brand if they have had success selling the menswear, and end-consumers will have existing **brand awareness**.

If the company decided to utilize their established brand name in a completely different and unrelated market such as adventure travel then this would be termed brand stretching ('diversification' in Ansoff's Matrix). Missoni did this by creating the Missoni Home Collection as well as opening the former Hotel Missoni in Edinburgh, Scotland, and in Kuwait. When considering a brand stretching strategy it is important that there is a strong conceptual fit between the original brand and the new market. Missoni, for example, is a brand built around luxurious mixes of colour, texture and pattern that translate well into the arena of interior design.

Brand licensing

Brand licensing is a strategy that can be utilized by a business for brand extension. **Licensing** is a business arrangement where

"Successful brand licensing can have a very positive effect on the overall perception and value of the brand... However, it is not an easy proposition and failure to manage licensing effectively might weaken or permanently damage the brand."

Sean Chiles

Below left
Hotel Missoni in Edinburgh.

Below right
Missoni women's ready-to-wear Spring/ Summer 2009.

Designs for a colourful world

Agatha Ruiz de la Prada

The Spanish fashion designer Agatha Ruiz de la Prada is known for her vibrant use of colour, bold graphic prints and for the extraordinary funky shapes shown in her catwalk collections. Early in her career, de la Prada realized that she could not build her brand without collaborating with a big-name company. The breakthrough came with a deal to design a collection under her name for the Spanish department store chain El Corte Inglés. Since then the Agatha Ruiz de la Prada brand has expanded into a wide array of product areas through partnerships and licensing agreements with a range of manufacturers and globally renowned brands. The Agatha Ruiz de la Prada heart motif has become a distinctive trademark and has been used in many collaborations, including a chemical-free dress for Greenpeace, a special crocodile logo for French leisurewear brand Lacoste and a brooch for car maker Audi. Collaborations such as these have provided de la Prada with the investment required to expand her branded empire while at the same time enabling her to focus on design.

Above
Spanish designer Agatha Ruiz de la Prada.

Right
The heart motif is a signature of the brand and is used in wonderfully surreal ways within the collections. The heart also features on a wide range of other Agatha Ruiz de la Prada products such as sunglasses, stationery and kitchenware.

a brand company sells the right to use their name to another company who can then develop, manufacture and market specified branded merchandise under licence. Brand owners use licensing as a way of extending their brand into other product areas such as accessories, eyewear, intimate apparel, footwear, fragrances and beauty products, watches and homeware, or to expand into new geographic territories. Fila Luxembourg signed an agreement with US company Berkshire Fashions, for example, for the design, manufacture and sale of Fila branded accessories in the US market. This type of arrangement is known as **licensing out** and the manufacturing or distributing company (the **licensee**) will pay a royalty fee to the brand owner (the **licensor**). Royalty rates vary. The exact percentage is dependent on the time-frame of the agreement, the type of product involved, the financial investment, the time it takes to develop the product, and the volumes of merchandise predicted to sell. Licensing provides a means of diversification for a fashion brand, allowing it to expand into other markets and reach a broader audience. The general view is that less financial risk is attached to licensing compared to brand stretching because the brand company is not responsible for the capital investment or the costs involved in producing, distributing or marketing the licensed product. It is important therefore that licensing agreements are signed with companies with the correct expertise in manufacturing and marketing specific products.

Fashion licensing is meant to be invisible to the consumer, who should not know or notice that a licensee is making the products that carry a designer's name. However, a lack of control over the licensing can damage the identity and value of a brand. Calvin Klein and Burberry have suffered from this in the past.

Another growing licensing model is two trademark owners collaborating to create a new product with shared brand values. Examples include the collaboration between Harris Tweed and Clarks shoes; French designer Christian Lacroix launching a furniture collection with Italian art mosaic manufacturer Sicis; and Spanish designer Agatha Ruiz de la Prada designing vacuums for Dyson.

The most common form of licensing is the licensing out model, as explained above. There is another approach known as **licensing in**. A fashion brand pays for the rights to use the recognizable designs, images or intellectual property of another brand. An example is a clothing company buying the rights to use a Disney character on a T-shirt. This type of licensing is most common at the lower end of the market, but a new trend of licensing in is gaining momentum at the higher end. Gossip Girl by Romeo & Juliet Couture, inspired by the *Gossip Girl* television series, is one such tie-in.

A return to core values

....

Mr. Hare

Mr. Hare is the London-based men's contemporary shoe brand created and run by Marc Hare. He believes in running an ethical business with a focused range of essential products.

Marc Hare launched his business in 2008 as a one-man band. By 2014 the business had grown considerably. Marc realized that he needed to reassess the future direction of his brand. To start, he initiated a situation analysis of the business, carrying out market research and SWOT analysis as well as assessment of the Mr. Hare brand identity and an evaluation of consumers. The results identified a lack of product focus, with too many styles and colours, a lack of marketing focus, and a diversion from the brand's original roots. An opportunity to expand into the Asian market was identified, particularly Japan, where traditional and authentic footwear was a prevailing trend. Japanese consumers were particularly interested in the provenance and craftsmanship of the shoes. However, consumers there didn't always understand the nuances of the Mr. Hare brand, so it was time to reposition.

The Autumn/Winter 2014 collection returned to the core values of Mr. Hare. It was designed to target international, motivated and cultured male customers looking for professional style. The fresh positioning focused on styles that were contemporary, luxurious, high quality, timeless and black!

Below left
The Autumn/Winter 2014 collection of shoes and boots; almost entirely black, the contemporary Italian-crafted footwear is designed to appeal to style-conscious customers.

Below right
Marc Hare, the man behind the brand.

POSITIONING MAP FOR MR. HARE

This initial positioning map created by Marc Hare shows what he termed 'the brandscape'. The map identified the position of the Mr. Hare brand relative to other brands in the men's classic and contemporary shoe market.

Marc analysed the market in detail, including assessing the business model and production strategies of competitor brands.

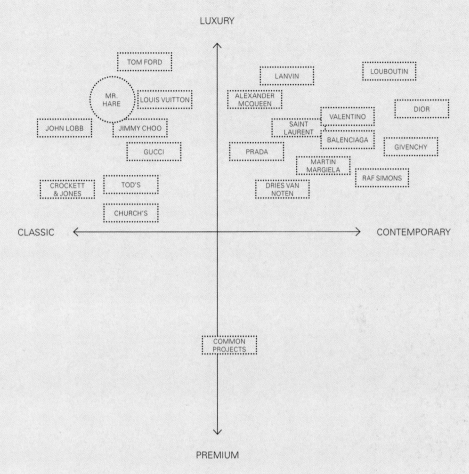

REPOSITIONING MAP

After analysing the brandscape, a new map was compiled to show the strategic approach and pricing of brands in each sector of the market.

Mr. Hare is not a vertically integrated brand with its own factory, so reviewing the market like this revealed that the brand competed with designer brands that manufactured in Italy. The strategic positioning of Mr. Hare was updated based on this observation.

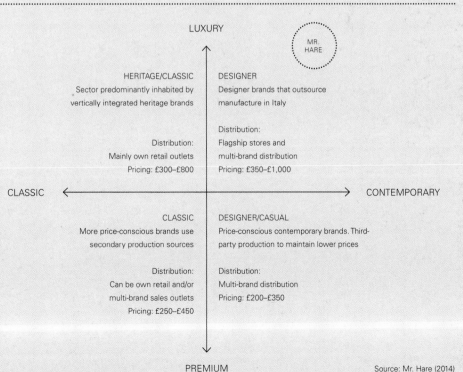

Source: Mr. Hare (2014)

A fresh visual identity for an established business

Greenwoods

Greenwoods are a menswear specialist retailer and suit hire business established in 1860 by Willie Greenwood. The company, which has generations of experience in the menswear business, was family owned until 2009 when it was bought by a Chinese company, Harvest Fancy Hong Kong Ltd., a unit of Bosideng International Fashion Ltd. Greenwoods trades online and from approximately 85 stores, situated mainly in the northern regions of the UK. It also has a suit hire business (www.1860.com) that specializes in traditional men's eveningwear, morningwear and Highlandwear for formal occasions and weddings.

In 2009 an independent graphic design consultancy, Studio Ten and a Half, were commissioned to revitalize and update the Greenwood brand identity. Footfall had gone down and Greenwoods were losing existing customers to competitors on the UK high street. The Greenwoods retail environment no longer looked fresh, the brand identity and message had become unclear and the brand personality was tired. There was a lack of coherence between the visual identity, the product on offer, the pricing strategy and the overall look of the retail environment. The bottom line was being affected

and Greenwoods were struggling to compete. Research revealed that consumers valued Greenwoods for its heritage and specialist menswear knowledge, and they valued the individual attention and service offered by staff. They also thought of the brand as masculine and trustworthy. The new visual identity created by Studio Ten and a Half was designed to ensure that Greenwoods could capitalize on the tradition, heritage and trust that consumers so valued. The rebranding package included an updated design for the logo, a new store fit, a refreshed look for the fascia, new swing tickets, in-store signage, stationery and carrier bags.

The makeover of Greenwoods achieved by design consultancy Studio Ten and a Half illustrates the importance of having the right visual style for a brand. The new logo, signage and fascia build upon the original heritage of the brand. Traditional elements such as the gold lettering were retained, but the introduction of a more refined and modern typeface brought the overall look and feel of the brand up to date. The clean but traditional typeface creates a fresh and contemporary brand identity, and a simple palette using Greenwoods' trademark green, gold, cream and grey ensures a balance between classic and modern. The brand's long-standing heritage is communicated clearly by the use of the statement, 'Menswear since 1860'.

Licensing agreements need to be considered with care, because you are selling the right to use your brand name. If your business is own-brand jeans and T-shirts and you sell the rights to use your brand name to a big manufacturer in this product area, it would be shrewd to retain the rights for other products such as dresses or accessories, leaving your options open for other deals in the future.

Brand repositioning

Brand repositioning is the process of redefining the identity of an existing brand or product in order to shift the position it holds in consumers' minds relative to that of competitors. A brand organization may decide to alter its strategic direction and reposition a brand if the current **brand positioning** is no longer relevant or effective. This decision might be a response to:

> » A brand losing market share

> » Changes in the macro or micro marketing environment

> » New brands entering the market

> » Repositioning of competitor brands

> » Shifts in consumer demand

Repositioning does not usually entail a change of brand name but might include updating and modernizing the existing logo.

On pages 166–67 and 168 are two examples of repositioning. The first illustrates how streamlining the product ranges was used to reposition a brand. The second example shows how a brand updated its visual identity by modernizing its logo, store **fascia**, in-store design and packaging.

Rebranding

Rebranding is a type of brand repositioning, but it goes further to encompass a complete change of name and logo, usually underpinned by a significant change in ethos and business strategy. This usually occurs in response to a company takeover and could include radical internal restructuring. Total rebranding generally occurs in industries such as banking and insurance; it is unusual within fashion, although it can occur within garment manufacturing or in the chemical fibre industry. One notable example, however, is the transformation of the French fashion conglomerate PPR into a new brand named Kering.

A brand transformation

Kering

In 2013 the Paris-based retail conglomerate PPR (Pinault-Printemps-Redoute) was relaunched as Kering. The strategic rebranding occurred to highlight the company's metamorphosis from a mass distribution concern into a luxury fashion and lifestyle group. The new name, pronounced 'caring', derives from the Breton dialect word ker, meaning hearth and home. It was chosen to reflect the group's protective and nurturing role in relation to its family of brands, which include Gucci, Balenciaga, Saint Laurent, Stella McCartney, Alexander McQueen, Christopher Kane and sports brands Puma, Tretorn and Volcom. Kering allows its subsidiaries a high level of autonomy. The benefit to the brands is that they can learn from each other, share resources and adopt best operating and business practices identified within the group.

The new logo is a stylized owl hovering over the Kering name. The owl with its sharp vision stands for Kering's ability to spot potential and anticipate trends; a heart framing its face represents Kering's human values. The sans serif typography is light and airy.

The rebranding campaign was broadcasted via social media platforms. Kering saw the change of name as an opportunity to launch a series of short films, *Kering Stories*, created in collaboration with renowned fashion blogger Garance Doré.

> *"We take something immaterial – imagination – which is absolutely fundamental to the luxury business and the sports business, and turn it into something tangible."*
>
> Louise Beveridge,
> Senior Vice-President of Communications

Chief Executive Officer François-Henri Pinault unveils the new Kering emblem and logo. In China the brand goes under the name of Kering Kai Yun, meaning 'open sky', a synonym for good luck.

6

Fashion Promotion

"Half the money I spend on advertising is wasted; the trouble is I don't know which half." *John Wanamaker*

Fashion promotion is a key element of the marketing mix. The task of promotion is to communicate with customers and publicize products and services. Promotional activities such as advertising, public relations and sales promotions have become increasingly more engaging and interactive. Dominic Walsh, Managing Director at Landor in Sydney, Australia, suggests that there is a new paradigm of Social Branding driven by technology. This is reflected across a wide range of promotional campaigns that use social media to generate consumer participation. Promotion is used to build a brand's status, enhance perception of a brand, increase desire for products, raise awareness of what's on offer and inform consumers about benefits or services. The ultimate aim of promotion is, of course, to support sales and persuade consumers to purchase.

The promotional mix

The promotional mix refers to the combination of promotional tools used by a company to promote their brand products and services and communicate their message to consumers. The four standard elements of the mix are advertising, sales promotion, public relations or PR, and personal selling. Similar to the concept of the marketing mix, the promotional mix simplifies a vast array of potential promotional possibilities into four overarching headings. This simplification masks the full range of promotional opportunities that might be employed, especially the wide variety of interactive social media campaigns, contests and promotions that invite consumer participation online. These campaigns often generate a global audience and can help consumers feel as if they are shaping the story behind the brand. In addition, there are specific promotional channels within the fashion industry such as the fashion press, seasonal catwalk shows, window displays and visual merchandising.

The fashion press

The press plays an important role in fashion promotion. Fashion magazines, both print and digital, and respected fashion bloggers perform a vital role in fashion promotion in terms of advertising and editorial. They report on the designer collections and premier new season styles in their fashion editorial; give details of key fashion looks; and profile hot trends for the season. Important to fashion promotion is the press obsession with celebrity. Acres of print are devoted to celebrity goings-on. Weekly celebrity gossip magazines keep readers updated with the latest celebrity news, fashion trends and must-have items available in-store and online. National newspapers also cover celebrities, the designer catwalk shows and report on seasonal and day-to-day developments within the industry.

Fashion shows

Fashion shows are an integral part of the industry and provide significant PR and publicity for designers. The major international designer catwalk shows take place twice a year during London, Paris, Milan and New York Fashion Week when design houses, designers and luxury fashion brands show their ready-to-wear collections for the forthcoming season. There are also fashion weeks in India, Sri Lanka, Indonesia, Brazil, Australia, Hong Kong, China, Germany and Spain. While these might not be as well known as those in London, Paris, Milan or New York, they are gaining global recognition and are equally important for the relevant regions' designers, press and buyers. A catwalk show is expensive to produce and only a selection of designers will be invited to join the schedule for Fashion Week, but for those who show it is an important opportunity. A fashion show is a great opportunity for promotion and many brands are now gaining press coverage for the ingenuity of their digital presentation. Shows used to be invitation-only events. Now designers can connect with their customers using live-streaming and updates from the show. Burberry were a pioneer of live-streaming, broadcasting the show on a giant screen on London's Piccadilly Circus. They then went global with outdoor screens in New York, Hong Kong and Beijing. The show, along with additional content, was disseminated via Instagram, Facebook, Twitter, Google+, YouTube, Pinterest, LinkedIn, Japan's Sumally and China's Sina Weibo, Douban and Youku.

Retailers might also choose to put on a fashion show as part of their PR campaign or press day, or they might hold a special in-store event and fashion show to reward loyal customers and social media followers. Fashion shows are often the favoured choice of those organizing charity fundraiser events, especially if high-profile retailers, designers and models lend their support, which helps publicity and potential ticket sales.

Window displays

Windows provide a fantastic canvas and major marketing opportunity for retailers. Inspirational and eye-catching windows act as a powerful magnet, drawing customers in and enticing them to visit the store or website. Displays can be used to reinforce brand identity, attract press attention or to provide information on products, prices and promotions. Zara, for example, does not advertise, preferring to use their expansive windows and stylish displays to promote the brand. Windows can be used to promote special seasonal events, the holiday season and Christmas usually being the most important. Or they can be used to tell a fashion story showcasing a hot new seasonal trend or designer collection. Many retailers use digital media in their displays. The Liberty of London 'Scan to See' window campaign entertained viewers with clues about products sold in the store. Each window featured a large QR code which linked to an online brochure revealing the story behind the product's manufacture.

Visual merchandising and signage

Once a customer is inside a store, then it is **visual merchandising** and signage that become important for communication, promotion

Below
A window display at DKNY to celebrate the 25th anniversary of the brand.

Bottom
The underwater theme and props from Chanel's Spring/Summer 2012 Paris show were used for window displays worldwide.

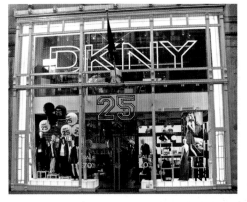

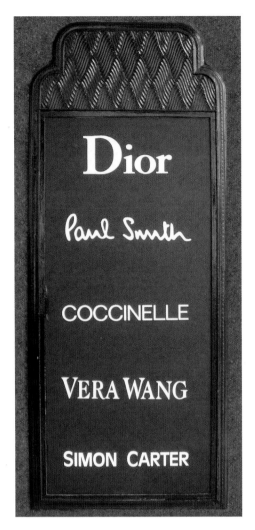

Above
Signage on the outside of a department
store is used to indicate noteworthy
brands carried inside on the fashion floors.

and visual drama. Visual merchandising (VM) is used to create internal displays, put key looks together and outfit-build. It should be used to highlight specific looks and products that store owners or buyers wish to promote, and it is important that visual merchandisers are aware of products that are scheduled to be promoted in the press so that these items are given prominence. Signage can be used within the store to guide customers and identify departments, zones or specific collections. Externally, signage can be used to indicate which brands and labels are carried. Some retailers use windows or an internal wall near the front of the store to promote what is inside.

Fashion advertising and digital campaigns

Advertising can be an expensive mode of promotion, but for big global brands with sizeable budgets, it is an important and highly visible facet of a promotional campaign and one of the primary methods used to transmit brand identity and communicate brand message.

Traditional advertising is considered a non-personal form of promotion; in other words it is a one-way communication from a brand to its audience. However digital and social media have made advertising and promotion campaigns more interactive and participatory. The principal objectives of advertising are to raise awareness, inform, persuade and encourage consumer engagement with the brand. The ultimate aim is, of course, to generate sales, but under the surface advertising endeavours to:

> » Reinforce a brand's image
> » Communicate a brand's position in the market
> » Embed specific meanings into the consumer psyche
> » Tap into consumer aspirations
> » Create desire for the brand and its products
> » Generate conversation and consumer engagement

Most adverts developed to promote fashion aim to generate desire and tap into consumer aspirations. In general, they do this by reinforcing the idea that you will be desirable, sexy, beautiful and alluring or young, cool, hip or cutting edge if you buy into a brand and purchase its clothing, accessory, fragrance, jewellery or make-up products. For men the most common messages relate to being successful, attractive, powerful, sexy, rugged, cool and so on. The dominant media for fashion advertising is the press, particularly within magazines, so the key to communicating these attributes lies in developing powerful and impactful visual imagery that can be decoded by consumers.

Fashion magazines

Magazines such as *Vogue* and *Harper's Bazaar* make their profits by selling page space to advertisers. The amount a magazine can charge for advertising is determined by the size of its circulation, made up from subscription sales and retail sales. The September issue of any fashion magazine is usually the largest of the year, with many more ad pages, because it features the launch of the autumn or fall collections and marks the start of the Christmas shopping season.

The premium spot for print advertising is the back cover, also known as the **fourth cover**. This is because many people carry a magazine rolled up with the back cover on show, and when a magazine is placed on a table there is a 50 per cent chance that the back cover is uppermost. The next most prominent position is inside the front cover. For digital, it is important to have a banner advert at the top of the screen or to be *above the fold*. This means that the advert is viewable without the user having to scroll down. The challenge for digital developers is the need for content to fit the screens on a range of devices of different sizes. The goal is to produce *device-neutral* solutions so that digital content works well on every device.

Content marketing

Content marketing is the creation and sharing of digital content with the aim of promoting and selling a brand, product or service. The traditional channel for promoting new season designs was advertising and editorial in a major magazine. Now, with an ever-increasing array of digital promotion options, fashion brands and retailers seek to provide consumers with a seamless digital media and shopping experience that means they can click and buy direct from videos, Pinterest or Instagram. This is called **shoppable content**. Social shopping site Lyst.com has a tie-up with Pinterest. Consumers who 'pin' products straight from the catwalk will be notified when any of those products are available to purchase. In-store, the top pinned items are displayed with the red Pinterest logo, merging the online and in-store experience.

Video content is one of fashion's most successful modes of digital promotion. Gucci, Juicy Couture, Barneys, Neiman Marcus and ASOS were all early adopters of the shoppable video. For its global Christmas 2012 campaign, *Best Night Ever*, ASOS released three interactive shoppable videos – a fashion video with US model

"The company is now just as much a content generator as it is a design house."

Christopher Bailey

Charlotte Free and two music videos featuring singers Azealia Banks and Ellie Goulding. The combination of video, music, celebrity and instant shoppability drove an extra £5 million in sales for ASOS.

As you may now be aware, marketers love to create marketing models such as the 7P Marketing Mix. Now there are the 4Cs of Content. The four Cs are a good complement to the AIDA model used in advertising (*see* page 128), and present a logical flow from the creation of content through to consumer conversion or action. There are several variations. Mine is shown in the diagram below.

When creating digital content for marketing campaigns it is important to consider its exact purpose and context. There is no point if the topic does not interest followers. Social media representation must be in keeping with a brand's business strategy, brand and values. Digital content is great for telling a powerful story, offering a peek behind the scenes and keeping followers updated. The aim is to increase desire for the brand and its products. If consumers and followers take action, sign up for an email newsletter, join a voucher scheme, 'Like' a product on Facebook, re-pin an image on Pinterest or retweet, then the message will spread and this should raise the likelihood of consumers converting (clicking through to purchase).

Celebrity endorsement

Employing a celebrity to become the 'face' of a brand or campaign is a technique used by an increasing number of the world's most prestigious or high-profile fashion brands. Over the years a vast array

RELATIONSHIP BETWEEN 4CS OF CONTENT AND AIDA

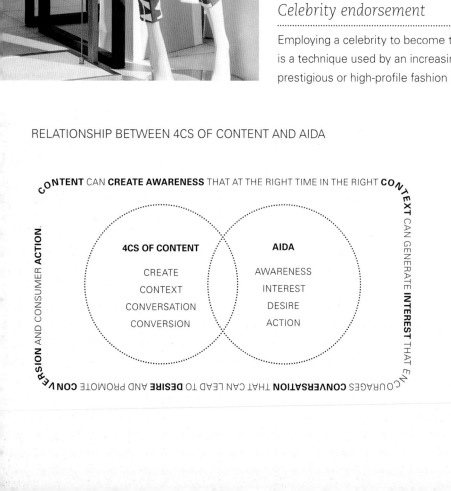

CONTENT CAN CREATE AWARENESS THAT AT THE RIGHT TIME IN THE RIGHT CONTEXT CAN GENERATE INTEREST THAT ENCOURAGES CONVERSATION THAT CAN LEAD TO DESIRE AND PROMOTE CONVERSION AND CONSUMER ACTION.

4CS OF CONTENT

CREATE
CONTEXT
CONVERSATION
CONVERSION

AIDA

AWARENESS
INTEREST
DESIRE
ACTION

The interrelationship between AIDA and a more recent marketing model known as the 4Cs of Content illustrates the purpose of advertising. In many ways the processes of marketing have not changed radically; it is the methods of communication that have altered dramatically.

of famous personalities from the worlds of film and music have signed deals to promote branded fashion, accessories, cosmetics and perfume. Beyoncé was the face of H&M; Scarlett Johansson advertised Dolce & Gabbana make-up and Desire fragrance; Rihanna featured in an Armani Jeans campaign; and Lara Stone did the same for Calvin Klein Jeans. Male celebrity endorsements include Garrett Hedlund as the face of Yves Saint Laurent's La Nuit De L'Homme, Romeo Beckham for Burberry and Justin Bieber becoming global style icon for adidas.

The aim of **celebrity endorsement** is that the cachet and sparkle of the celebrity personality will become directly associated with the brand and that this will reinforce the brand's image and position in the marketplace. The right choice of celebrity is crucial. The Davie-Brown Index (DBI) developed by the talent division of Davie Brown Entertainment (DBE) helps advertising agencies and brands assess the suitability of a celebrity. The index has eight criteria for which the celebrity is scored and the final result is analysed using a sophisticated database. Access to this system of evaluation costs a considerable sum but if viewed as a percentage of the payment the celebrity receives, the actual cost could be considered relatively small. The eight criteria are: appeal, notice, influence, trust, endorsement, trendsetting, aspiration, awareness. They are worth considering even without the addition of complicated number crunching or analysis, as they help illuminate the essential factors that establish a celebrity's suitability to become a brand ambassador.

Opposite
Marking a significant milestone in a brand's history can provide excellent marketing opportunities. British department store John Lewis celebrated its 150th anniversary with special merchandise and product displays.

Below
Milla Jovovich presents the Tommy Hilfiger limited-edition bag in a window advertisement at the Coin store in Milan, Italy. The advert combines both image and text to deliver its message.

When designing an advert or campaign, determine what will make it distinctive and how it will attract consumer attention. The message must be decided upon and an understanding of how it will be relevant and meaningful to consumers will be needed. Will the advert provide a talking point, have a story to tell, communicate ideas directly or work more obliquely through a visual subtext? Should a celebrity be linked with the campaign and will budgets allow for this? Also consider the skills that might be required and personnel needed; will there be a need for a stylist, photographer, art director or film director, or will a fashion illustrator have to be commissioned?

d Edition Bag

Tommy Hilfiger & Milla Jovovich

for Breast Health International

TOMMY ▬ HILFIGER

DIGITAL PROMOTION

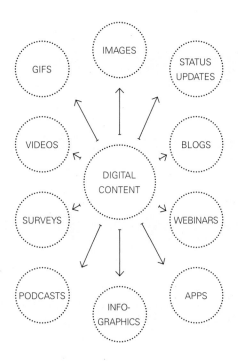

Appeal and notice relate to the celebrity's popularity, appeal and ubiquity within their specialist field and the media. Influence, trust and endorsement act as a measure of how strong the celebrity might be as a spokesperson or icon of the brand. Trendsetting and aspiration are concerned with how consumers might aspire to have the trendsetting lifestyle of the celebrity in question. Consumer awareness of the celebrity is, of course, essential for the endorsement to be effective.

In general, campaigns using celebrities are not designed to shock or be controversial as it is important for both parties to keep their reputations intact. There are instances, however, of fashion advertising that pushes boundaries or subverts normal messages. Kate Moss caused a sensation when she starred in a series of risqué and erotic promotional films, *The Four Dreams of Miss X*, for lingerie brand Agent Provocateur, and Italian fashion house Dolce & Gabbana came under fire back in 2007 for its use of controversial and sexually explicit imagery in a print campaign published in the Spanish press. The advert, showing a man pinning a woman to the ground by her wrist, was withdrawn after complaints that it was sexist and promoted gender-related violence. However, as you will see in the example opposite, it is possible to build a strong brand image through the use of provocative and unconventional advertising.

Components of an advertising campaign

Advertising is comprised of several components. There is the **advertising message** being communicated, the medium or **channel** used to display the advert and the timing and **exposure** of the advert or campaign. The following section explains each of these elements with particular focus on the message and the medium, which are of key importance to any campaign.

The message

It should already be apparent that the message is a crucial element of any advertising campaign. It is therefore vital that the purpose of the advert and its overt and subliminal messages are considered carefully. Who is the advert aiming to attract and what is it trying to communicate? What type of message will be relevant to the audience but also be coherent with the purpose of the campaign and the values of the brand? Seth Godin, author of *Purple Cow*, mentioned in Chapter 1, believes that marketing ideas must be 'remarkable' in order to stand out and get a foothold in consumer consciousness. Malcolm Gladwell in his book *The Tipping Point* takes this further, stating that the message itself or the product it is

Fashion brands must utilize a diverse range of digital formats in order to disseminate brand information and media content and engage effectively with target audiences. Use the QR code below and go to 'Associated material' to access further information.

promoting must be 'memorable'. Gladwell introduces what he calls the 'stickiness factor'; for an idea or marketing message to spread it must 'stick'. Something about the message, its content or how it is delivered must remain active in the recipient's mind – it must be remarkable, memorable and worth talking about. The mantra is 'ideas that spread win'.

A unique approach to fashion advertising

The United Colors of Benetton

Since its inception the United Colors of Benetton advertising initiative has used the Benetton brand name as a platform for comment on many significant global issues such as racism, war or world hunger. During its early years Benetton stocked an extensive range of sweaters in a dizzying array of colours – the original advertising slogan was 'All the colors of the world'. This was later altered to become the now legendary 'United Colors of Benetton'. The company believed the United Colors concept to be so strong and its metaphor for diversity to have such potential that the slogan became an official trademark.

Top
The Africa Works global communication campaign run by the United Colors of Benetton. The adverts were designed to promote the Birima microcredit programme in Senegal. The photograph by James Mollison features Senegalese workers who have used micro loans to start small businesses. Additional graphics include the United Colors of Benetton and Birima logos and the Africa Works campaign slogan developed by Fabrica, the Benetton Group's communication research centre.

Above
The Victims advert shows a Tibetan monk and Chinese soldier bowing in peace.

Benetton advertising campaigns capitalize on the power of the photographic image to convey strong emotional messages and raise awareness of universal issues.

When deciding upon the message the following points should be considered:

» What is the purpose of the advert? Is it to raise awareness, inform, reinforce brand values or provoke action?

» What if the most important message the advert needs to convey?

» Will the message be communicated directly or indirectly?

» What media would be best for communicating the message?

Consider if the message should be direct and to the point – 20 per cent off all products in a coming sale, for example – or will it be more subtle, provocative and challenging? Another issue to consider is how the message will be conveyed visually – will it be via video, photographic image, fashion illustration, product illustration or other graphic image? Will the advert need additional written information in order to get the message across? Should there be a slogan,

Advertising features and benefits

Blackspot shoes

Based in Vancouver, Canada, *Adbusters* is a not-for-profit magazine with a circulation of around 60,000. The activist magazine offers its readers philosophical articles and commentary that address social, cultural and economic global issues. The aim is to promote change in the way business is conducted and create a stronger balance between economy and ecology. To that end *Adbusters* decided to do something concrete that could challenge the status quo – so they became the first magazine to manufacture and sell a shoe.

The classic V1 Blackspot sneaker and the V2 Unswoosher boot are marketed as 'The most earth-friendly shoes in the world'. The soles are made from recycled car tyres and both styles have organic hemp uppers. The shoes are ethical, anti-sweatshop, anti-logo and pro-environment as well as what Adbusters call 'pro-grass roots capitalism'. Every pair of Blackspots comes with a Blackspot Shareholder Document. The certificate, included in the box with the shoes, has a unique login number that allows the purchaser to log into the members' zone on the Adbusters/Blackspot website and participate in shareholder online forums. Anyone buying a pair of the shoes automatically becomes a member of the Blackspot 'Anti-corporation' and receives the right to vote on a selection of company issues.

The Blackspot sneaker is a deliberate subversion of the Converse Chuck Taylor All-Star. The advertisement draws attention to the specific features and benefits of this ethical, anti-logo sneaker.

strapline or written text to accompany the image? Could the message be communicated without any image at all, or perhaps all that is needed is some written text?

The advertising medium or channel

Once the message and purpose of the advert is established, the next issue to consider is the medium. The medium, or channel, is the vehicle by which an advert is presented and reaches the public. Traditional mass media advertising channels are print, cinema, television, outdoor advertising and radio. Then there is digital media; websites, video, blogs and social media. Most fashion brands will use a combination of channels. For example, Michael Kors runs print ads and billboard advertising as well as destinationkors.com featuring campaign videos, Kors TV and Michael's Notes where the designer posts comments and photographs. In addition the brand has accounts on all major social media and was the first to launch an advert on Instagram at the end of 2013. The network announced that it would roll out further adverts from brands such as Burberry, Levi's and Macy's.

Cinema and television These mainstream channels are expensive so are generally only used by global brands. They can be effective for building brand consciousness and television can be used to reach national and local audiences. Film advertising allows brands to tell a story. Scarlett Johansson starred in a cinema campaign for Dolce & Gabbana perfume, while Natalie Portman advertised Miss Dior perfume on television.

Radio This is a less favoured choice for fashion, which is more suited to visual media. However, adverts on local radio stations are a cost-effective way to advertise sales or promotions, store openings, local fashion events or celebrity appearances.

Below
Orla Kiely advertises on buses in London and in Hong Kong. Here a London bus is decorated with the distinctive trademark Orla Kiely 'Stem' pattern.

Bottom
David and Victoria Beckham advertise Emporio Armani underwear. The traffic-stopping advert displayed on a massive billboard in the centre of Milan caused a sensation.

"I have found that after Google, Facebook actually ranks second as being the avenue that brings the most traffic to my website. It is a powerful tool. Also it allows me to communicate on a personal level with my customers and keep them updated for free with what's been happening in the shop."

Hannah Jennings

Outside media Outside media or ambient advertising refers to billboards, large-scale building wraps, posters and adverts on the side of buses or taxis. Armani is famous for its 310-sq-m (3,337-sq-ft) billboard located at the junction of Via Cusani and Via Broletto in Milan. Italian brand Ermenegildo Zegna 'wrapped' the One Peking building in Hong Kong, targeting affluent consumers in this Asian market.

Online media Online adverts can raise audience engagement and viral propagation of the advert or brand message. Advertising campaigns designed to run on a variety of digital platforms are often referred to as pay-per-click. Fashion companies and brands place pay-per-click adverts on fashion blogs or Facebook pages. When someone clicks on the advert they will be taken to the brand website and the blogger or Facebook page owner will receive a small payment.

Big data

Social networking, digital interactions and e-commerce means a vast increase in digital data. Known as **big data**, this information can reveal societal trends that can help analysts predict future trends with more accuracy. Big data offers significant potential for the fashion industry, where success hinges on picking the right fabrics, colours, patterns and silhouettes ahead of each season. There is now a trend for fashion businesses, particularly retailers such as ASOS, Gap or Target, to analyse real-time data and therefore understand consumer behaviour in far more depth than ever before. Big data can help companies to do the following:

» Identify demand more accurately

» Gauge consumer response to products

» Create better consumer experience

Timing and exposure

The next issue to consider is the timing of an advert – how long it will be published, placed on television or viewable online. A company needs to balance the spread of media used with the time-frame and costs of exposure. A fashion brand might choose to advertise twice a year with campaigns timed to coincide with the launch of the Spring and Autumn seasons. A concentrated campaign using an intense burst of advertising might be suitable to announce the launch of a new brand or product. Adverts can also be used at strategic times to promote mid-season or end-of-season sales.

A permanent advertising presence is expensive, so continuous campaigns are most likely to be used by the large global brands with sizeable advertising budgets. Each advert can be considered in terms of its **advertising reach** or coverage – the number of people within the target market exposed to the advert over a specific length of time – and frequency, or the number of times someone is likely to view the advert during the time-frame. For television advertising it is believed that a viewer needs to see an advert between five and seven times for its message to take hold. Another issue to consider is which media will have the most impact on the target audience. The key factors when deciding upon the most suitable media are:

» **The target audience:** which media are most suitable to attract desired consumers?

» **The reach:** how many people are likely to be exposed to the advert?

» **The frequency:** how often or how many times is the target consumer likely to be exposed to the advert?

» **The impact:** which media or combination of media will provide most impact?

» **The cost:** what are the cost implications of each medium, how will the advertising budget be best employed?

Below
A hoarding outside the BCBGMaxazria store in Vancouver, Canada, is used to advertise the fashion brand during store renovations.

Planning advertising and promotional campaigns

As with all aspects of marketing, thorough research, planning and clarity of purpose are essential when developing an advert or larger campaign. The first step in the planning process is to set objectives for the advertising campaign. Is the purpose to inform about something specific such as a sale, special promotion or product launch? Or is it to maintain brand awareness and keep the brand in consumers' consciousness? Or perhaps it is to persuade a new target audience to adopt the brand. When the objective is clear it should then be possible to take the next steps and determine suitable media, consider the exact message of the advert and decide upon its style and content. It will also be necessary to calculate a budget and decide if the campaign can be carried out in-house or if an agency will need to be appointed. A simple advert might be handled in-house on a limited budget. A more complicated advert, integrated digital promotion or global campaign will usually require the expertise of an advertising or digital communications agency. In summary the steps of the planning process are:

» Set advertising objectives
» Determine suitable media platforms
» Decide who will devise the campaign
» Set budget and time-frame
» Confirm content, style and advertising message

Below

A Levi's store in Bangalore, India. The US jeans brand is offering Indian shoppers the opportunity to purchase a $30 pair of jeans by paying in three instalments. This age-old sales promotion technique is more commonly used to sell white goods like washing machines, but Levi's has embraced the concept to tempt Indian customers with limited budgets.

Empowering the whole fashion community

ModCloth

Co-founders of ModCloth, Susan Gregg Koger and Eric Koger, transformed a hobby into a business. ModCloth started as an outlet for Susan's love of fashion and vintage. Its aim is to reinvent the way that a fashion brand and its customers relate to one another. With more than 1.6 million orders shipping in 2013, their growth has been pretty spectacular; ModCloth now has over 500 employees and is one of the fastest-growing online retailers in the US.

Nurturing the relationship with customers

ModCloth uses two simple yet highly effective ways of nurturing the relationship with their community. First, the diversity of platforms that ModCloth uses reflects the differing ways in which customers want to connect with the brand and one another. Then, and crucially, the brand uses a single voice, in a personal style, in all its consumer interactions. This is "the fashion company that you're friends with," in the words of Susan and Eric, not a corporate entity. So the blog, for example, covers a wide range of subjects from art and design to travel and beauty.

Collaboration and curation

ModCloth were early and enthusiastic adopters of social media. Their following is massive with over 2.3 million on Pinterest, for example. ModCloth is set up for use on all mobile devices, with mobile traffic reaching 50 per cent in 2013, proving that investment in relationship building translates into customer loyalty, word of mouth and sales.

ModCloth have been market leaders in the concept of curation. They invite their community to be collaborators and contributors, engaging their customers significantly more than a typical online retailer. Campaigns include Make the Cut, where community members submitted their own designs; Name It and Win It, a product-naming competition; Something ModCloth, Something You, a wedding-themed competition on Pinterest; and Be the Buyer, to help select online products. Marketers at ModCloth use insights from these customer interactions, as well as polls, quizzes and keyword analysis, to create yet more features and content. This in turn strengthens the ModCloth community further.

The Make the Cut contest invites followers to submit designs for prints and garments. The ModCloth development team select their top 20 and the winner is voted by the ModCloth community on the Be the Buyer section of the site. The winning design will go into production and be sold online.

Top
Store windows are used to promote
seasonal sales or special promotions.

Above
An in-store display and matching floral
carpet to promote an Erdem collection.

Sales promotion

Sales promotion, also known as below the line marketing, works to increase demand and boost sales of specific products or services. The aim of a sales promotion is to make a brand and its merchandise or services more attractive to customers by offering additional inducements to purchase, such as a price reduction, giving a product away for free, offering an extra benefit or service with a purchase, or offering a prize. Promotions usually run for a limited and very specific time-frame and there may be certain conditions attached, such as a minimum spend. Sales promotions directed at the end-consumer are termed consumer sales promotions; those aimed at retailers, wholesalers or manufacturers are known as trade sales promotions. Trade sales promotions by apparel and textile wholesalers or suppliers and manufacturers are offered to encourage business customers to purchase or place forward orders.

Promotions directed towards the ultimate consumer employ what can be termed as **pull strategies**, the idea being that the offer creates demand and entices or pulls the customer in, encouraging them to visit the store or website and ultimately make a purchase. **Push strategies** are geared towards trade distributors and retailers and are designed to encourage them to promote or push a brand or particular product and sell it on to the end-consumer.

The key types of consumer sales promotions are discussed below with indications as to how each might be used. The advantages of each technique and its benefit to consumers are given, as well as points to consider when planning sales promotion campaigns. Information outlining the essentials of trade sales promotions is given at the end.

Consumer sales promotions

The purpose of sales promotions directed at the end-consumer is to generate an increase in the volume of sales in the short term, with a positive effect on overall business in the long term. Promotions generally appeal to several basic consumer instincts – to save money, get something for free, buy something unique hopefully for a reduced price, or win a prize. For retailers, the motivation for sales promotions is to increase the number of consumers visiting the store or website and increase the conversion rate; that is, the number of visitors converted into purchasers. The advantage of sales promotion campaigns is that they achieve results quickly and usually cost less than high-profile advertising.

Fashion brands and retailers use a variety of promotional activities, the most common being:

» Price reductions
» Special offers
» Gift with purchase
» Coupons and vouchers
» Competitions and prize draws

Price reductions

Price reductions are most commonly used to shift slow-selling stock. The aim is to boost sales volumes as quickly as possible by reducing the price of selected merchandise. This helps to sell stock through, brings cash into the business and frees up retail space for new product. A price reduction should help to increase volume sales but it will also reduce the margin and affect profit. Price reductions employed during seasonal sales will normally be planned as part of the buying and merchandising strategy. Reductions will usually be in the region of 10–30 per cent; however, in a harsh trading climate retailers may be forced to offer reductions of 50–70 per cent.

Special offers

The main objective of special offers is to increase sales but they can also be employed as a technique to create desire for a brand or product or as a way to develop or reward customer loyalty. Special offers can be designed in a variety of formats; the exact nature will be dependent on the situation that needs to be addressed and the market level of the retailer. Offers such as 'two for the price of one' (known as a 2-4) or 'buy one get one free' (BOGOF) are typically used by high-street or volume retailers as a way to move old-season stock or lower-priced merchandise that is underperforming. An example would be, 'Buy a camisole and get one free'. This type of promotion could be used to shift camisoles in old-season colours so that fresh stock can be brought into the store. Another option is for retailers to offer customers a discount on a specific item when they make a purchase. A men's retailer might, for example, offer certain slow-selling tie designs at half price when a customer purchases a shirt. The advantage of a promotion such as this is twofold; it should help to improve sales of both the ties and the full-price shirts. Sales can be maximized if the offer is accompanied by clear signage and an eye-catching display. This will alert customers, inform which items are being promoted and detail prices and time-frames. Promoted merchandise can be featured on mannequins, presented on a selling table or highlighted through use of in-store posters, banners, display boards or marketing materials. **Point-of-sale**

Above
The British handbag and accessory brand Radley produce regular limited editions. Each season they design and produce a unique bag featuring an illustrated scene incorporating their signature little black dog. These bags have become collectors' items; many customers return season after season to purchase the latest version of the series.

displays placed by till points can be used to encourage customers to purchase a special offer before they leave the store.

Special offers can also be used to promote a specific brand. A department store or boutique might run a campaign to introduce a new brand or create an offer to push a brand that is not performing as well as expected. An option in this instance would be to run a co-operative promotion where the retailer and the fashion brand develop a campaign together and share the costs. Special offers may be used to encourage customers to shop in-store rather than online, or alternatively to tempt customers to purchase online, sign up to a loyalty scheme or to reward loyal customers who spend over a specified amount.

Limited editions

One way that a designer, brand or retailer can increase their kudos and create desire for their merchandise is to offer customers the opportunity to purchase limited-edition product. For many consumers it can be an attractive proposition to know that only a restricted number of people will have the same item. There are several ways to approach the concept of limited editions. One way is to develop a special one-off item available in limited quantity for a limited time-frame. Another option is to create a limited-edition collection rather than just one item. Christopher Kane designed an exclusive nine-piece cruise collection for Net-a-Porter in 2013, and Gap offered a limited-edition menswear collection by four emerging designers voted Best New Menswear Designers in America 2014 by *GQ* Magazine. Yet another approach is to produce a special edition as a series that comes onto the market at regular intervals.

High-profile designer and high-street retail collaborations

Collaborations between high-profile designers and high-street retailers is a promotional trend that has grown rapidly in recent years, although it is not a completely new phenomenon; the UK department store Debenhams pioneered the idea in the 1990s with its Designers at Debenhams collections. The collaboration concept really took off in November 2004 when the Swedish fast-fashion giant H&M teamed up with Karl Lagerfeld to produce the Lagerfeld for H&M collection, consisting of womenswear, menswear, a fragrance and accessories. The collection was limited to 20 out of the 32 global markets in which H&M operated. Since then H&M has worked with many designers including Stella McCartney, Viktor & Rolf, Roberto Cavalli, Finnish brand Marimekko, Comme des

Below
Rihanna promotes black and beige ankle boots sold as part of her Rihanna for River Island collection.

A celebratory special offer

Diesel Dirty Thirty

Fashion companies develop limited editions as a way to differentiate them from competitors and to offer exclusive product to their customers. To celebrate their thirtieth birthday, the Italian jeans company Diesel developed an exclusive special offer to thank fans for their loyalty to the brand. The Diesel Dirty Thirty campaign offered customers the chance to purchase a pair of limited-edition jeans in either the Heeven style for men or Matic for women. Only 30,000 pairs were made available in 160 stores worldwide. Priced at £30 (€30 or $50) the premium jeans were affordable and highly desirable. Designed with several distinctive features, each pair came with a commemorative xXx back patch (the Xs representing 30 in Roman numerals), a hand-made repair patch and an embroidered 'Dirty Thirty 1978–2008' stitched on the side seam. They were also finished with a special 'dirty' wash treatment. The Diesel promotion also had a limited and very specific time-frame – one day only from 10 a.m. As an added incentive, the first ten customers purchasing the jeans at each store were invited to attend one of the Diesel xXx global parties that took place simultaneously in 17 locations around the world. The Dirty Thirty promotion illustrates several important elements that go towards creating a successful special offer:

> » A desirable product with unique features
>
> » Limited availability
>
> » A limited and specified time-frame
>
> » A promotional price reduction

When developing a special offer, it is important to ensure that the offer is in keeping with the ethos and market level of a brand or retailer. Great special offers such as the Diesel Dirty Thirty promotion should raise the profile of the brand and achieve a sales boost in the short term but must not undermine or cheapen the image of a brand and drive customers away in the long term.

Above

The limited-edition jeans included unique design features such as a leather back patch with the distinctive Diesel xXx sign, a hand-made repair patch and embroidery celebrating Diesel's thirtieth anniversary.

Right

Daisy Lowe models the women's Matic style Dirty Thirty jeans.

The O'Neill brand was born on the beaches of California and is an international label recognized for selling youthful surf and sport lifestyle clothing. The company's mission is to inject a new sense of creativity into the youth lifestyle market; to that end O'Neill have set up a collaborative initiative known as The Collective. O'Neill understand the significance of graphic art within the sports apparel and youth market, so they teamed up with Dutch artist Boxie (real name Marco van Boxtel) to create an exciting limited-edition range specifically designed for the brand. They have also collaborated with British fashion designer, Luella Bartley, who has produced surf wear and winter sportswear for the brand.

Below
Boxie designs for O'Neill.

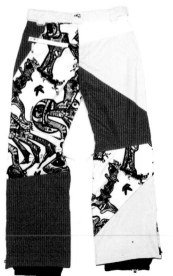

Garçons, Matthew Williamson, Maison Martin Margiela, Lanvin and Isabel Marant. Massive crowds gather prior to a launch, storming the store when the doors open, and stock sells out in hours or days. Another retailer that collaborates with designers is the US discount store Target. The brand promise is, 'Expect More. Pay Less.®' Target delivers on this promise with its 'Design for All®' offering. Alliances with fashion designers including accessory designer Anya Hindmarch, shoe brand Sigerson Morrison, and fashion brands such as Isaac Mizrahi, Phillip Lim, Peter Pilotto and Prabal Gurung have allowed Target to offer customers designer product at affordable price points.

A variation on the collaborative theme is for a retailer to team up with a celebrity; H&M have done this with pop icons Madonna and Kylie and more recently teamed with David Beckham to launch a range of Beckham-branded underwear and bodywear. UK high-street retailer Topshop has developed an ongoing relationship with the globally famous Kate Moss. Moss works closely with the Topshop in-house design team so that they can interpret her individual and eclectic fashion sensibility, translating it into the desirable and commercially successful Kate Moss for Topshop collection. It is understood implicitly that the celebrity does not design the garments themselves, they merely provide the inspirational style and lend their name to the enterprise. There is a risk to this kind of arrangement as celebrity status can be fickle – a chosen personality can go out of fashion or lose favour with the public. The key issue with celebrity collaborations is to ensure that the face fits, that the chosen celebrity enhances the profile of the brand and that target consumers connect with that person's style.

Other collaborations

The potential of collaborative initiatives continues to be harnessed by a diversity of clothing companies. Design collaborations and strategic alliances have flourished, particularly between designers or celebrities and sports brands. Each one manages to take an individual and innovative approach to the collaborative concept, utilizing its possibilities to generate new ideas and develop products designed to appeal to the targeted consumer. Puma was a pioneer of the sport-fashion collaboration, joining with model Christy Turlington as early as 2000 to produce her Nuala yoga and lifestyle collection. Puma and Turlington extended their association by developing Mahanuala, a technically focused yoga apparel, footwear and accessories collection. Adidas launched its Y-3 collection, created as a strategic alliance between the German sports brand and the Japanese fashion designer Yohji Yamamoto. A key purpose of this partnership was to establish a strong fashion element within the adidas brand, giving it a distinctive platform for differentiation; the sports brand went on to develop a further partnership with Stella McCartney to launch the fashion directional sports collection, adidas by Stella McCartney. Fashion and art are another mix for collaborative cross-fertilization, as evidenced when artist Damien Hirst designed a range of scarves with distinctive kaleidoscopic prints for Alexander McQueen. Bloggers are also getting in on the action. Super blogger Leandra Medine, the brain behind The Man Repeller, designed a capsule collection of shoes for trendy trainer brand Superga and debuted a clothing collection in collaboration with contemporary label PJK.

As can be seen from the variety of collaborations featured, it certainly appears that there is mileage in creative associations and opportunity for other fruitful alliances to blossom. The growth of this phenomenon indicates that it is a beneficial strategy for brand awareness, promotion and product diversification.

The benefits of collaborations

The general format for collaborations is for a large, well-known brand or retailer to join forces with a more exclusive design-led company, individual designer, celebrity designer, musician or blogger. For the venture to work and be profitable, each partner must gain something from the relationship. It is also important to ensure that the association does not alienate existing customers. Collaborations between high-profile designers and high-street retailers provide considerable benefits to all parties concerned. The designer or brand gets wider exposure and should be able to attract a new audience that previously might have been excluded, usually because of the high price or exclusivity of the designer label. For the retailer, the arrangement allows them to offer increased choice, keep relevant and up to date and attract new fashion-conscious customers. In short, the high-street retailer gains prestige, the designer company is exposed to a new market, and consumers are able to buy designer fashion at an affordable price in a store that they are familiar with or in which they feel comfortable. Successful collaborative partnerships manage to build upon the power and recognition associated with each contributor, merging their strengths to accomplish something unique that could not have been achieved by each partner on their own. Collaborations allow a brand or designer to:

» Attract new customers
» Gain credibility in a new market
» Enhance kudos and prestige
» Innovate and develop alternative creative approaches

Below
Luella Bartley designs for O'Neill.

Above
British luxury leather goods and stationery brand, Smythson, teamed with Erdem to create notebooks (above) lined with printed silk from Erdem's Resort 2010 collection (top).

» Generate new business opportunities
» Share resources
» Reduce the risk of going it alone
» Create a buzz and attract press coverage

Limited editions and collaborative associations have become two of the foremost sales promotional tools utilized within the fashion industry. Other options that can be contemplated are offering a gift with purchase, setting up a competition of some sort or organizing a coupon or voucher promotion.

Gift with purchase

A gift with purchase promotion is widely used by the cosmetics and perfume industry, where trial size make-up or skincare items are given away when a customer purchases a specified number of products. Women's fashion magazines also give away free gifts with an issue. Gift with purchase promotions can be a useful tool for fashion retailers but it is vital to factor in the cost of the gift item relative to how much a consumer must spend before they are entitled to receive it. Referring back to the example of the slow-selling men's ties on page 187, a retailer might consider a gift promotion of a free tie when a customer buys a high-priced item such as a suit or spends over a certain amount. Giving a gift with a purchase could also be an effective promotion to use if launching a new brand such as a new perfume. In this instance a small sample of the fragrance could be given away. Overall a gift must be desirable, in keeping with the brand or retailer's image, and the scheme must have potential to increase sales.

Coupons and vouchers

Promotions using coupons or vouchers offering a discount to customers are another option. Traditionally, schemes such as this have been operated between a magazine or newspaper and a fashion retailer. Customers usually receive a discount in the region of 10 or 20 per cent when they redeem their coupon in a participating store. This type of promotion benefits the retailer and the magazine with the potential of boosting circulation for the magazine and increasing sales for the retailer. Nowadays most coupons or voucher promotions are available online or via smartphone. There are many coupon sites providing voucher codes or discounts on designer fashion and high-street brands.

Consumers can also register to have **text codes** or mobile barcodes sent to their phone. The latest schemes allow consumers to scan

QR (quick response) **codes** or photograph barcodes on swing tickets, print ads or store windows. Barcodes or QR codes can also be sent straight to a consumer's smartphone to be scanned by a retailer when the shopper wants to make a purchase or claim a promotional discount. These types of promotions are effective in targeting a younger audience for whom the mobile phone is one of the main modes of communication. They also offer a retailer or brand the possibility of direct communication and interaction with consumers and the opportunity to gather useful data.

Competitions and prize draws

Another promotional device that retailers or fashion brands can consider is to run a competition or prize draw. Prize draws can be operated via the Internet, mobile phone or a printed entry form available in-store, in a magazine or newspaper or by direct mail. Basic competitions usually ask entrants to answer a simple question about the brand or company but competitions can be developed that are much more interesting and engaging – inviting consumers to customize or redesign garments, for example. The Nudie Jeans Empowerment Challenge invited customers to design a T-shirt print to illustrate 'Empowerment'. A donation of €10 from every T-shirt sold was donated to Amnesty International. Winners were rewarded with €1,000 and the honour of supporting Amnesty International and having their T-shirt produced.

Technology is changing radically the format possibilities for competitions. During London Fashion Week Autumn/Winter 2014, Topshop ran a 'Virtual Front Row' competition. Fans were invited to share their Fashion Week look on Twitter or Instagram, and winners got the chance to sit in the window of the London flagship store wearing virtual reality headsets to watch a 3D, 360-degree live stream of the Topshop Unique fashion show.

The key point about a competition is to ensure that the prize is enticing enough; consumers must feel that it is worthwhile entering. Also for consideration is the value and number of prizes on offer; in other words, will customers believe they have a reasonable chance to win and is the prize worth winning?

Planning consumer sales promotions

One of the main advantages of sales promotional offers is that they have the potential to achieve results quickly. They can increase consumer traffic in-store and online, boost sales and generally cost less than high-profile advertising. Campaigns can also be used to enhance consumer loyalty, often with the side benefit of collecting

Above
Smythson also worked with Giles Deacon to produce 300 boxes of couture correspondence cards, each embellished with exquisite, hand-engraved pen and ink sketches.

Above
The Nudie Jeans Empowerment
Challenge.

valuable data on consumers. Consumer sales promotions offer a company considerable scope but they will need to be planned with care; disadvantages can occur if a company over-relies on discounts or offers that could cheapen its image. Another problem, particularly in a tough trading climate, is that consumers cut back on normal spending and purchase only during a promotion. While this can be advantageous in keeping cash flowing through the business, it can devalue the overall financial position of the company. When planning a promotion, it is important to consider the following:

» Purpose of the promotion

» Target audience

» Type of scheme most appropriate

» How it will operate

» Time-frame

» Range or reach of the offer

» How to inform customers about the promotion

» Costs

» Potential tie-ins, additional events and
  co-operative partners

The first consideration should always be its purpose – what it should achieve for the company and what it should offer customers. Tied to this is the next key issue, what is the target audience for the campaign? With these two points in mind it should be possible to determine the most appropriate type of sales promotion and how it will operate. The time-frame of an offer needs to be thought through with care. It is important to fix a viable time limit, long enough to allow the promotion to have an effect but not so long that consumers delay purchasing. The cut-off date must be communicated clearly so that customers appreciate the offer is limited. Hopefully this will create desire and a sense of urgency. For a price reduction on slow-selling stock, the issue will be to calculate how much the selling price needs to be reduced in order to encourage customers to purchase while also ensuring the least damage to the overall margin and profit. For a special offer promotion on product designed or ordered in specifically for a promotion, the important issue will be judging the correct quantity, particularly if it is a limited edition like the Diesel's Dirty Thirty jeans. A fine balance must be achieved between limiting availability so that customers crave the product and ensuring that there is enough stock; running out too soon could disappoint loyal customers. Equally, over-ordering and having a large amount of unsold stock would be counterproductive. The range or reach of the offer should also be determined: will it be available in every store or retail channel or in selected channels or locations only?

Consumers will need to be alerted and informed about a promotion, so an advertising campaign may be required, or some form of public relations activity such as a teaser ad or video, announcement on the website, blog or Twitter feed. Information on a sales promotional campaign can also be disseminated within window displays or by using in-store and point-of-sale materials.

Finally there is the ever-important issue of cost and available budget. Price reduction promotions used to shift stock will be best handled with minimum extra costs, so promotional information is likely to be simple and informative point-of-sale or window signage. Planned special offers or limited editions that require a sizeable awareness campaign with possible advertising or PR support will have significant costs that will need to be budgeted. There may, however, be potential co-operative partners or tie-ins that could extend the scope of the promotion and present possibilities to share the costs.

There is one last point to mention in conclusion. There are legal regulations governing advertising and promotions. Prize draws and competitions in particular are subject to specific restrictions. Sales promotional schemes should therefore be created with care

ADVANTAGES AND DISADVANTAGES OF SALES PROMOTIONS

ADVANTAGES

» Creates desire and provides incentive to purchase

» Short-term increase in sales

» Brings customers in-store or to the website

» Supports consumer loyalty

» Improves conversion rate

» Can be used to target specific customer groups

» Lower cost compared to advertising campaigns

» Can be used to collect valuable data on consumers

DISADVANTAGES

» Only provides short-term results

» Could negatively affect brand image

» Could negatively affect full-price sales

» Might run out of promotional stock early and disappoint customers

» Must comply with government regulations

to ensure that all aspects comply with relevant law. Professional bodies such as the Institute of Sales Promotion (ISP), the Chartered Institute of Marketing (CIM) or the American Marketing Association (AMA) can assist with information on legal matters.

Trade sales promotions

So much of the focus within fashion is on retail and the end-consumer but business-to-business (B2B) trade and promotions are a highly important aspect of the industry. It is common practice for companies to offer promotions, such as discounts or extended payment terms, to business consumers as an incentive to purchase or place forward orders. Many companies offer special promotions at trade exhibitions, fairs or conferences to encourage customers onto a stand and place orders at the show. It is also usual to provide incremental price reductions for purchasing higher volumes. Free point-of-sale materials in the form of literature, display visuals or swing tickets with product information may also be offered by manufacturers as part of the deal. Negotiations might also take place to discuss the possibility of co-operative advertising between the supplier and a retailer, perhaps as a special campaign to promote a new product, fabric or garment technology. Promotional schemes can be used to develop an ongoing relationship with a customer or be tailored to match specific customer requirements. A promotional offer might help to finally close a sale with a customer who is wavering. Once again, it is important to consider the overall objectives of the company and its reasons for being at a fair or trade event and to ensure that promotions are fair and ethical.

Direct marketing

The aim of **direct marketing** is to establish a direct link between the business and the end-consumer. It might not be considered as high profile as advertising but it can be cost-effective and more easily controlled from within the company. Direct marketing is also effective in B2B situations; companies can send out new season catalogues to existing trade customers or send email information and updates. Direct marketing covers promotional activities such as:

» Direct mail via post or email
» Mail order catalogues
» Text message alerts
» Magazine inserts

In order to carry out direct marketing, a company will need to have a customer database (although this is not necessary for magazine inserts). This is why loyalty programmes such as store cards or

Above

The Superdry trade stand at the Bread & Butter trade fair. Fashion brands that sell wholesale will need to market and promote their merchandise to the many fashion buyers who visit the fair. It is standard practice to offer discounts on larger orders if placed during the fair. This acts as an incentive to the buyer to place an order there and then, rather than leave the stand and perhaps purchase from a competitor brand. Trade discounts are usually incremental, in other words the amount of discount offered increases in line with the size of order placed.

voucher clubs are so important to a business, because they collect useful data that can be used to connect with customers either by email, text message or social media. Also of importance are purchases made online, as this information will automatically be added to the database. Brochures or catalogues can be enclosed with monthly store card statements or sent out to customers who have ordered online.

Magazine inserts are beneficial in communicating with potential customers not yet on the database; although not targeted at a specific person they can be directed at the readership of particular magazines or newspapers. Uniqlo, for example, had a ten-page insert placed within a major UK newspaper's weekend colour supplement magazine. The insert was used primarily to promote the Spring menswear collection but it also informed readers that Uniqlo was due to open in Selfridges, gave a useful list of all other stores within the UK and promoted exclusive offers and 'first chance to buy' opportunities online. Direct marketing is a strategy also used in B2B situations. A business could pay to have an insert placed within an industry paper or magazine or carry out direct mailing. The London Edge trade fair, for example, sends out mailings to 30,000 international buyers.

Fashion PR and publicity

PR and publicity are another vital component of the fashion promotional mix. The overall aim of PR is to get media coverage and establish and generate a favourable image of an organization, brand or fashion label. Positive publicity and well-handled PR has a great advantage for fashion companies – not only does it have potential to enrich the image, kudos or reputation of the company or brand but it can be lower in cost compared to advertising. Advertising and PR do often achieve similar end results; however, companies have to pay substantial sums to place an advert in a major magazine or in the cinema or on TV. The costs incurred with PR on the other hand are generally much lower and relate either to the operational costs of running an internal PR department or paying a PR agency – they normally charge a monthly retainer and/or a fee for their work. PR helps to ensure that international, national and local press as well as influential bloggers feature garments and accessories and carry newsworthy stories attributed to a brand or fashion designer.

Dependent on the requirement and the size of a company, it can be possible to handle publicity and PR in-house. Smaller companies with lower budgets may find they can manage most of the day-to-day aspects of publicity themselves via their website and social media. They may consider appointing a freelance PR person to help them get coverage in the national press or to handle special projects or events. Larger companies may employ a specialist PR agency or they may be able to afford to run their own dedicated PR or press department. Other companies may generally use outside PR agencies and employ a communications manager to oversee projects and liaise with the agency.

A brand behind the scenes

DKNY PR GIRL®

Aliza Licht, aka DKNY PR GIRL®, is Senior Vice-President of Global Communications at Donna Karan International. Her job is to produce the runway shows, dress celebrities and get press on the brand's clothing and accessories. In 2009 she came up with the idea of a Twitter account looking at the world of DKNY through the lens of PR.

Licht explains in a TED talk that in the early days the DKNY PR GIRL® was a creation – a twenty-something fashion girl who lived downtown and loved yoga – merged with Licht's real account of her PR role and life at Donna Karan. Later, realizing that authenticity is key, she exposed herself as the real DKNY PR GIRL®. Since then Licht and the Twitter handle @dkny have become part of the Donna Karan brand DNA. According to Executive Vice-President of Global Communications, Patti Cohen, "Everyone loves behind the scenes, it's the perfect insider's view… Our customers and followers love engaging with her." Licht shares real-time dramas and is open about the frustrations she and her team face. Licht offers her 480,000-plus followers something more than the commercial agenda. However, social media does have an effect on sales. As Licht reports, "Someone tweeted to ask if we sell the DKNY Cozy at the Atlanta International airport and I responded. Within just four tweets, she was posting a picture of her new DKNY Cozy".

Above
The DKNY PR GIRL® illustration by Dallas Shaw shows a twenty-something PR who gives the behind-the-scenes scoop from inside Donna Karan New York.

Right
Aliza Licht – the real DKNY PR GIRL®.

Basic PR techniques

The following section looks at a selection of basic techniques employed by fashion PR: product placement, celebrity seeding, events and product launches, fashion shows and press days.

Product placement

A company can raise awareness of its brand and products by having them feature in a film, television show, music video or digital game. Known as **product placement**, this form of promotion can generate considerable desire for a particular product. One of the most notable examples of fashion product placement was in the *Sex and the City* (SATC) television show and films. The first movie, which came out in May 2008, featured clothing by Vivienne Westwood, Prada, Jimmy Choo, Louis Vuitton, Christian Lacroix and Chanel to name but a few. Shoe designers Manolo Blahnik and Jimmy Choo became household names after their product first featured in the show. The association between the Blahnik and SATC brands became so integral to the concept that a link to the Blahnik website was included on the SATC movie website.

Product placement can have a dramatic effect on sales, as was evidenced when the movie *The Queen* was released in the United States in 2006. Immediately after the film opened in New York, visitor numbers at the Barbour by Peter Elliot store on Madison Avenue increased dramatically, as did demand for two classic Barbour jackets, the 'Beaufort' and 'Liddesdale', worn by the actress Helen Mirren when she portrayed the Queen in the film.

Product placement provides an important revenue stream for film financing, though companies do not always have to pay to have their products showcased. Karl Lagerfeld provided two custom-made white bouclé wool Chanel jackets with navy trim for Cate Blanchett to wear in the Woody Allen film *Blue Jasmine*. Costume designer Sandy Powell collaborated with Armani to create the power suit worn by Leonardo DiCaprio in Martin Scorsese's *Wolf of Wall Street*. In both cases, the outfits became talking points and were much written and blogged about.

Celebrity seeding or celebrity product placement

The cult of celebrity and its relationship to the world of fashion is becoming an increasingly important factor within fashion PR. Many agencies have had to add a dedicated celebrity division to handle 'buzz press', which refers to the new speed at which agencies

Below
This set of Louis Vuitton luggage featured in the Wes Anderson movie *The Darjeeling Limited*. The luggage was designed by Marc Jacobs with the help of Anderson's brother, Eric, who created the distinctive jungle pattern that decorated the surface of the cases. Not only did the luggage feature in the film, but it became the centrepiece of a window display at the Louis Vuitton store in New York.

Bottom
Musician Rita Ora wearing a Donna Karan Atelier silver-bugle-bead-embroidered dress for the Gabrielle's Angel Foundation Angel Ball 2013 in New York.

have to pump out stories concerning a brand's links with celebrities or what clothing or accessory brands famous personalities are wearing. One consequence of all this interest in celebrities is the PR activity known as **celebrity seeding** or celebrity product placement. As discussed earlier, celebrity product placement occurs when a celebrity signs a contract to become the face of a brand. Seeding, on the other hand, is when a designer or brand loans or donates product to a celebrity so that they will be seen wearing the brand's products. This is usually handled via a PR agency. The aim of celebrity endorsement is, of course, to choose a suitable celeb with a personality and reputation that enhances the brand's status. Usually this is someone who is regularly in the public eye, has a large social media following, posts 'selfies' wearing the brand's products or is constantly snapped by the paparazzi; the result should be massive social media and press coverage.

Press days

PR agencies and in-house press offices organize press days to showcase next season's collections to the fashion press. Magazines work on long lead-times so press days are held well in advance of the season so that editors can request samples from designers and start developing ideas for fashion shoots and editorial. Press days can be held to promote trade fairs or a group of designers; the British Fashion Council, for example, held a press event to promote estethica, their trade initiative for sustainable fashion, showcasing 23 ethical labels.

Special events

Special events are designed to suit a variety of situations that might include:

> » Product launches
> » Charity events
> » Sponsorship events
> » Fashion seminars and style clinics
> » Fashion shows
> » Private shopping evenings
> » Designer guest appearances

Special events can be aimed either at the press, industry professionals and business customers or at the end-consumer. They will either be organized by a PR agency or an in-house events office or press office. With product launches, the product need not necessarily be apparel or accessories but could be a trade initiative. For example, an evening drinks event was held in a prestigious hotel

A prestigious charity shopping event

Light Up the Holidays – Miracle on Madison Avenue

Hearst Magazines' *Town & Country* dedicated its December 2013 issue to philanthropy as part of a strategy to appeal to its core demographic. The magazine focused on charitable acts and the joy of giving during the holiday season. For this campaign, 'Light Up the Holidays', *Town & Country* sponsored two charity shopping events, in Beverly Hills and New York City. Participating stores held special events and donated 20 per cent of sales made during the event to a cancer charity.

Illustrations by Chesley McLaren promote Light Up the Holidays charity shopping events on Rodeo Drive in Beverly Hills and Madison Avenue in New York.

in the centre of Colombo in Sri Lanka to promote the Apparel South Asia Conference and two trade exhibitions, the Apparel Industry Suppliers Exhibition (AISEX) and Fabric and Accessory Suppliers Exhibition (FASE). Another example is the Hermès Festival des Métiers. This travelling exhibition toured cities in China, Europe and the US, giving visitors a chance to meet and watch artisans as they crafted Hermès leather goods, jewellery and watches. Special events aimed at end-consumers can be used to draw in new customers, to offer something engaging and extra special, to reward loyal customers or to promote sales or specific designers and brands. On top of this many special events include a charitable element such as a percentage from sales made at the event going to a not-for-profit organization. Organizing a special event will require a press release, announcements via social media and, if required, invitations to be sent to guests.

Measuring campaign effectiveness

Measuring the effectiveness of an advertising or promotional campaign is important to determine the extent to which a campaign has met its objectives and ascertaining whether the financial investment has been worthwhile. It is not always easy to gauge results. There may be several criteria by which the campaign can be evaluated in terms of its ability to:

> » Stimulate an increase in sales
> » Build brand awareness
> » Change consumer image and perception
>   of a brand and product
> » Target new consumers
> » Increase customer loyalty

Sales increases may result from a combination of factors such as pricing compared to competitors, or whether the product is also available online. The campaign could trend on social media or a celebrity seen wearing the brand might boost sales. Product placement in a popular TV show or film could also create demand. Determining if an advertising campaign has increased consumer awareness requires research to test consumer awareness before and after a campaign; similarly, detailed consumer analysis will be required to determine if an ad campaign was effective in changing consumer image of the brand. Measuring a campaign will also depend on the medium used.

Print advertising Costs can be evaluated using a **cost per thousand (CPT)** calculation. This is the average cost of reaching one thousand of the target audience. The cost of a full-page colour advert in American *Vogue* varies depending on its position within the magazine but it will be upwards of US$100,000. To calculate the CPT divide the cost by the circulation number and multiply by 1,000. So if the circulation were 1.2 million, the CPT would be just over US$83 per thousand.

Television or radio Measuring the impact of a TV or radio commercial is achieved using what is known as **advertising impacts**. This refers to the total number of separate occasions when a TV or radio commercial is viewed or heard by a target audience. If an advertising campaign aired 100 times over four months and each time the advert was on air it achieved an average of one million viewers then the campaign would have received 100 million impacts with a monthly impact of 25 million.

Press articles The most traditional method to monitor the number of press articles (called press clippings) published as a result of a PR campaign is the **clip report**. Clip reports give details of which publications covered the story, the topic of the article published and the circulation of the publication. Measuring the amount of column inches printed can further refine this information. **Advertising value equivalent (AVE)** measures the benefit to a client of a PR campaign. AVE compares the cost of the column inches printed with how much the equivalent space would have cost as advertising. Another analysis is **share of voice**. This compares a company's press results with those of its main competitors and determines who got the most coverage.

A multi-media campaign A traditional metric for measuring a campaign is known as **opportunity to see (OTS)**. This represents the frequency of exposure of an advertisement. Average OTS gives a figure to indicate how many people from a target audience have had an opportunity to see, hear or read an advertisement. OTS is a rather blunt instrument of measurement, as it calculates only 'opportunities' to see, rather than the exact number of people that actually see an advertisement. Also it does not compare like with like – viewing an advert as a film or video is different to seeing it as a static print advert in a magazine. Gross OTS is a cumulative figure for a campaign, derived from adding results from different adverts within a campaign and from the various media such as TV, cinema, magazines, Internet and outdoor channels. OTS figures were originally gathered by using surveys, face-to-face interviews and through self-reporting, such as diaries kept by members of the target audience. Now sophisticated digital tools are used by tracking companies such as the global firm Nielsen.

Measurement of digital campaigns is similar to traditional media, but the number of people seeing an advert or content is known as

impressions and the number of people as the **reach**. There are three key areas of a campaign to evaluate: social media exposure, influence, and engagement, and there is an ever-increasing range of online tools that can be used to report on web analytics, measure the reach of social media and quantify social 'buzz'.

Above
Fabric buyers meet face to face with sales representatives from a textile company at Première Vision.

Personal selling

Finally we come to the last element of the Promotional Mix, known as personal selling. This refers to promotional or sales activities that take place face to face. There are two key interfaces for personal selling within the fashion industry. The first, most obviously, is in-store, where sales personnel interact directly with customers. The customer experience in-store can be a make-or-break factor in terms of whether customers purchase or not, so this element of personal selling is vital for the industry. This topic was discussed in Chapter 2 in terms of 'process' within the marketing mix (*see* pages 50–51). This concept views the entire process of purchasing from the consumer's point of view, of which personal selling will be a part. Many boutique owners know their customers intimately; they often purchase items directly from design houses and fashion retailers with a specific customer in mind and will call their most loyal customers to inform them that they have an item especially for them. There is report of a personal stylist ordering three Balenciaga cocktail dresses priced around £3,000 each for her various clients at a Harrods pre-season trunk show.

The other important area for personal selling is in business-to-business (B2B) situations. Much of the global fashion and textile industry operates at manufacturing and wholesale level, requiring sales representatives and agents to foster and develop profitable business relationships with appropriate buyers. Personal selling occurs at a variety of industry trade fairs for fabric, trimmings, apparel and accessories and other industry resources. Fibre manufacturers must sell their products to textile manufacturers, who in turn need to capture the imagination of, and sell fabrics to, fashion designers and retailers. Each of these businesses will utilize personal selling as a key promotional tool.

The advantage of personal selling is that it affords customers a high level of personal attention. Sales representatives can tailor their message and information to suit specific customers. Personal selling presents the opportunity to build a long-term business relationship, offer good technical advice and background information on products and services, and solve the numerous problems that occur within fashion design, manufacturing, supply and retail.

7

Careers in Fashion Marketing

"Customers pay their money for whatever it is that you, the retailer, sell to them, but there's so much more to the relationship than this exchange." *Martin Butler*

Fashion is an international industry with potential for employment across a wide range of disciplines. This final chapter outlines the key skills required to work as a professional within fashion design, fashion retail management and fashion marketing and promotion. It provides information on some of the day-to-day tasks and responsibilities involved to help you determine which options to explore further so you can decide upon a potential career direction.

Marketing is an essential function of the industry, and affects the entire supply chain, from production and wholesale of raw materials to the design, development, manufacture and promotion of fabrics, garments and accessories, right through to fashion retail and the sale of products to the end-consumer. Marketing is the common denominator linking all the processes together, so whatever role you intend to pursue within the industry, an understanding and appreciation of marketing is becoming an ever more essential skill.

FASHION AND TEXTILE SUPPLY CHAIN

This diagram shows how the fashion industry interfaces with other industries such as media, retail and the textile industry, which has links with both the chemical and agricultural industries.

Marketing operates along the entire fashion supply chain. At every stage, businesses need to develop, sell and market products and services that satisfy their business customers' requirements and meet the demands of the end-consumer.

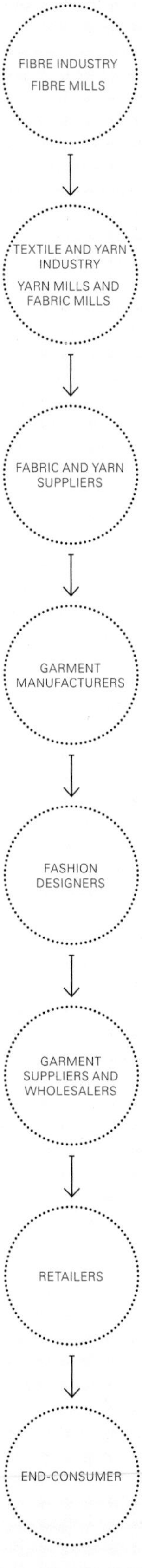

FIBRE INDUSTRY
FIBRE MILLS

↓

TEXTILE AND YARN INDUSTRY
YARN MILLS AND FABRIC MILLS

↓

FABRIC AND YARN SUPPLIERS

↓

GARMENT MANUFACTURERS

↓

FASHION DESIGNERS

↓

GARMENT SUPPLIERS AND WHOLESALERS

↓

RETAILERS

↓

END-CONSUMER

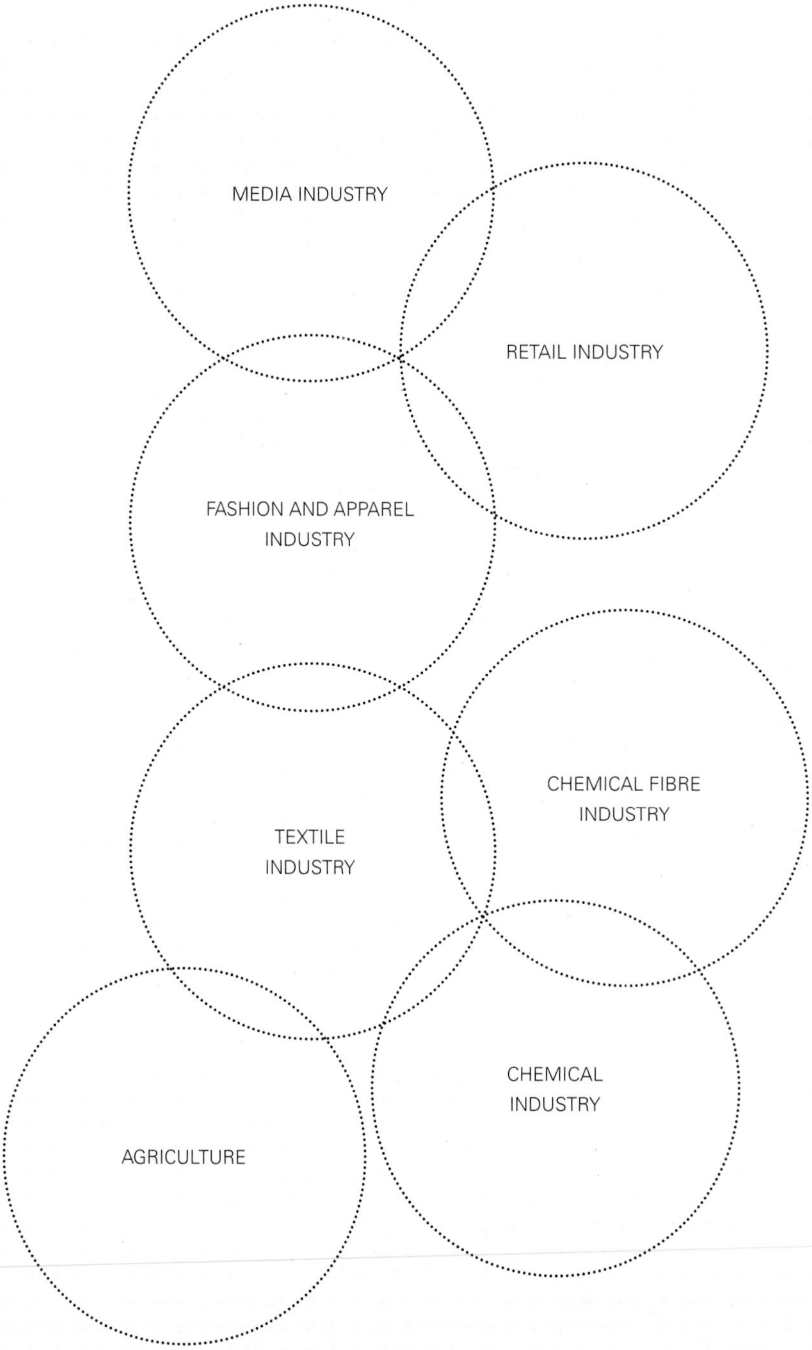

MEDIA INDUSTRY

RETAIL INDUSTRY

FASHION AND APPAREL INDUSTRY

CHEMICAL FIBRE INDUSTRY

TEXTILE INDUSTRY

CHEMICAL INDUSTRY

AGRICULTURE

Professional skills

Fashion can be glamorous and exciting, but it is important to remember that fundamentally it is a commercial business producing and selling fashion and textile products. These must satisfy customer demand and produce profit for the business concerned. To work in the industry you need to be ambitious, self-motivated, creative, energetic and passionate about fashion and have a working knowledge of marketing and business. Employment within fashion is very competitive and you will find that you are required to work at a much faster pace than you did as a student. If you are lucky enough to land a job you should be prepared to put in long hours and be willing to deal with the constant barrage of tight deadlines that most fashion professionals accept as the norm. It is also likely that you will work on more than one project or fashion season at a time, so it is vital that you are organized, accurate and pay attention to detail. Employers will expect you to understand the market, be aware of customer requirements and work within set financial parameters.

An understanding of the target market No matter what role you take on within the industry, you will be expected to understand and grasp the particulars of the specific market targeted by the company for which you are working. Although you might not be required to carry out detailed consumer research yourself, you must make sure that you are informed and aware of relevant consumer and market trends and appreciate the way in which the identity and values of the brand are reflected in the product and services on offer to customers.

Commercial awareness If you remember back to the marketing definitions in Chapter 1, you will recall that "marketing is the management process responsible for identifying, anticipating and satisfying customer requirements profitably." The bottom line is that individual products, collections, marketing schemes and promotional strategies must all be commercially viable and contribute to the profitability of the company. It is important therefore that you grasp the bigger picture and ensure that your creative ideas are also commercial and profitable.

Awareness of corporate business objectives Whether you work for yourself or for a company, you will always have a desired outcome or specific objectives to achieve and there may be key performance indicators set by the company by which you will be judged. It is vital that you always have the business objectives and company strategy in mind when you develop designs or propose schemes for marketing and promotion.

Above
Confidence in communicating ideas and presenting collections is essential for fashion. Jason Wu presents his collection to Anna Wintour, Editor-in-chief of American *Vogue*.

Communication and presentation skills Presentations and meetings are an essential part of professional life so it is important to develop competent skills in this area. The fashion industry operates on long lead-times – product can take anywhere from 1–18 months to be developed. This means that the textiles, garments or accessories under discussion might not actually exist yet, so excellent communication skills, both visual and verbal, will be required in order to explain ideas, discuss concepts and describe products accurately during meetings. Designers, product development teams and buyers developing own-label collections for high-street retailers or purchasing for department stores will be expected to present their product ranges, explain the rationale behind their designs and communicate how the collection and pricing strategy will achieve the company's overall strategic and financial objectives. It may also be necessary to present to key suppliers and manufacturers so they are aware of the types of styles, detailing and fabrications that they will be required to source, produce or supply. In a marketing role, you too are likely to have to present ideas and be able to explain how plans and strategies for campaigns will achieve set targets.

Team-work Getting on with and working alongside others is a key professional skill and whatever role you are employed in within the industry, team-work and good communication will be required. Even the most talented designer or marketer will not be able to make it totally alone. Even if it is their name on the label or they are the figurehead of a brand or business, they still rely on a team of professionals across a wide selection of disciplines, including pattern cutting, sewing, managing production, sales, promotion, social media, business and marketing.

Skills required to progress within the fashion industry

» Creative flair and commercial awareness

» Evaluating market and business trends

» Strategic thinking and awareness of corporate business objectives

» Ability to research trends and to intuit future fashion and market direction

» Team-working skills and ability to work with others

» Ability to negotiate and network

» Strong organizational skills and ability to work to tight deadlines

» Presentation skills and ability to communicate information clearly

» A proactive and flexible approach

» Ability to multitask and work on more than one project or fashion season at a time

» Problem-solving, creative process management and project planning

Career choices

This section shows how an understanding of marketing principles is integral to many key job roles within the fashion industry.

Fashion design

Jobs exist within fashion design at every level of the industry from haute couture and designer ready-to-wear through to high-street fashion or designing for a garment manufacturer. Designers will usually specialize in womenswear, menswear, accessories or childrenswear, although it is possible to work in more than one area. They also tend to stick to a particular market level such as couture, luxury, streetwear or the denim market. Designers working for a large organization may work for a specific department, such as casual wear, knitwear, outerwear, formal wear or separates. Depending on the type of market and the direction you wish to take you can be employed as a designer or as a fashion and trend forecaster.

Below
The ability to work as a team is another vital skill. Designers rely on a team of skilled technicians to help them realize their creative ideas.

» Professional knowledge of fabrics
   and materials

» Ability to illustrate and draw technical
   details accurately

» Creative flair and commercial awareness

» Good eye for proportion and colour

» Self-motivated

» Ability to research and monitor trends

Below
The team behind the streetwear
label Durkl working in their studio
in Washington, DC.

ROLES AND DEPARTMENTS
THAT INTERFACE WITH DESIGN

Fashion designer

The fashion designer's role is to design and develop individual fashion products or product ranges appropriate for a specified target market. It is important for designers to have a clear understanding of trends in the overall fashion market as well as solid background knowledge of their particular market and target consumer. This knowledge should assist the designer in determining the correct design concept, product details, fabrications and pricing for their proposed collection or product range.

Typical work activities:

» Reviewing sales results from current and previous season

» Researching trends and undertaking inspirational shopping trips

» Developing and presenting concepts for the new season

» Sourcing fabrics, materials, components, trims and embellishments

» Designing and developing product ranges

» Overseeing creation of prototypes, producing accurate product specifications for samples and production

» Managing sampling process and fittings

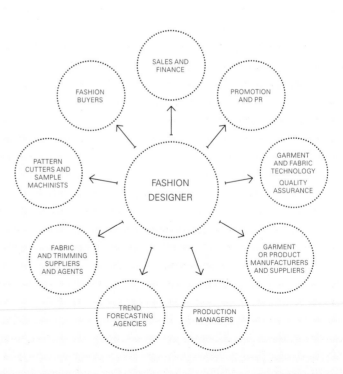

» Liaising with manufacturers and suppliers for sampling and production

» Confirming range selection with management, buyers and other relevant personnel. Presenting final range to internal staff or external buyers

» Approving final colours, bulk fabric and trimmings

» Presenting ranges to management, sales staff and buyers

Fashion and trend forecaster

Fashion and trend forecasters work approximately 18 months to two years ahead of the season in order to develop and compile trend and market reports purchased by the industry. Fashion forecasting and prediction agencies provide information on current and developing consumer trends and emerging fashion and textile trends in womenswear, menswear and childrenswear. They produce presentations and printed and/or online reports that include colour palettes, design illustrations, print and fabric designs and technical flat drawings of product so that companies who purchase their services can see how the predicted trends will translate into product designs.

Trend forecaster: key skills

» Self-motivated and ability to research

» Awareness of what is going on culturally in music, art, street fashion and film

» Creative flair and commercial awareness

» Good eye for colour

» Ability to produce fashion illustration and technical flat drawings to a high standard

» Good networking skills

» Ability to analyse trend data

ROLES AND DEPARTMENTS
THAT INTERFACE WITH FORECASTING

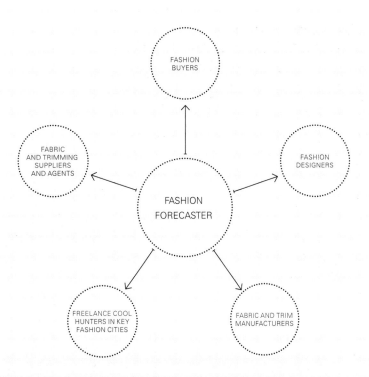

Typical work activities:

» Visiting trade fairs or working on an agency stand to sell prediction packages at fairs like Première Vision

» Travelling to research trends

» Monitoring street fashion trends

» Compiling visuals and colour palettes for key trends and fashion themes

» Researching technical developments in fabrics, materials, components, trims and embellishments

Fashion retail management

Retail culture is high pressure and demanding. Stores are open six or seven days a week, virtually 365 days a year. If you want to work in this sector you will need to be committed and proactive – retailing is never fully predictable and the situation changes daily so you will need to be able to respond to each challenge that arises. The head-office or behind-the-scenes jobs outlined in this section are retail buyer, merchandiser and visual merchandiser.

Retail buyer

Buyers source, develop and select product ranges. They must understand customer needs and predict consumer demand in order to select commercially viable ranges of merchandise that appeal to the target market. Career opportunities for fashion buyers exist in two main areas, either working for retailers selling their own label ranges or for an individual boutique, small boutique chain or department store selling wholesale and designer fashion labels and brands. Retail buyers have considerable responsibility to achieve a company's financial targets and create profit, so they must have a good head for business, be aware of current trends and shifts in consumer demand, keep up to date with what competitors are up to and respond effectively to change.

Above
Visitors to Première Vision look at fabric samples. Fashion designers, buyers and trend forecasters will all travel to relevant fabric and trade fairs to monitor trends, gather information or place orders.

Typical work activities:

» Researching fashion trends and analysing consumer buying patterns

» Attending fabric and trade fairs

» Sourcing, developing and selecting product ranges

Garment fitting and approval

Designers, buyers and product technicians usually work as a team to fit garments and approve product specifications.

At American outdoor brand, Nau, the team pay meticulous attention to key details as well as to the look, fit and feel of a garment. Every aspect of the jacket being fitted, right down to buttons, closures, pockets, zips and stitching, has to be approved and specified accurately. At Nau garments are specifically cut to increase ease of movement. Sleeves are cut longer than average, to ensure wrist coverage when reaching for a hold while climbing or holding bicycle handlebars, and tops are cut lower in the rear to keep wearers warm when bending. The designers also work closely with fabric suppliers to create new, more sustainably produced technical fabrics that deliver on performance, hand-feel and drape. It is worth thinking about the promotional possibilities of showing a behind-the-scenes video online of a fitting. This could demonstrate the care and attention the company goes to during product development.

....

Retail buyer: key skills

....

» Keen eye for fashion

» Excellent commercial awareness

» Strong communication and negotiation skills

» Numerate

» Accurate

» Ability to work to tight deadlines

» Ability to monitor fashion trends

» Awareness of competitors
   within the market

» Working with a merchandiser to create range plan

» Negotiating with suppliers and manufacturers

» Reviewing and analysing sales performance

» Managing supplier relationships and sourcing new suppliers

» Travelling to manufacturers in home market and overseas

» Visiting stores to review performance and meet managers

» Writing reports and presenting ranges to management

Right
Buyers placing orders with Danish label
nümph on their stand at the Bread &
Butter trade fair in Berlin.

ROLES AND DEPARTMENTS THAT INTERFACE WITH FASHION BUYING

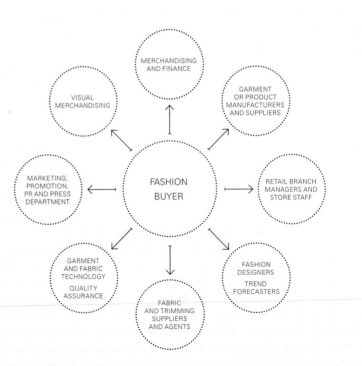

MERCHANDISING AND FINANCE

VISUAL MERCHANDISING

GARMENT OR PRODUCT MANUFACTURERS AND SUPPLIERS

MARKETING, PROMOTION, PR AND PRESS DEPARTMENT

FASHION BUYER

RETAIL BRANCH MANAGERS AND STORE STAFF

GARMENT AND FABRIC TECHNOLOGY QUALITY ASSURANCE

FABRIC AND TRIMMING SUPPLIERS AND AGENTS

FASHION DESIGNERS TREND FORECASTERS

Merchandiser

Merchandisers are responsible for the budget and work to maximize a retailer's profitability by ensuring that products appear in the right store at the appropriate time and in the correct quantities. Merchandisers work very closely with buyers to plan ranges and determine what quantity of each style should be bought. They must make sure the buyer stays within budget and that the range will achieve margin and profit targets. Merchandisers must also co-ordinate and liaise with suppliers to monitor deliveries and work with the distribution and warehouse departments to ensure the right amount of stock is sent to the correct stores. Merchandisers monitor the daily and weekly sales figures and must be proactive in devising markdown or promotion strategies. In a small company, the same person may have to do the buying and handle the merchandising.

Merchandiser: key skills

» Numerate with excellent analytical skills

» Accurate

» Strong computer skills and ability to use IT packages

» Understanding of product manufacturing

» Strong negotiation skills

Typical work activities:

» Budget planning

» Working with buyer to plan product ranges

» Liaising with buyers, suppliers, distribution, stores and management

» Analysing financial data

» Forecasting potential sales, profits and stock figures

ROLES AND DEPARTMENTS THAT
INTERFACE WITH FASHION MERCHANDISING

Visual merchandiser: key skills

Visual merchandiser: key skills

» Creative flair and good eye for composition, proportion and colour

» Understanding of how to communicate brand identity within visual displays

» Good knowledge of fashion trends

» Strong display techniques

» Ability to work to tight deadlines

ROLES AND DEPARTMENTS
THAT INTERFACE WITH
VISUAL MERCHANDISING

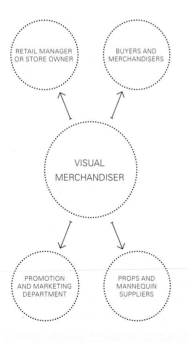

» Devising markdown and promotional strategies to mitigate losses and maximize sales and profit

» Presenting financial data, sales forecasts and stock information to management

» Negotiating delivery dates and stock quantities with suppliers

» Travelling with buyers to visit manufacturers

Visual merchandiser

A visual merchandiser is responsible for creating and installing schemes for windows and in-store displays with the aim of drawing customers into the store, promoting merchandise and maximizing potential sales. Displays and promotions will be designed to fit in with important annual events such as the launch of the Spring and Autumn seasons and Christmas, Valentine's Day or Easter. Large and medium-sized companies may employ their own visual merchandising (VM) team, but they could also use the services of a specialist retail or VM consultancy. Owners of smaller businesses may 'do it themselves' or use the skills of a freelancer. If you are interested in working in VM, then be prepared to lift and carry props and mannequins, climb ladders, adjust lighting and paint backdrops. You may also be required to travel, usually from store to store, and work unsocial hours – changes in displays and installations usually take place at night when the store is closed to avoid disruption or loss of sales.

Typical work activities:

» Researching and devising display concepts and schemes

» Creating concept boards and presenting schemes to colleagues

» Technical drawing by hand or CAD of windows and floor plans

» Sourcing materials and display elements, such as lighting, props and accessories

» Installing and dismantling displays

» Dressing mannequins

» Creating VM informational packs sent out to stores

» Visiting stores and training sales staff

Fashion marketing and promotion

Describing the career options within fashion marketing is somewhat complicated by the fact that interpretations of exactly what comes under the banner of marketing vary considerably depending on the requirements and structural set-up of a particular company. This makes it much harder to define individual job roles, as some view marketing as a sales-related role, others regard it as a management function, and there are those that consider it to mean promotion and PR, so job options could be in any of the following:

» Sales and marketing

» Brand management/product management

» Promotion and PR

To work in sales, marketing or promotion you will need to be a people person and a good communicator with strong verbal and written communication skills. You should enjoy networking and be willing to socialize as part of your work. You should also be proactive, organized and flexible.

Opposite
Window displays are an important element of the visual merchandiser's job. This dramatic scheme for Harvey Nichols in London illustrates how colour can be used to promote summer merchandise.

Below
Behind the scenes the team prepare for London Fashion Week.

» Highly analytical

» Numerate with strong skills in maths

» Knowledge of apparel manufacturing

» Ability to analyse and utilize data from sales, production and fashion forecasts

» Well-organized

» Attention to detail

» Ability to deal with pressure and tight deadlines

» Ability to present and communicate detailed information to others

» Good negotiation skills

Brand management/product management

Brand management focuses on the strategic management of a brand and the development and maintenance of the brand identity. Marketing management encompasses a variety of roles and again these will be dependent on each company's requirements. If you check recruitment agency websites for fashion marketing jobs you will notice adverts for product management. Product managers are responsible for overseeing the overall process of developing product and bringing it to market. They usually handle a specific product or product category, overseeing the entire process of conceptualization, design, production, selling and distribution of a manufacturer or designer's products. With so much responsibility it is no surprise that a product manager is a senior level job; you will probably need to start in an assistant position and work up. You will also need a degree in business administration, marketing, or apparel production. As product managers gain extensive experience and knowledge of the manufacturer's operations, they can be promoted into an executive leadership position.

Typical work activities:

» Working with a technical team on product design, construction and manufacture

» Sourcing manufacturers and negotiating production contracts

» Planning production and delivery schedules

» Negotiating distribution rights

» Writing detailed marketing and business reports

» Reviewing sales results and analysing data

» Monitoring fashion and market trends

» Forecasting and preparing monthly and annual sales targets for specific regions

» Researching and developing new product lines

» Travelling to visit overseas manufacturers and distributors

Promotion and PR

Fashion PR is about promotion and image. The aim of PR is to gain media coverage to promote and generate a favourable image of an organization, brand or fashion label. To work in PR you will need to get on well with a broad spectrum of people, be sociable, a good networker and competent with social media. PR people need to build strong working relationships with their clients and with members of the fashion press.

Typical work activities:

» Managing and maintaining social media

» Writing blog, Facebook and Twitter posts. Uploading images to Instagram and Pinterest

» Writing press releases and handling press enquiries

» Creating press packs and goodie bags for fashion shows and events

» Sending garments out to magazines or bloggers to be featured in fashion shoots and editorial

» Creating look books and style books to give to press and buyers

» Running press days to view collections

» Developing and managing product launches, special events or parties

» Managing the guest lists for fashion shows, events, store openings, shopping evenings, retail events or product launches

» Managing business communication or news stories concerning announcements on trading figures

» Informing press of newsworthy stories, sponsorship deals, celebrity endorsements or designer collaborations

» Handling negative news stories and limiting any damage that might be caused

Above right
PR personnel are responsible for sending sample garments out to the fashion and national press so they can be featured in editorial fashion spreads or in articles on key trends or what's hot in the shops.

Promotion and PR: key skills

» Strong verbal and written communication skills

» Good networker and confident in social situations

» Proactive, organized and flexible

ROLES AND DEPARTMENTS THAT INTERFACE WITH FASHION PR

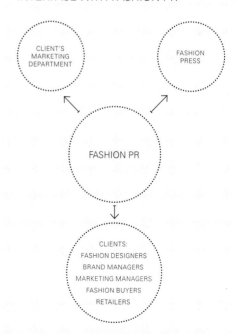

CLIENT'S MARKETING DEPARTMENT

FASHION PRESS

FASHION PR

CLIENTS:
FASHION DESIGNERS
BRAND MANAGERS
MARKETING MANAGERS
FASHION BUYERS
RETAILERS

Work placements and internships

Work placements and internships have become an essential first step for a career in fashion. They can be beneficial for both students and employers, preparing students for working life and giving the employer valuable support. Consider how you will benefit from gaining first-hand industry knowledge and how this might help you attain your academic goals. Many fashion courses include a work placement, which can vary from a few weeks to a whole year working for one or more companies. If a placement is included in your course, the company is not obliged to pay you, but they should agree to guide and mentor you and offer suitable experience. An internship is a period of voluntary or paid work experience offered to students and graduates. It is usually short-term and project-led. Many fashion companies take on interns to assist with completing a collection or a major marketing campaign.

Working life is usually much faster paced than your college studies, particularly if there are tight schedules. There may be long days before a deadline or during an unexpected crisis. Some tasks may be boring or repetitive, but it is worth persevering, as industry experience will help you learn how to work in a professional manner and, of course, is helpful on your CV. Some of the benefits identified by students after work experience are:

> » It helps put theory into practice
>
> » I understand the jargon now
>
> » I have more confidence and motivation
>
> » It helped me develop a 9–5 routine
>
> » I gained practice in applying for jobs and being interviewed
>
> » I am clearer about my intended career direction
>
> » I realize how competitive the workplace can be
>
> » I've built a network of industry contacts

Internships can be worthwhile after graduation if finding a job is proving a challenge. You may need to do several but they will help you gain confidence and widen your professional network, and, of course, an internship may lead to a full-time job. Be open-minded. It is not always possible to intern in the most prestigious fashion brands, but there are many smaller labels, wholesalers or design-led suppliers where you could gain invaluable experience.

Tip: Get involved

Try volunteering at fashion-related events. You can work backstage at a fashion show as a dresser or help on a trade-show stand for a design company or individual designer. They may value an extra pair of hands to help with setting up and occasional cover for them during the show. Any involvement could help you develop industry contacts and you can include your stints as a volunteer on your CV and LinkedIn page.

Applying for a placement or internship

Consider the type of organization you wish to approach and which level of the market your skills are best suited to. Are you happy to work in a corporate environment, or are you more independently minded and would prefer a smaller organization? Take a look at the company mission statement, brand values and objectives. Do you fit here? If the company has a press section on their website, look at the most recent press releases, and, of course, keep an eye on their social media output. Once you have identified a company you would like to work for, research them and their target customers. Think about answers to these questions. Why do you want to work for this company and not their competitor? Can you identify their brand proposition and values? How do these values relate to your personal views on fashion and business? What excites and interests you about the work this company does? Consider all aspects from the content and tone of their social media output, the clients they represent if they are a PR company or the fashion collections they produce and sell if they are retail brand or designer label.

Think about the best approach. You could send a formal letter or contact them via LinkedIn or Facebook; some companies do recruit via social media. Find out about internships and employment opportunities from:

> » Company websites and social media
>
> » Contacting companies directly by calling their HR department and sending your CV and a covering letter
>
> » Recruitment agencies
>
> » Trade fairs, exhibitions and graduate employment fairs
>
> » College and university careers departments
>
> » Appointment sections in industry publications such as *Drapers* or *Retail Week*
>
> » Networking on social media and in person

If your placement is part of a degree you should get help finding a company, but you may be expected to make enquiries yourself. If you are applying for an internship alone, double-check and agree terms and conditions with the employer and be sure that you understand their expectations. Legally you must be paid if you undertake an internship unless it is an official element of an accredited course, or the internship could be considered as training and is for your benefit. Employment law, of course, differs from country to country so make sure you know the law in your area.

Interview tips

» Prepare thoroughly, research the company and gather background information on the skills required for the job.

» Research the latest industry developments and trends so that you are knowledgeable and informed if asked during your interview.

» Confirm beforehand if you are expected to take anything with you, such as examples of previous work or a portfolio.

» Make sure you know exactly where to go, how to get there and allow enough time for transport problems or hold-ups. It is better to be early than late. Try to arrive about ten minutes ahead of your interview time so that you can take time to breathe and unwind from the journey.

» Think about a suitable outfit to wear and make sure it is clean, presentable and still fits! It's a good idea to try your outfit on well before the day of the interview, check for missing buttons, holes or dropped hems.

» Take a copy of the job application and your CV with you. You can read these in preparation while travelling or waiting.

It is important to note that there are distinctions between an intern, a worker and an employee. If an intern works set hours, is left to work unsupervised, is given deadlines or required to manage staff, and the work they are doing would usually be carried out by a paid employee, then the intern can legally be termed as a worker. A worker is not an employee (and therefore not entitled to employee benefits or protection), but should be paid a minimum wage.

Interviews

Interviews vary enormously depending on the job role, the level of the job and the type of company involved. The interview may be an informal chat or could involve a panel of interviewers, you might be expected to make a presentation, or the recruitment process might be conducted in a group with other candidates.

Informal interview These may be carried out by telephone or Skype or in a public place like a hotel lounge or café. A company might ask for an initial meeting if they wish to talk to someone informally to learn more about them and see if they might fit into their organization.

Pre-screening Companies may use a recruitment agency or someone within their own Human Resources department to conduct an interview to pre-screen candidates. This could take place in person or on the telephone or Skype; the purpose is to verify details of your CV and check you have the minimum qualifications required.

Selection interview This is the next step in the process. Interviewers already know that pre-screened candidates have the right skills, so are looking to see who has the right attitude and personality and could fit in with other employees within the organization. Interviews may be carried out by one person, a series of different people who each interview the candidate one by one, or by an interview panel. If successful, you may be offered the job or invited back for a second interview.

Panel interview Panel interviews are conducted by several people at once. The panel is usually made of managers from departments you will work with if you get the job. Members of the interview panel will take it in turn to ask you questions. Keep calm and make eye contact with each panel member when you respond to him or her.

Group interviews and assessment centres Candidates may be interviewed as a group; this allows an organization to see how candidates interact with each other and assess if they are team players or have leadership potential. Assessment centres are special recruitment days where candidates perform a series of tasks and exercises such as group discussions, presentations and leadership exercises.

You should get an opportunity to ask questions at the end of the interview. Start with questions about training and appraisals. You can ask about career prospects and opportunities for growth and clarify any queries about job specification and responsibilities. Save questions about pay and holidays until last or, even better, double-check details with Human Resources before or after the interview. Find out when you can expect to hear if you have been successful, and don't forget to thank the interviewer for their time before you leave.

It is worth considering the type of language you use within a professional situation. On the next page is a list of positive words and action words you might find useful when compiling your CV or attending an interview. Make sure you choose ones that are suitable, relevant and true to you.

POSITIVE WORDS

Accurate
Adaptable
Ambitious
Analytical
Articulate
Assertive
Astute
Bright
Calm
Capable
Competent
Confident
Consistent
Co-operative
Creative
Decisive

Dedicated
Dependable
Diligent
Diplomatic
Dynamic
Educated
Effective
Efficient
Energetic
Enthusiastic
Experienced
Expert
Fast
Flexible
Friendly
Hard-working

Honest
Imaginative
Independent
Informed
Innovative
Intelligent
Inventive
Knowledgeable
Literate
Mature
Motivated
Objective
Open-minded
Organized
Outgoing
Patient

Perceptive
Persistent
Personable
Practical
Precise
Productive
Professional
Proficient
Punctual
Qualified
Quick-thinking
Rational
Realistic
Resourceful
Responsible
Self-assured

Self-confident
Self-motivated
Self-reliant
Serious
Skilled
Smart
Talented
Tenacious
Thorough
Trustworthy
Versatile
Willing

ACTION WORDS

Achieved
Administered
Advised
Analysed
Arranged
Assisted
Attended
Broadened
Collaborated
Communicated
Completed
Conceived
Conducted
Controlled
Co-ordinated
Created
Delegated

Demonstrated
Designed
Developed
Devised
Directed
Edited
Effected
Established
Evaluated
Expanded
Explored
Facilitated
Formulated
Founded
Generated
Guided
Handled

Headed
Identified
Implemented
Improved
Increased
Initiated
Installed
Instructed
Invented
Investigated
Launched
Led
Liaised
Maintained
Managed
Marketed
Monitored

Motivated
Negotiated
Opened
Operated
Organized
Oversaw
Participated
Performed
Pioneered
Planned
Prepared
Presented
Processed
Produced
Programmed
Promoted
Proposed

Recommended
Recruited
Reorganized
Researched
Resolved
Restructured
Reviewed
Revised
Scheduled
Secured
Set up
Solved
Structured

Source: The Careers Department, Plymouth College of Art

Further reading

Allen P. Adamson. *The Edge: 50 Tips from Brands that Lead*, Palgrave Macmillan, 2013

D. Adcock, A. Halborg, C. Ross. *Marketing: Principles and Practice*, Financial Times/Prentice Hall, 2001

Teri Agins. *The End of Fashion*, HarperCollins, 2000

Michael J. Baker. *The Marketing Book*, Financial Times/Prentice Hall, 2001

J.A. Bell. *Silent Selling: Best Practices and Effective Strategies in Visual Merchandising*, Fairchild, 2006

Sandy Black. *Eco-chic: The Fashion Paradox*, Black Dog Publishing, 2008

Sandy Black. *Knitwear in Fashion*, Thames & Hudson, 2002

Sandy Black. *The Sustainable Fashion Handbook*, Thames & Hudson, 2012

Sarah E. Braddock Clarke and Marie O'Mahony. *Techno Textiles 2: Revolutionary Textiles for Fashion and Design: Book 2*, Thames & Hudson, 2007

Evelyn L. Brannon. *Fashion Forecasting: Research, Analysis, and Presentation*, Fairchild Books, 2nd revised edition, 2005

Michael Braungart and William McDonough. *Cradle to Cradle: Remaking the Way We Make Things*, Vintage, 2009

Martin Butler. *People Don't Buy What You Sell: They Buy What You Stand For*, Management Books 2000 Ltd, 2005

Leslie de Chernatony and Malcolm McDonald. *Creating Powerful Brands*, Butterworth-Heinemann, 3rd edition, 2003

Michel Chevalier and Gerald Mazzalovo. *Luxury Brand Management*, John Wiley & Sons, 2008

Peter Chisnall. *Marketing Research*, McGraw-Hill Education, 2004

Pamela N. Danziger. *Let Them Eat Cake: Marketing Luxury to the Masses – As Well as the Classes*, Dearborn Trade Publishing, 2005

Scott M. Davis and Michael Dunn. *Building the Brand-driven Business*, Jossey-Bass, 2002

Kate Fletcher and Lynda Grose. *Fashion and Sustainability: Design for Change*, Laurence King Publishing, 2012

Kate Fletcher. *Sustainable Fashion and Textiles: Design Journeys*, Earthscan Publications Ltd, 2008

Mary Gehlhar. *The Fashion Designer Survival Guide: An Insider's Look at Starting and Running Your Own Fashion Business*, Kaplan Publishing, 2005

Malcolm Gladwell. *The Tipping Point*, Abacus, 2000

Seth Godin. *Purple Cow*, Penguin Books, 2005

Helen Goworek. *Careers in Fashion & Textiles*, Blackwell Publishing, 2006

Helen Goworek. *Fashion Buying*, Blackwell Science, 2001

Kaled K. Hameide. *Fashion Branding Unravelled*, Fairchild Books, 2011

Joseph Hancock. *Brand/Story: Ralph, Vera, Johnny, Billy, and Other Adventures in Fashion Branding*, Fairchild Books, 2009

Eric von Hippel. *Democratizing Innovation*, MIT Press, 2005

Jeff Howe. *Crowdsourcing: Why the Power of the Crowd is Driving the Future of Business*, Crown Business, 2008

Neil Howe and William Strauss. *Millennials Rising*, Vintage Books, 2000

Mark Hughes. *Buzzmarketing: Get People to Talk About Your Stuff*, Portfolio, 2005

Tim Jackson and David Shaw. *Mastering Fashion Buying and Merchandising Management*, Palgrave Macmillan, 2001

Tim Jackson and David Shaw. *The Fashion Handbook*, Routledge, 2006

Sue Jenkyn Jones. *Fashion Design*, Laurence King Publishing, 3rd edition, 2011

Richard M. Jones. *The Apparel Industry*, Blackwell Publishing Ltd, 2nd edition, 2006

Jean-Noël Kapferer. *Strategic Brand Management*, The Free Press, 1992

J.N. Kapferer and V. Bastien. *The Luxury Strategy: Break the Rules of Marketing to Build Luxury Brands*, Kogan Page, 2009

Philip Kotler. *FAQs on Marketing*, Marshall Cavendish Business, 2008

Philip Kotler. *Marketing Management: Analysis, Planning, Implementation and Control*, Prentice Hall, 1994

P. Kotler, G. Armstrong, V. Wong, J. Saunders. *Principles of Marketing*, Financial Times/Prentice Hall, 2008

Gaynor Lea-Greenwood. *Fashion Marketing Communications*, John Wiley & Sons Ltd, 2013

Suzanne Lee, Warren du Preez. *Fashioning the Future: Tomorrow's Wardrobe*, Thames & Hudson, 2007

Martin Lindstrom. *Buyology: How Everything We Believe About Why We Buy Is Wrong*, Random House Business, 2008

Naresh K. Malhotra, David F. Birks, Peter Wills. *Marketing Research: An Applied Approach*, Pearson, 4th edition, 2012

Margaret McAlpine. *So You Want to Work in Fashion?*, Hodder Wayland, 2005

Malcolm McDonald. *On Marketing Planning: Understanding Marketing Plans and Strategy*, Kogan Page, 2007

Toby Meadows. *How to Set Up and Run a Fashion Label*, Laurence King Publishing, 2nd edition, 2012

Geoffrey Miller. *Spent: Sex, Evolution and the Secrets of Consumerism*, William Heinemann Ltd, 2009

Safia Minney. *Naked Fashion*, New Internationalist Publications Ltd, 2011

David Meerman Scott. *The New Rules of Marketing & PR*, John Wiley & Sons, 2007

Gwyneth Moore. *Fashion Promotion: Building a Brand Through Marketing and Communication*, AVA Publishing SA, 2012

Tony Morgan. *Visual Merchandising: Window and In-store Displays for Retail*, Laurence King Publishing, 2nd edition, 2011

Bethan Morris. *Fashion Illustrator*, Laurence King Publishing, 2nd edition, 2010

Don Tapscott. *Grown-up Digital*, McGraw-Hill, 2009

Uche Okonkwo. *Luxury Fashion Branding: Trends, Tactics, Techniques*, Palgrave Macmillan, 2007

Wally Olins. *Wally Olins: The Brand Handbook*, Thames & Hudson, 2008

Trade publications and magazines

Faith Popcorn. *EVEolution: The Eight Truths of Marketing to Women*, HarperCollins Business, 2001

Martin Raymond. *The Trend Forecaster's Handbook*, Laurence King Publishing, 2010

Doug Richard. *How to Start a Creative Business*, David and Charles, 2013

A. Ries and J. Trout. *Positioning: The Battle for Your Mind*, McGraw-Hill Professional, 2001

Lon Safko and David K. Brake. *The Social Media Bible: Tactics, Tools and Strategies for Business Success*, John Wiley & Sons, 2009

Marian Salzman and Ira Matathia. *Next Now: Trends for the Future*, Palgrave Macmillan, 2008

Bernd H. Schmitt. *Experiential Marketing*, The Free Press, 1999

Robert Scoble and Shel Israel. *Naked Conversations: How Blogs are Changing the Way Businesses Talk with Customers*, John Wiley & Sons, 2006

Simon Seivewright. *Basics Fashion Design: Research and Design*, AVA Publishing, 2007

Sophie Sheikh. *The Pocket Guide to Fashion PR*, Preo Publishing, 2009

Michael R. Solomon and Nancy J. Rabolt. *Consumer Behaviour in Fashion*, Prentice Hall, 2008

Mark Tungate. *Fashion Brands*, Kogan Page, 3rd edition 2012

Rosemary Varley. *Retail Product Management*, Routledge, 2002

Rosemary Varley and Mohammed Rafiq. *Principles of Retail Management*, Palgrave Macmillan, 2004

Peter Vogt. *Career Opportunities in the Fashion Industry*, Checkmark Books, 2nd edition, 2007

Alina Wheeler. *Designing Brand Identity*, John Wiley & Sons, 4th edition, 2013

Nicola White and Ian Griffiths. *The Fashion Business. Theory, Practice, Image*, Berg, 2000

Judy Zaccagnini and Irene M. Foster. *Research Methods for the Fashion Industry*, Fairchild, 2009

Adbusters
Advertising Age
Adweek
Amelia's Magazine
AnOther
Arena
Auxiliary Magazine
Bloom
Brand Republic
Dansk
Dazed and Confused
Drapers: The Fashion Business
The Economist
Elle
Encens
Fantastic Man
Flaunt
GQ
Harper's Bazaar
i-D
InStyle
International Textiles
L'Officiel
Marketing Week
Nylon
Oh Comely
Plastic Rhino
Pop
Purple
Retail Week
Selvedge
Sneaker Freaker
SOMA
Tank
Textile View
V
View on Colour
Viewpoint
Visionaire
Vogue
Women's Wear Daily (WWD)
Zoom on Fashion Trends

Quotation references

p4   Teri Agins quote: *The End of Fashion*, HarperCollins, 2000.

p5   Mark Tungate quote: *Fashion Brands*, Kogan Page, 3rd edition 2012.

1
The Fashion Market

p9   Philip Kotler quote: *FAQs on Marketing*, Marshall Cavendish Business, 2008.

p28   Philip Kotler quotes: *Principles of Marketing*, Financial Times/Prentice Hall, 2008.

p29   Martin Butler quote: *People don't buy what you sell: They buy what you stand for*, Management Books 2000 Ltd, 2005.

p30   Seth Godin quote: *Purple Cow*, Penguin Books, 2005.

p32   Mark Hughes quote: *Buzzmarketing: Get People to Talk About Your Stuff*, Portfolio, 2005.

2
Marketing Strategy

p39   Tige Savage quote: 'Macy's Adds Scan-and-Shop App to Holiday Season Arsenal', posted on brandchannel.com by Sheila Shayon, 2013. Tige Savage is a partner at venture capital firm Revolution.

p41   Neil H. Borden quote: 'The Concept of the Marketing Mix', *Journal of Advertising Research*, Cambridge University Press, 1964.

p55   Martin Butler quote: *People Don't Buy What You Sell: They Buy What You Stand For*, Management Books 2000 Ltd, 2005.

p56   Ries & Trout quote: *Positioning: The Battle for Your Mind*, McGraw-Hill Professional, 2001.

The concept of Positioning was developed by Ries & Trout and first took hold in 1972 with a series of articles entitled *The Positioning Era*, published in *Advertising Age*.

3
Research and Planning

p65   Faith Popcorn quote: Faith Popcorn's Brain Reserve, www.faithpopcorn.com. Faith Popcorn is a futurist and author of *The Popcorn Report*.

p66   Philip Kotler quote cited by G. Lancaster & P. Reynolds. *Management of Marketing* (2005).

p71   Douglas Cordeaux quote: *The Mail on Sunday* (05.11.2012). Fox Brothers & Co. are British manufacturers of woollen, worsted, cashmere and flannel cloth.

4
Understanding the Customer

p107 John Rocha quote: *The Times Magazine* (22.09.07).

p112 Erdem Moralioglu quoted in *Elle Magazine*, 2007.

p114 Quote by Douglas Coupland posted on www.jonathanpontell.com. Jonathan Pontell is a cultural historian and writer whose website has a section devoted to information on Generation Jones.

p122 Jennings sourced information from *Drapers* article: 'Portas Says Future is Bright for UK's Indies', Khabi Mirza (24.11.07).

5
Introduction to Branding

p139 Definition of a brand: *How Brands Work*, Chartered Institute of Marketing. www.cim.co.uk.

p141 Allen Adamson, Chairman Landor Associates North America. www.landor.com.

p144 Clamor Gieske quote: *The Economic Importance of Brands – Seven Reasons Why Brands Really Matter*, The British Brands Group, 2004.

p155 Elizabeth Schofield quote: Posted in an article by Kayla Hutzler on Luxury Daily (www.luxurydaily.com) in 2011.

p161 Pamela N. Danziger quote: *Let Them Eat Cake: Marketing Luxury to the Masses – As Well as the Classes*, Dearborn Trade Publishing, 2005.

p163 Quotation by Sean Chiles of IPincubator, specializing in brand development and licensing.

p170 Louise Beveridge quote: 'Why Did PPR Change Its Name to Kering?', posted by Vikram Alexei Kansara on businessoffashion.com, 2013.

6
Fashion Promotion

p171 This famous quote is most usually attributed to John Wanamaker who opened Philadelphia's first department store, Wanamaker's, in the second half of the 19th century. Wanamaker developed the first ever copyrighted store advertisements in 1874.

p175 Quote by Christopher Bailey, Chief Creative and Chief Executive Officer of Burberry, 2013.

p182 Hannah Jennings, owner-buyer of Starburst Boutique, Dartmouth UK. Interviewed by the author.

7
Careers in Fashion Marketing

p205 Martin Butler quote: *People Don't Buy What You Sell: They Buy What You Stand For*, Management Books 2000 Ltd, 2005

Useful addresses

UK

The British Fashion Council (BFC)
Somerset House, South Wing
Strand
London WC2R 1LA
tel +44 (0)20 7759 1999
www.britishfashioncouncil.com

The British Fashion Council provides support to emerging British fashion designers with schemes ranging from business mentoring and seminars to competitions and sponsorship.

Organizes the annual fashion awards and supports initiatives such as estethica, Fashion Forward and NEWGEN.

Fashion Awareness Direct (FAD)
10a Wellesley Terrace
London N1 7NA
tel/fax +44 (0)20 7490 3946
www.fad.org.uk

A charitable organization committed to helping young designers succeed in their careers by bringing students and professionals together at introductory events.

UKFT – UK Fashion & Textile Association
3 Queen Square
London WC1N 3AR
tel +44 (0)20 7843 9460
fax +44 (0)20 7843 9478
www.ukft.org

UKFT advises members on running a business and supplying clothing and knitwear to the global marketplace.

US

Council of Fashion Designers of America (CFDA)
65 Bleecker St, 11th Floor
New York, NY 10012
tel +1 212 302 1821
www.cfda.com

The CFDA is a not-for-profit trade association whose membership consists of more than 400 of America's foremost womenswear, menswear, jewellery and accessory designers.

The American Apparel and Footwear Association (AAFA)
1601 North Kent Street
Suite 1200
Arlington VA 22209
tel + 1 703 524 1864
https://www.wewear.org

The AAFA is a national trade association representing apparel and footwear companies and their suppliers.

United States Small Business Administration
409 3rd St, SW
Washington DC 20416
tel +1 800-827-5722
www.sba.gov

The SBA assists with small business start-up and development.

Additional resources

International fashion and textile trade fairs

The Accessories Show
New York & Las Vegas
www.accessoriestheshow.com

Atelier
Accessories and apparel trade show.
New York
www.atelierdesigners.com

Bread & Butter
Street and urban wear.
Berlin, Germany
www.breadandbutter.com

CPD – Düsseldorf
International trade fair for
womenswear and accessories.
Düsseldorf, Germany
www.the-gallery-dusseldorf.com

CPH Vision
Exhibits established and up-and-coming
contemporary fashion brands.
Copenhagen, Denmark
www.cphvision.dk

CURVExpo
Designer lingerie and swimwear.
New York & Las Vegas
www.curvexpo.com

Ethical Fashion Show Berlin
www.ethicalfashionshowberlin.com

Expofil
Yarn, fibre and knitwear show.
Paris
www.expofil.com

Futurmoda
Leather and footwear trade show.
Alicante, Spain
www.futurmoda.es

Lineapelle
Trade fair for leather, accessories and
components for footwear, leather goods,
garments and furniture.
Bologna, Italy
www.lineapelle-fair.it

London Edge
Street and clubwear trade show.
London
www.londonedge.com

The Los Angeles International Textile Show (L.A. Textile)
Cutting-edge fashion direction,
textiles and creative design resources
from around the globe.
Los Angeles
www.californiamarketcenter.com

Modafabriek
Womenswear, menswear and children's
fashion.
Amsterdam
www.modefabriek.nl

Pitti Immagine
Organize a wide range of fashion and textile
fairs including:
Pitti Bimbo – childrenswear
Pitti Filati – yarn show
Pitti Uomo – menswear
Pitti W – women's pre-collection
All the above in Florence, Italy.
Modaprima – apparel and accessories. Milan
www.pittimmagine.com

Première Vision
International fabric trade fair.
Paris
www.premierevision.com

Pulse
Gifts, interior and fashion accessories.
London
www.pulse-london.com

Pure London
Womenswear, accessories and footwear.
London
www.purelondon.com

Spinexpo New York
International textile, yarns, fibres and
knitwear exhibition.
www.spinexpo.com

Texworld (US, China, France, Turkey)
International trade fairs for fabrics, trims,
accessories.
www.messefrankfurt.com

The London Textile Fair
Fashion fabrics and clothing accessories.
www.thelondontextilefair.co.uk

Top Drawer
Gifts, interior and fashion accessories.
London
www.topdrawer.co.uk

Marketing, advertising and promotion associations

Advertising Research Foundation (ARF)
www.thearf.org

The American Marketing Association (AMA)
www.ama.org

Chartered Institute of Marketing (CIM)
www.cim.co.uk

European Association of Communications Agencies (EACA)
www.eaca.eu

IAB Europe
www.iabeurope.eu

Institute of Direct Marketing (IDM)
www.theidm.com

Institute of Practitioners in Advertising
www.ipa.co.uk

Institute for Public Relations (IPR)
www.instituteforpr.org

Institute of Sales Promotion (ISP)
www.theipm.org.uk

International Licensing Industry Merchandisers' Association (LIMA)
www.licensing.org

The Internet Advertising Bureau
www.iabuk.net

Marketing Agencies Association Worldwide (MAAW)
www.maaw.org

World Advertising Research Centre (WARC)
www.warc.com

Trend forecasting and fashion intelligence

BrainReserve (Faith Popcorn)
www.faithpopcorn.com

The Carlin Group
www.carlin-groupe.fr

Committee for Colour and Trends
www.colourandtrends.com

The Future Laboratory
www.thefuturelaboratory.com

Li Edelkoort
www.trendunion.com

Nelly Rodi
www.nellyrodi.com

Pantone Inc
www.pantone.com

Peclers Paris
www.peclersparis.com

Promostyl
www.promostyl.com

Style.com
www.style.com

Stylesight
www.stylesight.com

Trendstop
www.trendstop.com

Trendwatching
www.trendwatching.com

Trendzine
www.fashioninformation.com

WGSN
www.wgsn.com

Geraldine Wharry
www.geraldinewharry.com

Fashion and textile market information

American Apparel and Footwear Association
www.apparelandfootwear.org

Business of Fashion (BoF)
www.businessoffashion.com

Clothesource
www.clothesource.com

Cotton Incorporated
www.cottoninc.com

The Doneger Group
www.doneger.com

Drapers
www.drapersonline.com

Euromonitor International
www.euromonitor.com

Fashion Incubator
Industry information.
www.fashion-incubator.com

Fashion Infomat
www.infomat.com

Fibre2fashion
www.fibre2fashion.com

First Research
www.firstresearch.com

Just-style
www.just-style.com

Mintel Reports
www.mintel.com

My Fashion Life
Industry analysis and news.
www.myfashionlife.com

TNS Worldpanel Fashion
www.tnsglobal.com

The Tobé Report
www.tobereport.com

Verdict Research
www.verdict.co.uk

Women's Wear Daily
www.wwd.com

Marketing, branding, advertising and retail information

Advertising Age
http://adage.com

Adweek
www.adweek.com

Brand Republic
www.brandrepublic.com

Fashion Marketing Group
http://fashionmarketinggroup.tumblr.com

Fashion Windows
Visual merchandising.
www.fashionwindows.com

The Gallup Organization
www.gallup.com

Interbrand Brandchannel
www.brandchannel.com

Landor & Associates
www.landor.com

The Market Research Society
www.mrs.org.uk

The Retail Bulletin
Fashion merchandising.
www.theretailbulletin.com

Retail Week
www.retail-week.com

Unity Marketing
www.unitymarketingonline.com

Visual Store
Visual merchandising.
www.visualstore.com

Wally Olins
www.wallyolins.com

World Luxury Association
www.worldluxuryassociation.org

Blogs, social networking and street fashion

Collage Vintage
www.collagevintage.com

Garance Doré
www.garancedore.fr

The Gentleman Blogger
www.thegentlemanblogger.com

HypeBeast
http://hypebeast.com

I'm Koo
www.koo.im

Jag Lever
www.jaglever.com

Japanese Streets
www.japanesestreets.com

Kenzas
www.kenzas.se

Lookbook
www.lookbook.nu

Man Repeller
www.manrepeller.com

Mariano Di Vaio Style
www.mdvstyle.com

Rachel Martino
www.rachmartino.com

The Sartorialist
www.thesartorialist.blogspot.com

She Wears Fashion
www.shewearsfashion.com

Shine by Three
www.shinebythree.com

Streetgeist
www.streetgeist.com

Style Bubble
www.stylebubble.co.uk

A Suitable Wardrobe
www.asuitablewardrobe.net

Tavi Gevinson
www.thestylerookie.com

Sustainability and eco-fashion

Better Cotton Initiative
www.bettercotton.org

British Association for Fair Trade Shops and Suppliers
www.bafts.org.uk

Eco Fashion World
www.ecofashionworld.com

Environmental Justice Foundation
www.ejfoundation.org

Ethical Fashion Forum
www.ethicalfashionforum.com

Ethical Trading Initiative (ETI)
www.ethicaltrade.org

Fair Wear Foundation
www.fairwear.org

Fashioning an Ethical Industry
www.fashioninganethicalindustry.eu

Futerra Sustainability Communications
www.futerra.co.uk

Global Organic Cotton Community Platform
www.organiccotton.org

Global Organic Textile Standard (GOTS)
www.global-standard.org

International Labour Organization
www.ilo.org

Material ConneXion
www.materialconnexion.com

National Association of Sustainable Fashion Designers
www.sustainabledesigners.org

New Economics Foundation
www.neweconomics.org

OEKO-TEX
Sets standards for manufacture.
www.oeko-tex.com

Pesticide Action Network
www.pan-uk.org

Soil Association
www.soilassociation.org

Sustainable Cotton
www.sustainablecotton.org

United Nations – Global Compact
www.unglobalcompact.org

World Fair Trade Organization (WFTO)
www.wfto.com

Company profiles & data

Dun and Bradstreet
www.dnb.co.uk

First Research
www.firstresearch.com

Hoover's
www.hoovers.com

LexisNexis
www.lexisnexis.co.uk

Zandl Group
www.zandlgroup.com

Government census and trade data

UK Office for National Statistics
www.statistics.gov.uk

US Census Data
www.census.gov

Information on starting a fashion business

Design Trust
www.thedesigntrust.co.uk

Fashion Angel
www.fashion-angel.co.uk

Fashion Capital
www.fashioncapital.co.uk

Skillfast
www.skillfast-uk.org

Fashion recruitment agencies

Arts Thread
Student and industry website.
www.artsthread.com

Fashion Personnel
www.fashionpersonnel.co.uk

Fusion Consulting
www.fusion-consulting.com

Indesign Recruitment
www.indesignrecruitment.co.uk

Jobs in Fashion
www.jobsinfashion.com

People Marketing
www.peoplemarketing.co.uk

Retail Choice
www.retailchoice.com

Smith and Pye
www.smithandpye.com

Vanessa Denza
www.denza.co.uk

Glossary

Advertising channel The medium by which an advert reaches the public, for example, cinema, magazine, Internet or newspaper.

Advertising exposure The length of time an audience is exposed to an advert.

Advertising impacts The total number of separate occasions that a TV or radio commercial is viewed or heard by a target audience.

Advertising message The message conveyed by an advert.

Advertising reach The number of people within a target market exposed to an advert over a specific length of time.

Advertising value equivalent (AVE) Measurement to compare the cost effectiveness of PR against advertising.

Audience sentiment Audience opinion relating to a particular brand, advertising or PR campaign.

Big data Massive and complex sets of data that are rapidly changing and adapting as new online data are generated and collected.

Brand A trademark name that distinguishes a product or brand company from others in the market.

Brand architecture The way a company structures and names its brands.

Brand awareness The number of customers or potential customers with awareness of a particular brand.

Brand equity A brand is a valuable asset to a company. The power of the brand name and any accumulated goodwill towards a brand make an extra value known as brand equity.

Brand essence The essential nature of a brand. The core or heart of the brand expressed in clear and simple terms.

Brand experience The perception of, and responses to, a brand's action by an individual. It can be direct, through the individual's own interaction, or indirect, by the filtering and sharing of the experience of others. All interactions therefore come together to shape the consumer's experience of a brand.

Brand extension Expansion of a brand by developing and selling new products in a broadly similar market. The term 'brand stretching' is used if a brand takes its name into a very different and unrelated market.

Brand identity The elements of a brand that define its identity, for example, identifying colours, logo, product, window displays and advertising. The brand's identity is its fundamental means of consumer recognition and symbolizes the brand's differentiation from competitors.

Brand image The consumer's view and perception of a brand and its identity. For users of a brand this will be based on practical experience. For non-users it will be based on impressions gathered from media sources or the opinion of others.

Brand licensing A brand owner can lease the use of the brand name and logo to another company. A licensing fee or royalty rate will be agreed for the use of the brand name.

Brand loyalty Refers to how loyal consumers are to a brand. In the fashion market it is possible for consumers to be loyal to several brands simultaneously.

Brand management Strategic management of a brand. Brand managers ensure the identity and values of the brand are maintained.

Brand message This is the message that a brand organization wishes to communicate about the qualities and ideas behind the brand and its product. The message can be communicated via the logo, strapline, slogan and advertising as well as via the press.

Brand personality Brand personality works on the idea that a brand has a distinct personality and that it is possible to attribute human personality traits to a brand.

Brand positioning This is both the strategic management of a brand's position relative to competitors in the market as well as the perception of the brand's position in the mind of consumers. Positioning strategy is a key component of marketing and branding strategy.

Brand proposition Statement encapsulating what the brand offers its customers. It defines the brand benefits and what makes the brand unique.

Brand repositioning The process of redefining a brand's identity and position in the market.

Brand strategy Refers to the strategic plan used to enable the development of a brand so that it meets its business objectives. The brand strategy should influence the total operation of a business and be rooted in the brand's vision and values.

Brand touchpoints A brand touchpoint is a point of interaction between a brand and consumers, employees or stakeholders.

Brand values These form the code by which a brand operates. Internally, the brand values act as a benchmark to measure behaviours and performance. They should be connecting and engaging and can also be used to market and promote a brand to consumers.

Bricks and mortar retail Retail that takes place in-store as opposed to online.

Bridge line American term for diffusion line or a collection placed between designer and high-street fashion.

B2B (Business-to-business) Trading that takes place between one business and another.

B2C (Business-to-consumer) Trading that takes place between a business and the consumer.

Celebrity endorsement A celebrity signs a contract to act as a brand ambassador and to be seen wearing and advertising the brand.

Celebrity seeding A brand loans or donates product to a celebrity for free so that they are seen wearing the brand's products.

Clip report A report giving information on the effectiveness of a PR campaign. Indicates which publications covered the story and their circulation figures.

Co-brand or Partnership brand A brand created when two brand names work together. Y-3 by Yohji Yamamoto and adidas is an example.

Co-creation A company designs and creates its products with co-operation and input from consumers.

Comparative shopping (comp shop) Designers and fashion buyers research the marketplace to compare products and prices from competitors.

Competitive advantage A specific advantage one company or brand may have over competitors within the market.

Concession A store or department store leases space within their store to another brand.

Consideration set The set of potential brand or product choices a customer may consider when purchasing.

Consumer profile Description of a typical customer or targeted customer. The profile is derived from analysis of market research data.

Content All communications material, in whatever form, generated by brands. Now that all content is available digitally, whether in written, visual, audio or video format, the creation and distribution of content is a vital point of differentiation in brand building and awareness.

Cost per thousand (CPT) Calculation to determine the average cost of an advert reaching one thousand people within the target audience.

Country of origin effect (COO or COOE) The perception that products made in certain countries may be of better quality, for example French perfume or Italian leather.

Crowdfunding A primarily Web-based means of sourcing funding for a project, venture or business. Many individuals may contribute small amounts so it can also help build a community of engaged consumers.

Crowdsourcing A company outsources design or other functions to the public, usually via the Internet.

Customer pen portrait A written portrait used to describe a typical customer or core customer.

Customer segmentation Analysis of customers, grouping them into clusters with similar characteristics.

Demi-couture Luxury-level fashion positioned between couture and ready-to-wear.

Demographics Analysis of a population by gender, age, occupation and social class.

Differentiation Strategy used to ensure a brand and its products are distinct from those of competitors.

Diffusion line Collection developed by a designer or brand to be sold at a lower price than the main collection; allows a wider range of customers to buy into the brand.

Direct marketing When a company markets directly to the end-consumer via mail-outs, emails, text messages or magazine inserts.

Distribution channel Route by which product is distributed and reaches the market.

Eco-fashion Fashion designed, produced and marketed to minimize the environmental and social impact of the process, sourcing and production of garments.

End-consumer The eventual user or wearer of the product. It may not always be the customer: a baby may be the end-consumer but the mother might be the customer.

Endorsed brand Parent brand endorses one of its own sub-brands: Obsession by Calvin Klein, for example.

Experience marketing Focuses on experience as a way to create connection between a brand and its audience.

Fad A short-lived fashion that does not survive long enough to become a trend.

Fascia Shop front and signage displaying brand logo and name.

Fashionability A term used to describe a garment or brand in terms of how fashionable it is.

Flocking To add fine particles of natural or synthetic fibres to a surface to change the texture, feel and look of the original surface.

Focus group Products or collections shown to a test group of people in order to gain feedback on their opinions, perceptions and attitudes.

Fourth cover The outside back cover of a magazine. Since it has a high visibility to readers it typically carries a significant premium in advertising costs.

Franchise A type of business model where a parent company grants permission for an individual business to trade using the main company brand name. The franchisee pays a fee and percentage of profits to the parent company.

Geo-demographics A combination of geographic and demographic analysis used to classify customer types.

Haute couture French term for 'high sewing' meaning the highest quality of made-to-order clothing made in a studio known as an 'atelier'. Only design houses approved by the Chambre Syndicale de la Haute Couture in Paris may be classified as haute couture.

Impressions In digital marketing, the number of times that a page containing a particular ad is visited. Whether or not the ad has been seen by the visitor is not known, and therefore it represents a rather crude assessment of the visibility of a digital advertising campaign.

Lead-time Time between placing a fabric, component or garment order with a supplier or factory and delivery of the order.

Licensee The company purchasing the right to use the brand name.

Licensing A brand company sells the right for a company to produce and market branded product under licence. Most commonly used by fashion brands wishing to create a perfume, cosmetics or hosiery.

Licensing in A fashion company pays for the rights to use recognizable designs, images or intellectual property on their garments, such as a Disney character.

Licensing out A designer or brand grants a licence for their designs or logo to be used by a specialist product manufacturer, or where the licensee operates in a territory where the licensor does not have a presence.

Licensor The company selling the right to use a brand name.

Like-for-like (LFL) product comparison Direct comparison of similar product sold by a range of competitive brands. Product can be compared in terms of price, quality, fabrication and design.

Likert scale A system used for setting questions on a questionnaire using a five-point scale so answers can be numerically analysed.

Manufacturer brand Branded manufacturer goods, usually fibres or fabrics such as Lycra® by DuPont™.

Market research Research into a specific market including investigation of consumers.

Market segmentation A system of dividing a market into smaller subsections; segmentation enables a company to focus their marketing more accurately.

Market share The share a particular company or country has of a specific market. Market share figures are expressed as a percentage.

Marketing environment Refers to factors that impact on an organization and its marketing.

Marketing mix Refers to key elements that must be balanced in order to develop an organization's marketing. There are two versions: the 4P (product, price, place, promotion) and 7P with additional criteria (physical evidence, process and people).

Marketing plan A formalized plan outlining an organization's marketing strategy.

Marketing research The full range of aspects that must be researched in order to determine a marketing strategy.

Microblogging Sharing short texts, digital images and videos with others, typically using a service such as Twitter or Tumblr. For the fashion industry it has become a significant means of content distribution and consumer engagement.

Mystery shopping The process of researchers visiting stores anonymously to assess the quality of service and product on offer.

Online trunk show A means by which designers or brands allow consumers and clients to view and purchase new designs before they go on general sale or, in some cases, are produced.

Opportunity to see (OTS) Frequency of exposure of an advert; relates to how many people have the opportunity to see, hear or read the advertisement.

Own label, Own brand or Private brand When a department store or retailer creates their own in-house brands. Marks & Spencer's Autograph or Macy's I.N.C. are examples.

Peer marketing Recommendation and promotion of products among consumers.

Perceptual map A map showing consumer perception of a brand in comparison to competitor brands.

PEST analysis Investigation and analysis of political, economic, social and technological factors affecting a business and its marketing.

Point-of-sale (POS) The actual place where product is sold to the customer; usually used in reference to the till-point or in the case of point-of-sale marketing, material used within store.

Pop-up store A temporary store set up for a limited time. Pop-up stores often include some kind of special event designed to create a buzz.

Positioning The position a brand or product occupies in the market relative to competitors.

Positioning map A brand management tool used to indicate the current position or proposed future position of a brand in comparison to competitors in the market.

Pretailer A business model whereby new designers or established brands can minimize production costs by taking advance orders from customers buying online. Production runs are based on items sold.

Prêt-à-porter French term for ready-to-wear clothing.

Price architecture The way a company structures pricing across the product range balancing the offer of low-, medium- and high- priced product.

Price point Product within a collection or product range will be priced at various price points according to type of product, quality or exclusivity.

Primary research Research conducted first-hand by collecting data through observations, surveys, interviews and market research techniques.

Product attribute Refers to the features, functions and uses of a product.

Product benefit Relates to how a product's attributes or features might benefit the consumer.

Product placement A company raises awareness of its products by ensuring they are seen in films and television shows.

Promotional mix Refers to key types of promotion (advertising, sales promotion, PR and personal selling) that must be balanced in order to develop an organization's promotional strategy.

Psychographic segmentation Analysis of consumer type based on their lifestyle, personality, motivations and behaviour.

Pull strategy Sales promotions directed towards the end-consumer. The offer creates demand and entices the customer to the store or website.

Push strategy Sales promotions geared towards trade distributors or retailers with the aim of encouraging them to promote the brand to their customers.

QR code Machine-readable quick response code allowing quick access to websites and digital data via smartphone.

Reach A term used in a number of advertising contexts and increasingly referred to as a measure in digital marketing, with a common measure being the number of unique visitors per time period.

Ready-to-wear Fashion that is not couture or custom-made. *See also* Prêt-à-porter.

Relationship marketing Focuses on the relationship between a brand or business and its customers with the aim of building long-term relationships and loyalty.

Sales channel Route by which a product reaches the market and is made available to consumers.

Sales promotion Promotional offers designed to encourage consumers to purchase. Also termed below the line marketing.

Secondary research Also known as desk research, this utilizes existing data that may have been gathered for other purposes and is available in the public domain.

Segmentation Process of subdividing and classifying a market and consumers.

Segmentation variables Criteria used to analyse and classify markets or consumers.

Share of voice Comparison of a company's press results with those of its main competitors to determine which achieved most coverage.

Shoppable content Digital content, such as adverts, films or images, from which consumers can purchase fashion products directly.

Showrooming Where consumers visit retail stores to examine items, but then purchase online to get the best price.

Signature style A unique and identifiable style attributable to a particular designer, brand or label.

Situation analysis An audit of the internal situation within a company and analysis of the external market situation.

Social networking services (SNS) Platforms used to build social networks, including fashion photo-sharing apps.

Sourcing The search for, and procurement of, fabrics, materials, trims and manufacturing at required prices and delivery time-frames.

Specification sheet or Spec sheet A technical design drawing with measurements used to communicate precise details of a product's design and manufacture.

STP marketing strategy A strategy that makes use of segmentation, targeting and positioning.

Style tribe A group of individuals who dress in a common distinctive style.

Supply chain The network of suppliers, manufacturers, agents and distributors involved in the process of producing a garment.

SWOT analysis Analysis of the strengths and weaknesses of an organization and investigation of opportunities and threats in the marketplace. SWOT analysis is carried out as part of the development of a marketing plan.

Targeting The strategy of developing products or services specifically aimed to appeal to a particular group of consumers.

Text code A code sent by text to a consumer's mobile allowing them access to a promotional offer.

Tipping point The moment when a trend or idea crosses a significant threshold; it then spreads exponentially through a population.

Total product concept A model created by Theodore Levitt to explain the tangible and intangible elements of a product.

Trademark A logo, symbol, brand name, slogan or design detail protected by law as a registered trademark.

Trend scout Also known as a Cool hunter. A person who seeks out and reports on emerging trends in fashion, street fashion, music, design and culture.

Triple bottom line An ethical accounting system that measures a company's success in economic, social and environmental terms.

Trunk show Designers or sales representatives go on tour to show or preview collections to buyers, invited guests and customers. Trunk shows are usually held in boutiques or hotels.

Unique selling proposition (USP) Also known as unique selling point. The distinguishing factors that differentiate one brand from another.

Upcycle To use old or discarded clothing or textiles as a basis for a new, refashioned garment.

Vertical supply chain When one company or conglomerate owns all the manufacturing resources within the supply chain.

Viral marketing Marketing campaigns where the message is spread by consumers on the Internet.

Visual merchandising Promotion of fashion through window display, store layout and in-store product displays.

Webrooming Where consumers research items online prior to visiting a retail store in order to have the ease and immediacy of purchase.

Index

Picture credits

Key:
a=above, b=below, c=centre, l=left, r=right.

p4 Antonio de Moraes Barros Filho / WireImage/Getty Images. p7 Mel Risebrow. p8 Getty Images. p9 Karl Prouse/Catwalking. p11a Courtesy The Gentleman Blogger (www. thegentlemanblogger.com); Photo: Jeff Porto. p11b Celia Peterson/arabianEye/Getty Images. p12a Apic/Hulton Archive/Getty Images. p12b Advertising Archives. p13 Walter McBride/ Corbis. p14 Pau Berolini at Oui Management; Alex Mabille Haute Couture; Miss Bell dress from AW13. p15 Fairchild Photo Service/ Condé Nast/Corbis. p17a, ca, cb Karl Prouse/ Catwalking. p17b Kristian Dowling/Getty Images. p18 Courtesy Beacon's Closet; Photo: Carly Rabalais. p20 Courtesy Michelle Lowe-Holder; Photo: Polly Penrose. p21 Pierre Verdy/Getty Images. p22 Image courtesy of Cordings of Piccadilly (www.cordings.co.uk). p23 LondonEdge Ltd. p24 Courtesy Erdem. p25a Andrew H. Walker/Getty Images. p25b Fairchild Photo Service/Condé Nast/ Corbis. p27 Jonatan Fernström DR DENIM JEANSMAKERS. p28 Harriet Posner. p30 Courtesy LittleMissMatched. p31 Richard Valencia. p33 Ari Versluis and Ellie Uyttenbroek. p37 Ada Zaniton - Spring Summer 2014, Berlin Fashion Week. p39 Courtesy Orla Kiely. p40 Stuart Wilson/Getty Images. p42 Courtesy Regatta. p44a Theo Wargo/Wire Image/Getty Images. p44 Frederique Veysset/Sygma/ Corbis. p45 Angela Weiss/Getty Images. p47 Barry Brecheisen/Getty Images. p48 Mark A. Steele Photography, Columbis, OH. p49 Courtesy Massey & Rogers. p50a Courtesy Prey. p50b, p51 Harriet Posner. p52 Courtesy Alice + Olivia. p54 Courtesy Earnest Sewn. p61 Courtesy Orla Kiely. p63a Lipnitzki/Roger Viollet/Getty Images. p63c WWD/Condé Nast/Corbis. p63b François Guillot/AFP/Getty Images. p65 SIPA/PixelFormula/Rex. p66 Noah Seelman/AFP/Getty Images. p69 Scott Olson/Getty Images. p70 Bill Ray/Time & Life Pictures/Getty Images. p71a Frazer Harrison/ Getty Images. p71b Courtesy The Gentleman Blogger (www.thegentlemanblogger.com); Photo: Adam Tannous. p72 Image courtesy: Julien Fournié and Dassault Systèmes. p73a

China Photos/Getty Images. p73b Haszlo Regos, Berkley, Michigan. p77a Courtesy Stylitics, Inc. p77b Dave M. Bennett/Getty Images. p78 Silvia Olsen Photography. p80a Courtesy LuisaViaRoma. p80b Courtesy Colette. p81 Rob Loud/Getty Images. p82 John Shearer/Getty Images. p83a © ZACARIAS by S.C. Vizcarra. p83b Courtesy Rita Hazareno; Photo: S.S. de Guzman. p85 Draught Associates. p89a Courtesy Nudie Jeans. p89b Yoshikazu Tsuno/AFP/Getty Images. p91 Première Vision. p92 Courtesy OnePiece. p94 © SPINEXPO™ (www. spinexpo.com)/Sophie Steller Studio (www. sophiesteller.com). p95a SuperPier – Courtesy of LOT-EK. p95b Suzanne Plunkett/Reuters/ Corbis. p96 Alberto Buzzola/LightRocket via Getty Images. p98 David Gray/Reuters/Corbis. p99 Courtesy Marc Jacobs International. p100 Image courtesy Eugenia Alejos; Photography: Cristian di Stefano; Hair & Make Up: Marta Arce; Model: Sandra Rudio. p107 Courtesy Philli Wood; Photo: Simon Armstrong. p109 Hannah Markham. p111a Bloomberg/Getty Images. p111b Courtesy Gooey Wooey. p113 Guardian News & Media Ltd. 2009; Photo: David Newby. p114 Gamma-Keystone/Getty Images. p116 Photo: Josh Meister. p119 Laura-Michelle Moore. p120 Thomas Concordia/ Getty Images. p122–123 Ian Rummey. p127 Joy Prater. p129 Courtesy David Sevenoaks, Spaaza. p131 Courtesy Philli Wood; Photo: Simon Armstrong. p132 Courtesy Nudie Jeans. p136 James Hayes. p137a Harriet Posner. p137b James Hayes. p138 Courtesy Nimish Shah. p139 Vittorio Zunino Celotto/ Getty Images. p140a Mel Risebrow. p140b Noel Vasquez/Getty Images. p141 Courtesy adidas. p142al, bl Karl Prouse/Catwalking. p142r Alberto Tamargo/Getty Images. p143 Courtesy adidas. p144 Courtesy Australian Wool Innovation Limited. p145 Courtesy Meredith Wendell. p149 Designer: Sophie Taylor, Castlefield Bridal. p150 Courtesy David Delfín; Photo: Gorka Postigo. p153 Courtesy Nau; Photo (a): Eugénie Frerichs; Photo (b): Shawn Lineham. p154 Advertising Archives. p155a, b Oliver Knight/Alamy. p155c Harriet Posner. p156 Vittorio Zunino Celotto/Getty Images. p159 Hannah Markham. p163l Jeff.

J. Mitchell/Getty Images. p163r AFP/Getty Images. p164al Miquel Benitez/WireImage/ Getty Images. p164ar Bravo Press SA/Rex. p164br Agencia EFE/Rex. p166 Courtesy Mr. Hare. p168 Nick Turner, Sam Robinson; Fascia and interiors by Pope Wainwright (www. popewainwright.co.uk). p170 Eric Piermont/ AFP/Getty Images. p171, p172a Ian Gavan/ Getty Images. p172b Nick Harvey/WireImage/ Getty Images. p173 Mel Risebrow. p174 Harriet Posner. p176 Courtesy John Lewis Partnership. p177 Vittorio Zunino Celotto/ Getty Images. p179 Benetton Group; Photo (a): James Mollison; Photo (b): Erik Ravelo/ Fabrica and Piero Martinello/Fabrica. p180 Courtesy Adbuster/Blackspot. p181a Craig Morey; Licensed under the Creative Commons Attribution-ShareAlike 2.0 Generic License. p181b Raffaela Lepanto (www.nomads. com). p183 Mel Risebrow. p184 Dibyangshu Sarkar/AFP/Getty Images. p185 www. modcloth.com. p186a Harriet Posner. p186b Mel Risebrow. p187 Courtesy Radley + Co. p188 James McCauley/Rex. p189 Courtesy Diesel. p190–191 Courtesy O'Neill. p192–193 Courtesy Erdem. p194 Courtesy Nudie Jeans. p196 © Bread & Butter (www.breadandbutter. com). p198a twitter.com/dkny. p198b Astrid Stawiarz/Getty Images. p199a Mark Von Holden/WireImage/Getty Images. p199b Dimitrios Kambouris/Getty Images. p201 Miracle on Madison Avenue, 2013; Images courtesy of Town & Country; Artist: Chelsey McLaren. p204 © Première Vision. p205 Brendon Thorne/Getty Images. p208 Jason Kempin/WireImage/Getty Images. p209a Jean-Pierre Muller/AFP/Getty Images. p209b François Durand/Getty Images. p210 David S. Holloway/Getty Images. p212 © Première Vision. p213 Shawn Lineham. p214 Anna KO (www.myspace.com/annako) © Bread & Butter (www.breadandbutter.com). p216 Mel Risebrow. p217 Dan Kitwood/Getty Images. p219 Brendon Thorne/Getty Images.

Acknowledgements

Special thanks and gratitude go to all those who have contributed in so many different ways to the creation of this book. To Ursula Hudson for her years of friendship and for putting me forward for this project. To the team at Laurence King for their guidance and constant encouragement – Helen Rochester for commissioning the book, Anne Townley for steering me through the writing process with such grace and clarity, Clare Double and Alex Coco for facilitating this new second edition and Annalaura Palma and Louise Thomas for the picture research.

I wish to acknowledge Peter Lewis-Crown, Jane Barran, Vanessa Denza, Karin Koeppel and Caroline Morgan for the pivotal role each played in shaping my career in fashion, and students past and present who have helped me learn and grow as a teacher; it has been a joy to see your careers take root and blossom. In particular; Erdem Moralioglu, Hannah Jennings, Hannah Markham, James Hayes, Joy Prater, Laura Moore, Nimish Shah, Rita Nazareno and Britt Mansveld – thank you for your support and contribution to this book.

Thanks to friends and colleagues at Norwich University of the Arts, Istituto Marangoni, Amsterdam Fashion Academy and Kensington and Chelsea College for inspiration and support.

Special thanks go to all the companies and individuals who generously agreed to be interviewed, contribute material or put me in touch with someone who could help.

To all my friends and family who have cared enough to listen, been tough enough to push and kind enough to give me a hug when needed – thank you. And last, but in no way least, a very special mention and heartfelt gratitude to Mel for his patience, support, guidance and love – I couldn't have done this without you. Thank you for being by my side day in and day out through all the ups and downs of this project.